The Language of the Third Reich

TITLES IN THE BLOOMSBURY REVELATIONS SERIES

Some titles are not available in North America

The Language of the Third Reich

LTI – Lingua Tertii Imperii
A Philologist's Notebook

Victor Klemperer

Translated by Martin Brady

B L O O M S B U R Y
LONDON • NEW DELHI • NEW YORK • SYDNEY

Bloomsbury Academic
An imprint of Bloomsbury Publishing Plc

50 Bedford Square   1385 Broadway
London   New York
WC1B 3DP   NY 10018
UK   USA

www.bloomsbury.com

Bloomsbury is a registered trade mark of Bloomsbury Publishing Plc

Translated from *LTI Notizbuch eines* Philologen, 3rd edition
Published in Germany 1957 by Max Niemeyer Verlag, Halle (Saale)
© Reclam Verlag Leipzig 1975

This English Translation © The Athlone Press 2000

Bloomsbury Revelations edition first published in 2013 by
Bloomsbury Academic

The publishers wish to record their thanks to Inter Nationes for a grant towards the cost of translation

British Library Cataloguing-in-Publication Data
A catalogue record for this book is available from the British Library.

ISBN: PB: 978-1-4725-0721-1

Library of Congress Cataloging-in-Publication Data
Klemperer, Victor, 1881–1960.
[LTI, Notizbuch eines Philologen. English]
Language of the Third Reich: LTI: Lingua Tertii Imperii/Victor Klemperer;
Translated by Martin Brady. – Bloomsbury Revelations edition.
pages cm
Originally published in English: London; New Brunswick, N.J.: Athlone Press, 2000.
Published in German in Germany 1957 by Max Niemeyer Verlag, Halle (Saale)
Includes bibliographical references and index.
ISBN 978-1-4725-0721-1 (pbk.)
1. German language. 2. National socialism. 3.German language–Political aspects.
4. German language–20th century. 5. German language–Semantics. 6. Propaganda, German.
I. Brady, Martin, 1962– translator. II. Title.
PF3074.K613 2013
430'.9043–dc23
                                                          2013020244

Typeset by Deanta Global Publishing Services, Chennai, India

Translator's Note

I would like to express my heartfelt gratitude to Helen Hughes and Sigmund Laufer, without whose energetic support this translation would not have been possible.

Contents

To my wife Eva Klemperer

As long as twenty years ago, my dear Eva, I prefaced the dedication of a collection of essays with the remark that a dedication from me to you in the conventional sense of a present was out of the question, given that you were already co-owner of my books, since they were in every way the product of an intellectual community of property. This is still the same today.

But in this case things are rather different than with all my previous publications, this time I am even less entitled to present you with a dedication, and incomparably more compelled to do so than during those peaceful days in which we engaged in philology. But for you this book would not exist today, and its author, too, would have ceased to exist long ago. If I were to explain this in detail it would require copious, intimate pages. In place of this, please take the general observations of the philologist and pedagogue which open these sketches. You know, and even a blind man would be able to divine with his stick, to whom I am referring, when I speak to my audience of heroism.

VICTOR KLEMPERER
Dresden, Christmas 1946

LANGUAGE IS MORE THAN BLOOD.

Franz Rosenzweig

Heroism (Instead of an Introduction)

New demands led the language of the Third Reich to stimulate an increase in the use of the dissociating prefix *ent-* {de-} (though in each case it remains open to question whether we are dealing with completely new creations or the adoption by the common language of terms already familiar in specialist circles). Windows had to be blacked out {*verdunkelt*} because of enemy planes, which in turn led to the daily task of lifting the blackout {*des Entdunkelns*}. In the event of roof fires, the lofts had to be free of clutter that might get in the way of the firefighters – they were therefore de-cluttered {*entrümpelt*}. New sources of nourishment had to be tapped: the bitter horse-chestnut was de-bittered {*entbittert*} . . .

For a comprehensive definition of today's most important task, a word formed in an analogous manner has been widely adopted: Germany was almost destroyed by Nazism; the task of curing it of this fatal disease is today termed denazification {*Entnazifizierung*}. I hope, and indeed believe, that this dreadful word will only have a short life; it will fade away and lead no more than a historical existence as soon as it has performed its current duty.

The Second World War has on numerous occasions demonstrated to us the process whereby a currently highly fashionable expression, one apparently destined never to be expunged, suddenly goes silent: it disappears with the context that gave birth to it and one day will bear witness to it like a fossil. That was the fate of the *Blitzkrieg* and the associated adjective *schlagartig* {precipitous}, of the *Vernichtungsschlachten* {battles of extermination} and the related

Einkesselungen {encirclings}, and also of the *'wandernden Kessel* {shifting encirclement}' – already today this requires a gloss to the effect that it was the desperate attempt at retreat on the part of encircled divisions – and the *Nervenkrieg* {war of nerves}, and indeed eventually even of the *Endsieg* {final victory}. The *Landekopf* {bridgehead} survived from spring to summer 1944, and was still alive when it had swollen to a huge, shapeless mass; but then, when Paris fell and the whole of France had become a *Landekopf,* it was all of a sudden over and done with, and will only resurface as a fossil in history lessons at some point in the distant future.

And this too will be the fate of that most serious and decisive of words in our own epoch of transition: one day the word *Entnazifizierung* will have faded away because the situation it was intended to end will no longer exist.

But that won't be for some time yet, because it isn't only Nazi actions that have to vanish, but also the Nazi cast of mind, the typical Nazi way of thinking and its breeding-ground: the language of Nazism.

What a huge number of concepts and feelings it has corrupted and poisoned! At the so-called evening grammar school organized by the Dresden adult education centre, and in the discussions organized by the *Kulturbund* {Cultural Association} and the *Freie deutsche Jugend* {Free German Youth}, I have observed again and again how the young people in all innocence, and despite a sincere effort to fill the gaps and eliminate the errors in their neglected education, cling to Nazi thought processes. They don't realize they are doing it; the remnants of linguistic usage from the preceding epoch confuse and seduce them. We spoke about the meaning of culture, of humanitarianism, of democracy and I had the impression that they were beginning to see the light, and that certain things were being straightened out in their willing minds – and then, it was always just round the corner, someone spoke of some heroic behaviour or other, or of some heroic resistance, or simply of heroism *per se.* As soon as this concept was even touched upon, everything became blurred, and we were adrift once again in the fog of Nazism. And it wasn't only the young men who had just returned from the field or from captivity, and felt they were not receiving sufficient attention, let alone acclaim, no, even young women who had not seen any military service were thoroughly infatuated with the most dubious notion of heroism. The only thing that was beyond dispute, was that it was impossible to have a proper grasp of the true nature of humanitarianism, culture and democracy if one endorsed this kind of conception, or to be more precise misconception, of heroism.

But after all, in what contexts had this generation come across the word *'heroisch* {heroic}' and all its kindred spirits, a generation which in 1933 had barely mastered the alphabet? The principal answer was that it had always worn a uniform, three different uniforms, but had never been seen in civilian clothes.

Whenever Hitler's *Mein Kampf* sets out general principles of education, the physical aspect is always by far the most important. He loves the expression *'körperliche Ertüchtigung* {physical training}', which he gleaned from the dictionary of the Weimar conservatives, he extols the Wilhelmine army as the only healthy and life-giving institution in the otherwise decaying body of the nation, and military service he sees principally, indeed exclusively, in terms of a training to achieve maximum physical potential. For Hitler, the development of character quite explicitly has to take second place; in his view it evolves more or less automatically when the physical dominates education and quashes the workings of the mind. Last of all in his pedagogical programme, however, comes the training of the intellect and its provision with knowledge; it is only countenanced with reluctance, and is viewed with suspicion and despised. The fear of the thinking man and the hatred of the intellect are revealed in a constant stream of new expressions. When Hitler talks of his rise to power, his first successful rallies, he extols the fighting prowess of his guards, the small group out of which the SA[1] was soon to emerge, at least as fervently as his own gifts as a public speaker. The 'brown Storm Troopers', whose task is merely to exercise brute force, to assault political opponents at the rally and throw them onto the streets – they are his true allies in the battle for the hearts of the people, his first heroes, and he portrays them as the blood-soaked conquerors of a mighty enemy, the exemplary heroes of historic bar-room brawls. And similar descriptions, the same attitude and the same vocabulary are to be found when Goebbels describes the battle for Berlin. It isn't the spirit {*Geist*} which is victorious, the intention is not to convince, it isn't even the hoodwinking with rhetorical devices

---

[1]Abbreviation of *Sturmabteilung*, Storm Detachment. The Storm Troopers of the *Sturmabteilung* were the early private army of the Nazi Party.

which tips the balance in favour of the new doctrine, it is the heroism of the first members of the SA, the 'old guard'. In my own mind these reports of Hitler and Goebbels are supplemented by a professional distinction drawn by a friend of ours who at the time was a houseman in the hospital of a small industrial town in Saxony. 'In the evening when the injured were admitted following the rallies', she often told us, 'I always knew straightaway which party each one belonged to, even if he was already in bed without any clothes on: those with head wounds inflicted by beer mugs or chair legs were Nazis, and those with a stiletto wound in the lung were Communists.' As regards reputation the same can be said of the SA as of Italian literature, in both cases the greatest splendour is to be found in the early stages, a radiance that can never be attained again.

Chronologically the second uniform in which Nazi heroism clothed itself is the masked figure of the racing driver, his crash helmet, his goggles, his thick gloves. Nazism nurtured all kinds of sport, and purely linguistically it was influenced by boxing more than all the others put together; but the most memorable and widespread image of heroism in the mid-1930s is provided by the racing driver: following his fatal crash, the image of Bernd Rosemeyer was almost as cherished in the nation's popular imagination as Horst Wessel. (Note for my university colleagues: the most fascinating seminars can be spent investigating the reciprocal relationship between Goebbels's style and the memoirs of the aviator Elly Beinhorn: 'My Husband, the Racing Driver {*Mein Mann, der Rennfahrer*}'.) For some time the champions of international motor races were the most photographed heroes of the day, seated behind the steering wheels of their chariots, leaning against them or even buried beneath them. If a young man didn't glean his image of heroism from those sinewy warriors depicted on the latest posters or commemorative coins, naked or sporting SA uniforms, then he doubtless did so from racing drivers; what the two incarnations of heroism have in common is the glassy stare which expresses a hard and thrusting determination coupled with the will to succeed.

From 1939 the racing car was replaced by the tank, the racing driver by the tank driver. (This was the private's designation not only for the man at the wheel, but also the armoured infantrymen.) From the very first day of the war, right through to the demise of the Third Reich, anything and everything heroic on land, at sea and in the air wore a military uniform. During the First World War there was still civilian heroism behind the front line. But how much longer will there be a 'behind the front line'? How much longer a 'civilian life'? The doctrine of total war turns terrifyingly on its creators: the battlefield is everywhere, military heroism is stored in every factory, in every cellar; children, women and old people die one and the same heroic death in battle – often enough in the same uniform even – normally only befitting or attainable by young soldiers in the field.

For twelve years the concept and vocabulary of heroism are increasingly and ever more exclusively restricted to military bravery and foolhardy, death-defying behaviour in some military action or other. It is not for nothing that the language of Nazism introduced into common usage the word *'kämpferisch* {aggressive, belligerent}', a new and rarely used adjective associated with Neo-Romantic aesthetes, fashioning it into one of its favourite words. *Kriegerisch* {warlike} was too narrow, it only intimated things relating to war itself, it was also probably too candid, betraying an aggressive disposition and mania for conquering. *Kämpferisch* is quite a different matter! It denotes in a more general way that taut frame of mind and will which in any situation is focused on self-assertion through defence or attack, and which refuses to countenance any form of compromise. The abuse of *kämpferisch* corresponds perfectly to the excessive damage done to the word heroism when it is used inappropriately or wrongly.

'But you really are doing us an injustice, Herr Professor! By "us" I don't mean the Nazis, because I'm not one. But, with a few interruptions, I was in the field for all those years. Isn't it natural that during wartime there is much talk of heroism? And why does it have to be a false kind of heroism which emerges?'

'There's more to heroism than courage and putting your own life on the line. Any ruffian or criminal can summon up these qualities. The hero {*Heros*} was originally someone who performed deeds which benefited mankind. A war of conquest, and especially one which perpetrated such atrocities as Hitler's, has nothing to do with heroism.'

'But amongst my comrades there were so many who were not involved in any atrocities, and who were firmly convinced – we were never told otherwise after all – that, even when attacking and conquering, we were only engaged in a defensive war, and that our victory would also bring salvation to the world. We only discovered the truth much later, when it was already too late . . . And don't you accept that true heroism can be achieved in sport, that a sporting achievement can benefit mankind through its exemplary quality?' – 'Of course it's possible, and even in Nazi Germany there must undoubtedly have been a handful of true heroes amongst the sportsmen and soldiers. It's simply that I am sceptical precisely when it comes to the heroism of these two professional groups as a whole. In both cases the heroism is too strident, too profitable and too indulgently overweening to be authentic in most cases. It is undeniable that these racing drivers were literally industrial knights in shining armour, their daredevil speeds were meant to promote German factories and consequently the Fatherland, and perhaps they were even supposed to benefit society at large by contributing their experiences to the goal of perfecting automobile construction. But there was so much vanity, so much gladiatorial triumph involved! And the racing driver's wreaths and prizes are the soldier's medals and promotions. No, only in the rarest of cases am I convinced by heroism when it blows its own trumpet in public and makes sure that success is all-too-handsomely rewarded. Heroism is purer and more significant the quieter it is, the less audience it has, the less it furthers the hero himself, and the less it is decorated. My criticism of the Nazi concept of heroism is that it is always shackled to decoration and vainglorious. Officially Nazism didn't recognize any kind of decent, real heroism. It thereby perverted the whole notion and brought it into disrepute.'

'Do you deny that there was any quiet, real heroism during the Hitler years?'

'No, not during the Hitler years – on the contrary, they led to the purest kind of heroism, but on the other side so to speak. I am thinking of the many brave people in the concentration camps, of all those people who recklessly committed illegal acts. The mortal dangers and the suffering were incomparably greater than at the front, and the glory of decoration was nowhere to be seen! It wasn't the much-vaunted death on the "field of honour" which confronted one, rather, at the very best, death by guillotine. And yet – even though there was no decoration and this heroism was undoubtedly real – these heroes did possess a source of inner strength and solace: they too knew they were members of an army, they had a firm and unshakeable belief in the ultimate victory of their cause, they could take with them to the grave the proud conviction that their name would one day be resurrected all the more triumphantly the more ignominiously they were massacred.

But I also know of another kind of heroism that is much more wretched and much less audible, a heroism which was completely deprived of the support of being part of an army or a political group, of the hope of future glory, a heroism which was left to fend entirely for itself. These were the handful of Aryan wives (there were not that many of them), who resisted every pressure to separate from their Jewish husbands. And just imagine what everyday life was like for these women! What insults, threats, blows and spittle they endured, what privations they had to suffer if they shared the standard inadequacy of their food ration-cards with their husbands, who were on the sub-standard Jewish card {*Judenkarte*} whilst their Aryan colleagues at the factory received labourers' supplements. What a will to live they had to muster when they fell ill from all the humiliation and excruciating wretchedness, when the countless suicides around them pointed temptingly to everlasting relief from the Gestapo! They knew that their death would inevitably be followed by that of their Jewish husband, because he would be transported from the yet warm corpse of his wife into deadly exile. What stoicism, what a huge outlay of self-discipline was needed to give fresh heart over and over again to their exhausted, broken and desperate husbands. Amidst the grenade fire of the battlefield, surrounded by falling rubble in a collapsing bomb shelter, even confronted with the gallows, there is always a degree of pathos which affords some support – but in the debilitating nausea of everyday squalor, to be followed by an unforeseeable number of equally squalid days, what is there to keep you going? And to remain strong in this situation, strong enough to be able to embolden your partner the whole time, and convince him again and again that the hour would eventually come and that it is a matter of duty to wait for it, to remain this strong when one is left to cope entirely on one's own in lonely isolation, because the Jews' House does not constitute a community, despite the shared enemy and fate, and despite its common language – this is heroism {*Heroismus*} over and above any hero-worship {*Heldentum*}.

No, there was certainly no lack of hero-worship during the Hitler years, but in Hitlerism proper, amongst the community of Hitlerites, there was only a superficial, distorted and poisoned heroism, witness the flashy cups and clinking of medals, witness the bloated words of indulgent adoration, witness the relentless killing . . .'

Did the family of words associated with hero-worship {*Heldentum*} belong to the LTI? As a matter of fact yes, because it is extensive, and every individual example is characteristic of that specifically Nazi form of hypocrisy and brutality. It was also closely tied up with the exaltation of the Teutons as a chosen race: all heroism was the sole prerogative of the Teutonic race. And, as a matter of fact, no; because all these distortions and superficialities had clung often enough to this sonorous family of words prior to the Third Reich. This is why it can be mentioned here in the marginal terrain of the foreword.

One expression, however, must be registered as a specifically Nazi one. Not least on account of the consolation which stemmed from it. In December 1941 Paul K. returned from work one day beaming. *En route* he had read the military despatch. 'They are having a terrible time in Africa', he said. I asked whether they were really admitting it – usually they only report victories. 'They write: "Our troops who are fighting valiantly {*heldenhaft*}." *Heldenhaft* sounds like an obituary, you can be sure of that.'

Subsequently *heldenhaft* sounded like an obituary in many, many more bulletins and was never misleading.

Chapter 1
LTI

There was the BDM[1] and the HJ[2] and the DAF[3] and countless other abbreviations of this kind.

The label LTI first appears in my diary as a playful little piece of parody, almost immediately afterwards as a laconic *aide-mémoire,* like a knot in a handkerchief, and then very soon, and for the duration of those terrible years, as an act of self-defence, an SOS sent to myself. A tag with a nice erudite ring – the Third Reich itself after all delighted from time to time in the rich sonority of a foreign expression: *Garant* {guarantor} sounds much more persuasive than *Bürge* {supporter}, and *diffamieren* {defame} far more impressive than *schlechtmachen* {run down}. (Perhaps some people won't understand such words; they are precisely the ones who are most vulnerable.)

LTI: Lingua Tertii Imperii, the language of the Third Reich. Many a time I have been reminded of an old Berlin anecdote which was probably in my beautifully illustrated edition of Glaßbrenner, the humorist of the Revolution of 1848 – but where is my library now that I might check it? Would there be any point in my asking the Gestapo what has happened to it? . . . 'Father,' a young boy asks in the circus, 'what is the man up there on the tightrope doing with that pole?' – 'Silly boy, it's a balancing

---

[1] Abbreviation of *Bund deutscher Mädel* (usually BdM), League of German Girls. The girls' branch of the Nazi youth movement.

[2] Abbreviation of *Hitler Jugend,* Hitler Youth. The boys' branch of the Nazi youth movement.

[3] Abbreviation of *Deutsche Arbeitsfront,* German Labour Front. Allied to the National Socialist Party, the German Labour Front replaced the unions of the Weimar Republic.

pole, and it's what's holding him steady.' – 'Oh dear, father, what if he lets go of it?' – 'Silly boy, he's holding it steady of course!'

Again and again during these years my diary was my balancing pole, without which I would have fallen down a hundred times. In times of disgust and despondency, in the dreary monotony of endless routine factory work, at the bedside of the sick and the dying, at grave-sides, at times when I myself was in dire straits, at moments of utter ignominy and when my heart was literally breaking – at all these times I was invariably helped by the demand that I had made on myself: observe, study and memorize what is going on – by tomorrow everything will already look different, by tomorrow everything will already feel different; keep hold of how things reveal themselves at this very moment and what the effects are. And very soon this call to rise above the situation and to safeguard my inner freedom was concentrated into that consistently effective secret formula: LTI, LTI!

Indeed, if I had the intention (which I do not) to publish the entire diary for this period with all its observations of everyday life, I would give it this tag as a title. You could take it metaphorically. For just as it is customary to speak of the face of an age or of a country, so it is also usual to characterize the spirit of a particular epoch as its language. The Third Reich speaks with a terrible uniformity both in what it said at the time and in its legacy: through the unbounded exhibitionism of its grandiose architecture and through its ruins, through its unique brand of soldier, the men of the SA and SS[4] which it elevated to the status of ideal figures on myriad different and yet indistinguishable posters, and through its motorways and mass graves. All of this is the language of the Third Reich, and of course there will be mention of all these things in the following pages. But if you have practised your profession for decades, and practised it with great pleasure, then you are bound to have been shaped more by it than by anything else, and it was thus the language of the Third Reich, both literally and in a non-figurative, philological sense, which I clung to with absolute determination and which became my balancing pole across the monotony of every ten-hour shift in the factory, the horror of house searches, arrests, physical abuse, and so on.

---

[4]Abbreviation of *Schutzstaffel,* Elite Guard. The black-shirts were originally Hitler's personal guard. Under their leader Heinrich Himmler they served as the Nazi political police.

People are forever quoting Talleyrand's remark that language is only there in order to hide the thoughts of the diplomat (or for that matter of any other shrewd and dubious person). But in fact the very opposite is true. Whatever it is that people are determined to hide, be it only from others, or from themselves, even things they carry around unconsciously – language reveals all. That is no doubt the meaning of the aphorism *Le style c'est l'homme*; what a man says may be a pack of lies – but his true self is laid bare for all to see in the style of his utterances.

I had a strange time with this unique (philologically unique) language of the Third Reich.

Right at the outset, while I was still suffering no persecution, or at most a very mild form, I wanted to hear as little as possible of it. I had more than enough of it in the language of the window displays, the posters, the brown uniforms, the flags, the arms outstretched in the Hitler salute, the carefully trimmed Hitler moustaches. I took flight, I buried myself in my profession, I gave my lectures and desperately ignored the increasingly yawning gaps in the rows of seats in front of me, I exerted all my energies on my eighteenth-century French literature. Why should I sour my life still further by reading Nazi publications when it was already being ruined by what was happening around me? If by chance or mistake a Nazi book fell into my hands I would cast it aside after the first paragraph. If the voice of the Führer or his Propaganda Minister was blaring out of a loudspeaker on the street I would give it a wide berth, and when reading the newspaper I desperately tried to fish out the naked facts – forlorn enough in their nakedness – from the repulsive morass of speeches, commentaries and articles. When the civil service was purged and I no longer had my lectern to lean on, my initial reaction was to try to cut myself off from the present entirely. Those thoroughly unmodern Enlightenment thinkers, long since despised by anybody who thought they were anybody, had always been my favourites – Voltaire, Montesquieu and Diderot. I could now dedicate all my time and energy to my opus which was already well advanced; as far as the eighteenth century was concerned I was in clover in the Japanese Palace in Dresden; no German library, and perhaps not even the national library in Paris, could have served me better.

But then came the next blow in the form of the ban on library use, pulling my life's work away from under me. After that I was driven out of my own house and everything else followed, every day something new.

From that point on the balancing pole became my essential tool, the language of the period my paramount interest.

I observed ever more closely how the workers in the factory talked, how the beasts from the Gestapo spoke and how we Jews expressed ourselves, caged in like animals in a zoo. There were no great differences to be registered; no, in fact there were absolutely none at all. Without a doubt, supporters and opponents, beneficiaries and victims all conformed to the same models.

I tried to get a grip on these models, a task which in some respects was extremely simple, since everything that was printed or spoken in Germany was standardized to conform to the official party line; anything which deviated in any way from the accepted pattern did not make it into the public domain; books, newspapers, official communications and forms issued by administrative departments all swam in the same brown sauce, and it was this absolute uniformity of the written language which explained the homogeneity of the spoken language.

Yet whilst for thousands of other people it would have been child's play to consult these models, for me it was extremely difficult, invariably dangerous and sometimes utterly impossible. Anyone who bore the star was not allowed to buy or borrow any kind of book, journal or newspaper.

Anything which one secretly kept at home was dangerous and either hidden under cupboards and carpets, on ovens and pelmets, or stored along with the coal as kindling. Of course measures of this kind only helped if you were lucky.

Never – never in my whole life – has my head spun as much from a book as it did with Rosenberg's *Myth*.[5] Not because his writings were exceptionally profound, difficult to comprehend or emotionally overwhelming, but because Clemens hammered on my head with the book for minutes on end. (Clemens and Weser were the principal torturers of the Jews in Dresden, and they were generally differentiated as the Hitter and the Spitter.) 'How dare a Jewish pig like you presume to read a book of this kind?' Clemens yelled. To him it seemed like the desecration of a consecrated wafer. 'How dare you have a book here from the lending library.' Only the fact that the volume had demonstrably

---

[5]Alfred Rosenberg's magnum opus *Der Mythus des zwanzigsten Jahrhunderts,* The Myth of the Twentieth Century.

been borrowed in the name of my Aryan wife, and, moreover, that the sheet of notes which accompanied it was torn up without being deciphered, saved me at the time from the concentration camp.

All my material had to be procured surreptitiously and had to be exploited secretly. And there was so much that I couldn't get hold of at all! When I wanted to dig deep to the roots of a particular problem, in short whenever I needed specialist materials, I was left in the lurch by the private lending libraries, and I had no access to the public ones.

Perhaps some people may think that academic colleagues or older students who in the meantime had gained posts might have helped me out in my hour of need, that they might have acted as middlemen in the library lending system. Dear God! That would have been an act of personal bravery giving rise to considerable personal danger. There is a neat verse in Old French which I often used to quote from the lectern, but which I only really understood later during the period when I had not lectern. A writer who has hit hard times recalls wistfully the numerous *amis que vent emporte, et il ventait devant ma porte,* 'the friends chased away by the wind, and it was certainly windy at my door'. But I don't want to be unjust: I have found faithful and courageous friends, it is just that there happened not to be any close colleagues within my discipline or in related fields amongst them.

There are therefore again and again remarks such as the following in my notes and excerpts: Check later! . . . Amplify later! . . . To be answered later! . . . And then as the hope of experiencing any kind of 'later' begins to ebb: This would have to be tackled at a later date . . .

Today, when this 'later' has not yet quite arrived, but will do so when books emerge once again from the rubble and the traffic chaos (and when one can withdraw to the study with a good conscience from the communal *vita activa* of rebuilding) – today I know that I will not in fact be able to transform my sketch-like observations, reflections and questions on the language of the Third Reich into a well-knit academic work.

That would demand more knowledge, and indeed a longer life, than I or (for the time being) any other individual has at his disposal. For there is a lot of specialist work to be done in many different areas, Germanists and scholars of the Romance languages, English specialists and Slavonicists, historians and economists, lawyers and theologians, engineers and scientists will have to solve innumerable individual problems in excursuses and entire dissertations before it will be possible for a courageous and comprehensive mind to attempt to characterize the Lingua Tertii Imperii in its entirety, in its most pitiful and most wide-ranging entirety. But an initial groping around and probing of these things – things which cannot yet be pinned down because they are still in flux – the work of the first hour, as the French describe this kind of thing, will certainly always be of value for the real researchers who will follow, and I think it will also be useful for them to see their object of study still in the process of metamorphosis, half as a concrete report on lived experience and half within the conceptual framework of an academic study.

However, if that is the purpose of my publication, why am I not reproducing the philologist's notebook word for word, insofar as it could be extracted from the private and more general diary of those difficult years? Why are certain things outlined in a summary? Why is the perspective of those years so often accompanied by the perspective of today, the immediate post-Hitler era?

I want to give a precise answer to these questions. Because there is a particular intention at work here, because as well as pursuing a scientific goal I also have a pedagogical one.

So much is being said at present about eradicating the fascist mentality and so much is being done to that end. War criminals are being executed, 'little Pgs'[6] (the language of the Fourth Reich!) are being removed from office, nationalist books are being withdrawn from circulation, Hitler Squares and Göring Streets are being renamed, Hitler oaks are being felled. But it appears that the language of the Third Reich is to survive in the form of certain characteristic expressions; they have lodged themselves so deep below the surface that they appear to be becoming a permanent feature of the German language. For example, since May 1945 I have on countless occasions, in speeches broadcast on the wireless and passionately anti-fascist demonstrations, heard reference to such things as innate qualities 'of character' {'charakterlichen' Eigenschaften} and the 'aggressive {kämpferischen}' nature of democracy. Those are expressions from the heart – the Third Reich would say 'from the very lifeblood' – of the LTI. Is it just pedantry

---

[6]Abbreviation of Parteigenossen, party members.

on my part when I take exception to this, is it the schoolmaster, who apparently lurks deep within every philologist, making his appearance? I want to resolve this question with a second one.

What was the most powerful Hitlerian propaganda tool? Was it the individual speeches of Hitler and Goebbels, their pronouncements on this or that theme, their rabble-rousing against the Jews, against Bolshevism?

Certainly not, because a lot of this was not even understood by the masses, or it bored them in its endless repetitions. On many occasions in public houses, while I was still allowed to enter a public house without wearing a star, and later on many occasions in the factory during air raid protection duty – when the Aryans had their own room and the Jews theirs, and the radio was located in the Aryan room (along with the heating and the food) – on many occasions I heard the cards being slapped down noisily on the table, and loud discussions about the rationing of meat and tobacco and about the cinema, whilst the Führer or one of his henchmen was carrying on interminably. And the next day the papers claimed that the entire population had been hanging on their every word.

No, the most powerful influence was exerted neither by individual speeches nor by articles or flyers, posters or flags; it was not achieved by things which one had to absorb by conscious thought or conscious emotions.

Instead Nazism permeated the flesh and blood of the people through single words, idioms and sentence structures which were imposed on them in a million repetitions and taken on board mechanically and unconsciously. One tends to understand Schiller's distich on a 'cultivated language which writes and thinks for you' in purely aesthetic and, as it were, harmless terms. A successful verse in a 'cultivated language' says nothing about the literary strengths of its author; it is not particularly difficult to give oneself the air of a writer and thinker by using a highly cultivated turn of phrase.

But language does not simply write and think for me, it also increasingly dictates my feelings and governs my entire spiritual being the more unquestioningly and unconsciously I abandon myself to it. And what happens if the cultivated language is made up of poisonous elements or has been made the bearer of poisons? Words can be like tiny doses of arsenic: they are swallowed unnoticed, appear to have no effect, and then after a little time the toxic reaction sets in after all. If someone replaces the words 'heroic' and 'virtuous' with 'fanatical' for long enough, he will come to believe that a fanatic really is a virtuous hero, and that no one can be a hero without fanaticism. The Third Reich did not invent the words 'fanatical' and 'fanaticism', it just changed their value and used them more in one day than other epochs used them in years. The Third Reich coined only a very small number of the words in its language, perhaps – indeed probably – none at all. In many cases Nazi language points to foreign influences and appropriates much of the rest from the German language before Hitler. But it changes the value of words and the frequency of their occurrence, it makes common property out of what was previously the preserve of an individual or a tiny group, it commandeers for the party that which was previously common property and in the process steeps words and groups of words and sentence structures in its poison. Making language the servant of its dreadful system, it procures it as its most powerful, most public and most surreptitious means of advertising.

The task of making people aware of the poisonous nature of the LTI and warning them of its dangers is, I believe, not just schoolmasterish. If a piece of cutlery belonging to orthodox Jews has become ritually unclean, they purify it by burying it in the earth. Many words in common usage during the Nazi period should be committed to a mass grave for a very long time, some for ever.

Chapter 2
Prelude

On 8 June 1932 we saw the sound film *The Blue Angel,* 'already almost a classic' (as my diary would have it). Anything conceived and realized in epic form will always be coarsened and made into something altogether more lurid when adapted for the stage, and all the more so in the case of the cinema – thus Heinrich Mann's *Professor Unrat* is without doubt a greater work of art than *The Blue Angel*; but in terms of the artistic achievement of the actors this film was truly a masterpiece. The leading roles were played by Jannings, Marlene Dietrich and Rosa Valetti, and even the minor characters were remarkably vivid. And yet the events on the screen only managed to hold my attention, or even carry me away, for a few fleeting moments; a scene from the preceding newsreel kept creeping back into my mind: again the drum-major danced – and it is precisely the dancing which concerns me here – his way in and out of the cast of *The Blue Angel.*

The scene took place following Papen's assumption of office; it was entitled 'Anniversary of the Battle of Jutland, the Marine Guard of the Presidential Palace Marches through the Brandenburg Gate'.

I have seen many parades in my life, both in reality and on film; I know what Prussian goose-stepping is all about – when we were drilled on the Oberwiesenfeld in Munich the command was always: You've got to do it at least as well as they do it in Berlin! And yet never before, and, what is more, never again, have I seen anything to match what I saw that evening, despite all of the parades in front of the Führer and all the Nuremberg march-pasts. These men kicked their legs so high that the tips of their boots seemed to rise up above their noses, all in a single sweeping arc, all as one leg, and the posture of all of these bodies – no, this one body – was so convulsively taut that the whole movement appeared to freeze, in a way that the faces had already frozen, so that the troop as a whole gave the impression of being utterly lifeless and frenziedly animated at the same time. However, I had no time – or to be more precise I didn't have enough emotional reserves – to solve the mystery of this troop, because it formed only the backdrop to the figure on which all its attention, like mine, was focused: the drum-major.

Marching out in front, he had driven the outstretched fingers of his left hand hard into his hip, or rather he had arched his body into this supporting hand in an attempt to find his balance, whilst his right arm thrust the baton high up into the air and the tip of his boot appeared to reach up after it with every swing of his leg. The man hung there at an angle in mid-air, a monument without a plinth, mysteriously held erect by a cramp which stretched from head to toe paralysing his fingers and feet. His performance was not simply a drill, it was as much archaic dance as goose-stepping. The man was a fakir and a grenadier in one. Comparable tension and convulsive distortions could be seen in contemporary Expressionist paintings and heard in Expressionist literature of the period, but amidst the sober life of the most sober town its impact was that of unalloyed novelty. And it was highly contagious. A bellowing crowd pushed forward until it was almost touching the troops, frantically outstretched arms appeared to want to grab hold of them, a young man in the front row with eyes ablaze bore an expression of religious ecstasy.

The drum-major was my first truly shocking encounter with National Socialism, which, despite its rapid spread, had seemed to me up until this point a trivial and passing aberration on the part of immature malcontents. It was here that I saw for the first time that form of fanaticism unique to National Socialism; this mute figure forced me to confront the language of the Third Reich for the first time.

Chapter 3
Distinguishing Feature: Poverty

The LTI is destitute. Its poverty is a fundamental one; it is as if it had sworn a vow of poverty.

Mein Kampf, the bible of National Socialism, began to appear in 1925, and its publication literally fixed the essential features of its language. Following the Party's 'takeover {*Machtübernahme*}' in 1933 the language of a clique became the language of the people, i.e. it seized hold of all realms of public and private life: politics, the administration of justice, the economy, the arts, the sciences, schools, sport, the family, playschools and nurseries. (The language of a particular clique will invariably only encompass those areas which are relevant to the cohesion of the group and not the totality of life.) Of course the LTI also took hold of the army, indeed with particular zeal; there is, however, a reciprocal relationship between military language and the LTI. To be more precise, military language initially influenced the LTI and then military language itself was corrupted by the LTI. That is why I make special mention of this influence. A vast amount of literature of all kinds was published well into 1945, almost until the very last day – the *Reich*[1] still appeared when Germany had been reduced to ruins and Berlin was surrounded. Flyers, newspapers, magazines, schoolbooks, scientific and belletristic works.

---

[1]*Das Reich* was a weekly newspaper founded by Goebbels in 1940. It was intended that he should contribute an article to each issue.

In all this time and across all these areas the LTI remained impoverished and monotonous, and the word 'monotonous' should be taken as literally as the aforementioned 'fixed'. I often compared my reading habits to a trip in a free balloon forced to surrender itself to whatever winds come along and abandon any attempt at steering, so, when the opportunity to read them presented itself, I studied the *Myth of the Twentieth Century* followed by a *Pocket Yearbook for the Retail Trader,* leafed through a legal magazine here and a pharmaceutical one there, read the novels and poems which were permitted publication during these years, listened to workers whilst sweeping the streets and working in the machine room: it was always, be it printed or spoken, from the mouths of the educated or the uneducated, the same clichés and the same tone. And even in the case of those who were the most persecuted victims and of necessity mortal enemies of National Socialism, even amongst the Jews, the LTI was ubiquitous – in their conversations and letters, even in their books, insofar as they were still able to publish, it reigned supreme, as omnipotent as it was wretched, omnipotent indeed in its very poverty.

I have lived through three epochs of German history, the Wilhelmine era, the Weimar Republic and the Hitler period.

The Republic, almost suicidally, lifted all controls on freedom of expression; the National Socialists used to claim scornfully that they were only taking advantage of the rights granted them by the constitution when in their books and newspapers they mercilessly attacked the state and all its institutions and guiding principles using every available weapon of satire and belligerent sermonizing. There were no restraints whatsoever in the realm of the arts and sciences, aesthetics and philosophy. Nobody was bound to a particular moral dogma or ideal of beauty, everyone was free to choose. This motley intellectual freedom was celebrated as a tremendous and decisive leap forward compared with the imperial age.

But was the Wilhelmine period really so much less free?

During my studies of the French Enlightenment I have often been struck by a conspicuous affinity between the final decades of the *ancien régime* and the epoch of Wilhelm II. For sure, there was censorship under Louis XV and Louis XVI, and for enemies of the king and for unbelievers there was the Bastille and even the hangman; a series of very harsh judgements was passed, but spread out across the entire age there were not very many. And repeatedly, moreover often almost without hindrance, the enlightened thinkers were able to publish and distribute their writings, and each punishment meted out on one of their number merely gave rise to an intensification and expansion of the insurgent writings.

Similarly, an absolutist and moral austerity still officially prevailed under Wilhelm II; there were occasional trials on counts of lese-majesty or blasphemy or sexual impropriety. But the real sovereign over public opinion was *Simplizissimus*. When the Kaiser objected, Ludwig Fulda had to go without the Schiller Prize awarded to him for his *Talisman*; yet the theatre, press and satirical magazines indulged in attacks on the prevailing order which were a hundred times more aggressive than the tame *Talisman*. Under Wilhelm II one was also able to devote oneself freely to any of the intellectual currents from abroad and experiment in the realms of literature, philosophy and the arts without hindrance. It was only during the final years of the Empire that the war inevitably brought censorship. Following my release from hospital I worked for a long time as an assessor for the books inspectorate Ober-Ost, where the entire civil and military output of literature for this large administrative district was monitored according to special censorship regulations, which meant that the controls were considerably tighter than under the domestic censorship authorities. Yet how lenient the procedures were – even here a ban was very rarely decreed!

No, in the two eras that I can assess from personal experience, literary freedom was so far-reaching that the very few occasions on which people were silenced must be viewed as exceptions.

The result of all this was not only that there was a wholesale blossoming of the principal areas of language – encompassing spoken, written, journalistic, scientific and literary forms – not only that widespread literary currents such as Naturalism and Neo-Romanticism and Impressionism and Expressionism could prosper, but also that in all disciplines entirely individual linguistic styles could evolve.

This richness, which flourished until 1933, when it was abruptly stifled, must be recognized in order to grasp the true poverty of that uniform slavery which is a fundamental characteristic of the LTI.

The reason for this poverty appears to be as clear as day. In all its manifestations – and thus also in its language – the unadulterated character of National Socialist doctrine was guarded with a tyrannical resolve, sustained down to the last detail. Following the example of papal censorship there is a declaration on the title page of books dealing with Party matters: 'The NSDAP[2] has no reservations regarding the publication of this text. The President of the Official Party Board of Inspectors for the Protection of National Socialism {des NS}.' Only the membership of the Reich's Literary Chamber has a chance to make its voice heard and the entire press can only publish what is served up by central office, the most it can do is to take the text which is binding for everyone and slightly vary its wording – but these variations are restricted to varying the padding around the obligatory clichés. In the later years of the Third Reich the custom was established that on Friday evening Goebbels's latest article for the *Reich* would be read on Berlin Radio the day before the paper was published, thereby fixing each time the intellectual content of all the newspapers in the National Socialist sphere of influence for the coming week. Thus a mere handful of individuals provided the entire population with the one acceptable linguistic model. In fact it was perhaps ultimately only Goebbels himself who determined what was linguistically permissible, given that he not only had the benefit of clarity of expression over Hitler, but also continued to make regular pronouncements whilst the Führer gradually fell silent, partly in order to affect the pose of a silent deity and partly because he had nothing decisive left to say. The occasional personal nuances cultivated by people like Göring and Rosenberg were integrated by the Propaganda Minister into the tissue of his own language.

The absolute authority exercised by the linguistic prescriptions of this tiny group, or rather of this one man, extended across the entirety of German-speaking lands all the more thoroughly because the LTI did not draw a distinction between the spoken and the written language. Rather, everything was oration, had to be address, exhortation, invective. There was no stylistic difference between the speeches and the tracts of the Propaganda Minister, which explains why his tracts could so easily be declaimed. To declaim {*deklamieren*} literally means to talk sonorously on and on in a loud voice, even more literally: to scream out. The style binding for one and all was thus the style of the loud and vociferous rabble-rouser.

And here a more profound explanation for the impoverishment of the LTI opens up from beneath the obvious one. It was poor not only

---

[2]Abbreviation of *Nationalsozialistische deutsche Arbeiterpartei*, National Socialist German Workers' Party, the official title of the Nazi Party.

because everyone was forced to conform to the same pattern, but rather – and indeed more significantly – because in a measure of self-imposed constraint it only ever gave expression to one side of human existence.

Every language able to assert itself freely fulfils all human needs, it serves reason as well as emotion, it is communication and conversation, soliloquy and prayer, plea, command and invocation. The LTI only serves the cause of invocation. Regardless of whether a given subject properly belongs in a particular private or public domain – no, that's wrong, the LTI no more drew a distinction between private and public spheres than it did between written and spoken language – everything remains oral and everything remains public. One of their banners contends that 'You are nothing, your people is everything'. Which means that you are never alone with yourself, never alone with your nearest and dearest, you are always being watched by your own people.

It would therefore also be misleading if I were to claim that the LTI addressed itself in all cases exclusively to the will. For whoever appeals to the will always calls on the individual, even if he addresses himself to a general public made up of individuals. The sole purpose of the LTI is to strip everyone of their individuality, to paralyse them as personalities, to make them into unthinking and docile cattle in a herd driven and hounded in a particular direction, to turn them into atoms in a huge rolling block of stone. The LTI is the language of mass fanaticism. Where it addresses the individual - and not just his will but also his intellect – where it educates, it teaches means of breeding fanaticism and techniques of mass suggestion.

The French Enlightenment of the eighteenth century has two expressions, themes or scapegoats of which it is particularly fond: priestly deception and fanaticism. It doesn't believe in the genuineness of the priest's convictions, sees in every kind of cult a deceit aimed at making the community more fanatical and exploiting the resulting fanatics.

Never has a handbook of priestly deception been written with such shameless candour as Hitler's *Mein Kampf* – although the LTI calls it propaganda rather than priestly deception. For me it will always remain the greatest mystery of the Third Reich that this book could be promoted in public – indeed had to be – and that Hitler still came to power, and that he should have held sway for twelve years, despite the fact that this bible of National Socialism had been in circulation for years prior to the takeover. And never, at any point during the entire eighteenth century in France, was the word 'fanaticism' (together with its corresponding adjective) given such prominence and used so regularly – moreover in an entirely distorted sense – as was the case during the twelve years of the Third Reich.

Chapter 4
Partenau

During the second half of the 1920s I got to know a young man who had just signed up to join the officer training corps of the German army. His aunt by marriage, widow of a colleague at the university – she was politically far to the left and a passionate admirer of Soviet Russia – introduced him to us in a somewhat apologetic manner. She assured us that he was really an upright and good-natured young man and had chosen his career with an honest heart and without any trace of chauvinism or blood lust. For generations the sons of this family had become either priests or army officers; his late father had been a priest and his elder brother was already studying theology, and for this reason Georg – an excellent gymnast but a poor Latin scholar – saw the army as the right place for him; without doubt his men would one day be fortunate to have him as their superior.

Subsequently we often met up with Georg M. and felt that his aunt's judgement was thoroughly accurate.

Indeed he also turned out to be gentle and thoroughly decent at a time when things around him were no longer thoroughly decent. From his garrison at Stettin, where he was awaiting promotion to the rank of lieutenant, he visited us many times while we were living in Heringsdorf, despite the fact that National Socialist ideas were already catching on powerfully, with the result that prudent academics and officers were already avoiding coming into contact with both left-wing and, in particular, Jewish circles.

Soon afterwards M. was transferred, taking up the post of lieutenant in a Königsberg regiment, and for years we heard nothing more from him.

His aunt only referred to him on one occasion, reporting that he was now being trained as a pilot and was very happy to be a sportsman.

During the first year of the Hitler regime – I was still in my post and trying to avoid reading any Nazi literature – I came across a debut novel which had appeared in 1929, Max René Hesse's *Partenau*. I'm not sure if it was called 'The Novel of the German Army' in the title or only in the blurb, either way this general description stayed with me. Artistically speaking it was a weak book: a novella in the guise of a novel, a form the author had not yet mastered, too many shadowy figures who remained underdeveloped alongside the two protagonists, too many protracted military strategies which could only be of interest to someone with a professional involvement such as a budding general staff officer, overall an uneven work. The substance however, which was indeed intended to portray life in the German army, astounded me from the outset and later surfaced in my memory again and again: the friendship between Lieutenant Partenau and the Junker Kiebold. The lieutenant is a military genius, a stubborn patriot and a homosexual. The Junker only wants to be his disciple, not his lover, and the lieutenant shoots himself. He is undoubtedly conceived as a tragic figure: the sexual confusion is to some extent glorified as the heroic manifestation of genuine male friendship, and the unfulfilled patriotism is presumably meant to remind us of Heinrich von Kleist. The whole thing is written in the Expressionist style of the war years and early Weimar Republic, occasionally coloured with a rather precious inscrutability, somewhat in the manner of Fritz von Unruh. But Unruh and the German Expressionists of that period were lovers of peace, they were humanitarian and, despite their affection for their native homeland, thoroughly cosmopolitan. Partenau, on the other hand, is filled with thoughts of revenge, and his plans are anything but fantastical; he speaks of 'underground provinces' which are already in existence, of the underground formation of 'organized cells'. All that is missing is an outstanding leader. 'Only he who has more than the combined strength of a warrior and master builder will be able to forge their unseen slumbering powers into a mighty and responsive instrument.' If this glorious leader can be found he will give the Germans the space they need. This leader will transplant thirty-five million Czechs and other non-Germanic peoples to Siberia, and the European lands that they presently occupy will fall to the German people. They have a right to it on account of their superiority as human beings, even though their blood has been 'contaminated by Christianity' for two thousand years . . .

The Junker Kiebold is fired with enthusiasm by the ideas of his lieutenant. 'I would die tomorrow for Partenau's dreams and ideas', he declares; and to Partenau himself he later says, 'You were the first person I could safely ask what conscience, remorse and morality mean when set against notions of nationhood and soil, concepts which made us both shake our heads in profound incomprehension.'

As I said, this had already appeared as early as 1929. What an extraordinary anticipation of the language and the fundamental attitudes of the Third Reich! At that time, as I noted the crucial sentences in my diary, I could only have had a vague premonition. And I didn't believe it possible that these convictions could be put into action, that 'conscience, remorse and morality' could really be extinguished in a whole army and in a whole nation. It all appeared to me to be the undisciplined fantasy of someone who had lost their sense of proportion. And it must generally have been viewed in this way; otherwise it would be impossible to explain how such a virulent text came to be published in the Weimar Republic . . .

I gave our friend of the Soviet Union the book to read; she had just returned from a holiday in the country at her nephew's family home. After a couple of days she brought it back without a trace of surprise. She was familiar with it all already, both the style and the content; the author must have observed it all very accurately. 'Georg, that harmless young man who hasn't read a book in his life, has been writing in that style and toying with the same ideas for ages.'

How effortlessly people with harmless average dispositions adapt to their environment! With hindsight we remembered how in Heringsdorf the good-natured young man had already talked of a 'clean, cheerful war'. At the time we took it to be a cliché endorsed without so much as a second thought. But clichés do indeed soon take hold of us. 'Language which writes and thinks for you . . .'

On a number of subsequent occasions we heard the aunt report on her nephew's progress. As an air force officer he had become a man of considerable standing. Extravagant and unscrupulous, he was pervaded by his own sense of superiority and heroism. He splashed out on boots and clothes and expensive wines. It was his task to assign commissions for an officers' mess, and in the process a good deal of

what in lesser circles would be called bribe-money came his way. 'We
have every right to enjoy the good life,' he wrote, 'we put our lives on
the line every day.'

Not only his own: the good-natured young man was now also playing
with the lives of his men. Indeed he played with them so unscrupulously
that it even became too much for his teachers and role models. As
commander of a squadron he ordered a training flight in bad weather
which was so gruelling and dangerous that three people had to pay for
it with their lives. Given that the accident also destroyed two expensive
planes, the whole affair ended with the captain, as he had now become,
being put on trial. The sentence was expulsion from the army. Shortly
afterwards the war broke out; I have no idea what became of M., I
presume he was recalled to the army.

Partenau will barely receive even a mention in future literary histories;
it should however be granted all the greater a role in the history of
ideas. A major taproot of the LTI is embedded in the resentment and
aspirations of disappointed professional soldiers {*Landsknechte*}, to
whom a younger generation looked up as if they were tragic heroes.

Moreover they are specifically German professional soldiers. Prior
to the First World War there was a widespread joke about national
attitudes: representatives of different nations are given as a theme 'The
Elephant' and they can make of it what they will. The American writes
an essay 'How I shot my thousandth elephant', the German reports
'On the deployment of elephants in the second Punic war'. There are
a large number of Americanisms in the LTI as well as other foreign
ingredients, so many, indeed, that one can occasionally almost overlook
the German core. But it is there, terrifyingly and decisively there – no
one can claim apologetically that the problem was an infection which
flew in from abroad. Partenau the professional soldier was no figment
of the imagination, but rather a classically stylized portrait of countless
contemporaries and peers; he is well read, and not only at home in the
works of the German general staff: he has also read his Chamberlain
and his Nietzsche and Burckhardt's *Renaissance,* and so on.

Chapter 5
From the Diary of the First Year

A few pages showing how it all gradually but inexorably begins to permeate my life. Up until this point politics, the *vita publica,* has generally remained outside the domain of the diary. Since being appointed to the post of professor in Dresden I have now and again given myself a word of warning: you have now found your vocation, you must now dedicate yourself to your discipline – don't allow yourself to be distracted, concentrate! And now:

21 March 1933. Today the 'state ceremony' is being held in Potsdam. How can I work as if nothing was happening. I feel like Franz in *Götz:* 'The world at large, I know not how, forces me to heed it now.' But in fact I do know how. In Leipzig they have set up a commission to nationalize the university. On our university noticeboard there is a lengthy announcement (it is supposed to have been put up on all German university noticeboards): 'When a Jew writes German he lies'; in future he is to be forced to label books he publishes in German as 'translations from Hebrew'. The Congress of Psychologists was due to be held here in Dresden in April. The *Freiheitskampf* {Battle for Freedom} published an inflammatory article: 'What has happened to Wilhelm Wundt's discipline? . . . A real case of judaification . . . Get rid of them!' As a result the congress was cancelled . . . 'in order to avoid offence to individual participants'.

27 March. New words keep turning up, or old ones acquire new specialist meanings, or new combinations are formed which rapidly ossify into stereotypes. The SA is now known loftily – loftiness is indeed now perpetually *de rigueur,* for it is the done thing to be fervent – as the 'brown army'. Foreign Jews, particularly those from France, England and America, are today frequently referred to as 'global Jews {*Weltjuden*}'. Equally prevalent is the term 'international Jewry {*Internationales Judentum*}', with the global Jew and global Jewry {*Weltjudentum*} presumably constituting the German version. This is an ominous translation into German: does this mean that Jews are to be found everywhere on earth, except, that is, in Germany? And where are they within Germany itself? The global Jews disseminate 'atrocity propaganda' and spread 'horror stories', and if we report so much as a scrap of what happens here every day then we too are guilty of disseminating atrocity propaganda and are punished accordingly. Meanwhile the boycott of Jewish shops and doctors is in the offing. The distinction between 'Aryan' and 'non-Aryan' governs everything. One could draw up a dictionary of the new language.

In a toy shop I saw a child's ball with a swastika printed on it. Would a ball like this belong in the dictionary?

(Shortly thereafter a law was passed 'to protect national symbols' which prohibited decoration of this kind on toys and other such nonsense. However the question of how to delimit the LTI continued to preoccupy me.)

10 April. You are '*artfremd* {alien}' if you have 25 per cent non-Aryan blood. 'In borderline cases a ruling will be made by the expert in racial research.' *Limpieza de la sangre* as in sixteenth-century Spain. But at that time it was a matter of faith, while today it is zoology + business. Spain – that reminds me. It seems to me to be an ironic twist of world history that 'the Jew Einstein' is ostentatiously appointed to a chair at a Spanish university and accepts the post.

20 April. Yet again a new opportunity for celebration, a new national holiday for the people: Hitler's birthday. The term '*Volk* {people}' is now as customary in spoken and written language as salt at table, everything is spiced with a soupçon of *Volk: Volksfest* {festival of the people}, *Volksgenosse* {comrade of the people}, *Volksgemeinschaft* {community of the people}, *volksnah* {one of the people}, *volksfremd* {alien to the people}, *volksentstammt* {descended from the people} . . .

The conference of doctors in Wiesbaden was a pitiful affair! They thank Hitler solemnly and repeatedly as the 'Saviour of Germany' – even if the racial question hasn't yet quite been sorted out, even if 'foreigners' such as Wassermann, Ehrlich and Neißer have achieved great things.

Amongst my 'racial comrades {*Rassegenossen*}' there are those close to me who declare this double 'even if' to be an act of courage, and that is the most pitiful aspect of the whole thing. No, most pitiful of all is the fact that I am continually forced to confront the insanity of this distinction between Aryans and Semites, that I am repeatedly compelled to observe the frightful eclipse and enslavement of Germany from one point of view only, the Jewish one. It feels like a victory of Hitlerism over me personally. I do not wish to concede that victory.

17 June. What sort of a compatriot is Jan Kiepura? Recently he was banned from giving a concert in Berlin. At that time he was the Jew Kiepura. Then he appeared in a film produced by the Hugenberg Company. There he was 'the famous tenor from La Scala Milan'. Then he was whistled at in Prague for singing the song 'Tonight or Never!' in German. There he was the German singer Kiepura.

(It was only much later that I discovered that he was a Pole.)

9 July. A few weeks ago Hugenberg stood down and his German Nationalist Party 'disbanded'. Since then I have noticed that where we once had the 'national uprising' we now have the 'National Socialist revolution', that Hitler is being referred to more frequently than before as the 'People's Chancellor' and that there is talk of a 'total state'.

28 July. A ceremony has taken place at the graves of 'those who removed Rathenau'. There is so much disdain, amorality or trenchant master morality implicit in this expression, this promotion of murder to the status of a profession. And how sure of oneself one must feel when one uses language in this manner!

But do they really feel so sure of themselves? There is also a good deal of hysteria in the government's words and deeds. The hysteria of language should one day be studied as a phenomenon in itself. This perpetual threatening with the death penalty! And then recently the halting of all traffic between 12 o'clock and 12.40 to 'facilitate a nationwide search for couriers and publications hostile to the state'. Surely that is direct fear and indirect fear in equal measure. What I mean by this is that this artificial generation of suspense, copied from American cinema and thrillers, is obviously just as much a premeditated means of propaganda as the direct creation of fear, but that, on the other hand, only those who are themselves afraid turn to this kind of propaganda.

And what is the purpose of the endlessly repeated articles – endless repetition indeed appears to be one of the principal stylistic features of their language – about the victorious battle over unemployment in East Prussia. No one really needs to know that it is modelled on the *battaglia del grano* of the Italian Fascists; but even the most witless amongst us must be saying to himself that in rural areas there are few unemployed during harvest time and that you can't draw any conclusions about a general, lasting reduction in the number of unemployed from this short-lived fall in unemployment in East Prussia.

But I see the most obvious symptom of their inner insecurity in the public appearances of Hitler himself. Yesterday in the newsreel there was a sound film sequence: the Führer says a few words to a large gathering. He clenches his fists, he contorts his face, it is more a wild scream than a speech, an outburst of rage: 'On 30 January they (he means the Jews of course) laughed at me – that smile will be wiped off their faces . . .!' At the moment he appears to be omnipotent, perhaps he is; but this recording testifies to almost blind rage. But do you go on talking in that way about enduring for a thousand years and about annihilated enemies if you are so sure of this endurance and this annihilation? I left the cinema with what almost amounted to a glimmer of hope.

22 August. Signs that people are growing weary of Hitler are emerging from the most diverse strata of society. Trainee teacher Fl., not an especially bright spark but a decent young fellow, spoke to me on the street in civilian clothes: 'Don't be surprised if at some point you see me wearing my *Stahlhelm*[1] uniform with the swastika on the armband. I have to wear it – but this coercion doesn't change us in any way. A *Stahlhelm* remains a *Stahlhelm* and is certainly better than the SA. We, the German nationalists, will come to the rescue!' – Frau Krappmann, the deputy concierge, married to a postal inspector: 'Professor Klemperer, by 1 October the "Hospitality" club of the postal workers of section A 19 will be brought into line {*gleichgeschaltet*} by the Nazis. But they will not receive any of its capital; a sausage dinner will be organized for the gentlemen, followed by coffee and cake for the ladies.' – Annemarie, clinically blunt as ever, relates the remark of a colleague wearing an armband with a swastika: 'What is one supposed to do? It's like a lady's Camelia sanitary towel {*Cameliabinde*}.' – And Kuske, the

---

[1] The *Stahlhelm* was a Nationalist ex-servicemen's organization formed in 1918. From December 1933 all members under 35 had to join the SA.

grocer, recites the new evening prayer: 'Dear Lord, make me dumb, so that to Hohnstein I never come {*Lieber Gott, mach mich stumm, daß ich nicht nach Hohnstein kumm*}.' . . . Am I deceiving myself if I derive some hope from all this? This total madness cannot be sustained once the people's intoxication has worn off, once the hangover has begun.

25 August. What use are the symptoms of weariness? Everyone is afraid. It had been arranged that my piece entitled 'Germany's Image of France' would be published by Quelle & Meyer and would first appear in the *Neuphilologische Monatsschrift* (New Philological Monthly), edited by the Vice-Chancellor or Professor Hübner, a thoroughly moderate and decent schoolmaster. A few weeks ago he wrote to me in a dejected tone, asking whether I would at least be willing to hold back on publishing the study for the foreseeable future; he added that there were 'factory cells {*Betriebszellen*}' in the publishing house (a strange term combining the mechanical and the organic – this new language!), and that they wanted to preserve a good specialist journal, and that the political leaders were not so much interested in the actual discipline itself . . .

After that I turned to the Diesterweg publishing house, for whom my thoroughly factual piece, containing ample documentary material, ought to have been ideal fodder. The speediest of rejections followed; the reason given being that the study was 'entirely backward-looking' and was lacking 'the necessary national {*völkisch*} angles'. The opportunities for publishing have been cut off – when will they gag me? During the summer semester my status as a 'front line soldier' protected me – how long will the protection last?

28 August. I really must not lose heart, the people won't go along with it for long. It is said that Hitler relied in particular on the petty bourgeoisie, and that was clearly the case.

We went on a 'mystery tour'. Two complete coach loads, around eighty people, the most petty-bourgeois company imaginable, entirely amongst their own kind, completely homogeneous, not a hint of the working classes or of the more sophisticated, more free-thinking bourgeoisie. In Lübau there was a stop for coffee accompanied by cabaret-style speeches from the courier or steward; that is customary on these excursions. The compère begins with a pathos-ridden poem in praise of the Führer and saviour of Germany, of the new national community, and so on, right through the whole National Socialist rosary. Everyone is silent and apathetic, at the end you notice from the clapping of one single individual, from this completely isolated clapping, that the ovation is entirely absent. Then the man tells a story of what apparently happened to him at the hairdresser's. A Jewish woman wants to have her hair crimped. 'I regret madam that I am not allowed to.' – 'You are not allowed to?' 'Impossible! The Führer solemnly promised on the occasion of the boycott of the Jews – and, despite all horror stories to the contrary, it remains true right up to the present day – that no one is to harm a hair on a Jew's head.' This was followed by laughing and clapping which lasted several minutes. – Can I draw any conclusions from this? Surely this joke and its reception are important for any sociological and political study.

19 September. In the cinema scenes of the Nuremberg Rally. Hitler consecrates new SA colours by touching them with the Blood Banner {*Blutfahne*} of 1923. Each meeting of the flags is accompanied by cannon fire. If that isn't a mixture of religious and theatrical ceremony, I don't know what is! Never mind the action on stage – the word *'Blutfahne'* says it all. 'Noble brothers, look hither: we are suffering blood-soaked martyrdom!' This whole National Socialist business is lifted from the political realm to that of religion by the use of a single word. And the spectacle and the word undoubtedly work, people sit there piously rapt – no one sneezes or coughs, there is no rustling of sandwich paper, no sound of anyone sucking a sweet. The rally is a ritualistic action, National Socialism is a religion – and I would have myself believe that its roots are shallow and weak?

10 October. My colleague Robert Wilbrandt visited us. Would we like to receive a guest who is an enemy of the state? He had suddenly been dismissed. The dreaded phrase reads 'politically unreliable {*politisch unzuverlässig*}'. Someone had dug up the affair surrounding Gumbel, the pacifist he had stood up for in Marburg. And moreover: he had written a little book about Marx. He wants to head for South Germany and bury himself in his work in some remote village . . . If only I could do the same! Tyranny and insecurity are on the increase every day. Dismissals amongst professional colleagues with Jewish connections. Olschki in Heidelberg, Friedmann in Leipzig, Spitzer in Marburg, Lerch, the utterly Aryan Lerch, in Münster, because he lives 'in concubinage with a Jew'. The blond and blue-eyed Hatzfeld, a pious Catholic, asked me timidly whether I still held my post. In reply I wanted to know why he was afraid for his own entirely unSemitic self. He sent me an offprint of a piece of research; under his name was added in ink 'kind regards – 25%'.

The specialist philological periodicals and the journal of the Association of Universities are so replete with the jargon of the Third Reich that every page literally makes you want to be sick. 'Hitler's iron broom' – 'science on a National Socialist footing' – 'the Jewish spirit' – 'the Novembrists' (these are the revolutionaries of 1918).

23 October. A 'voluntary winter charity' donation has been deducted from my salary; no one asked me about it beforehand. It is apparently a new tax from which you can no more exempt yourself than you can with any other taxes; the voluntary aspect merely consists in the option to pay over and above the prescribed amount, and even this option constitutes for many a thinly disguised compulsion. And leaving the hypocritical adjective aside, isn't the noun itself a covert coercion, already itself a plea, an appeal to the feelings. Charity rather than tax: that is part of the national community {*Volksgemeinschaft*}. The jargon of the Third Reich sentimentalizes; that is always suspicious.

29 October. A sudden order from on high, with far-reaching implications for the university timetable: Tuesday afternoon is to be kept free of lectures, all students are to be trained during these hours in military sporting exercises. At almost exactly the same time I came across the word on a cigarette packet: Military Sport brand {*Marke Wehrsport*}. A half mask is the same as being half unmasked. Universal conscription is banned under the Treaty of Versailles; sport is allowed – officially we are not doing anything illegal, although we are a little bit, and we also make it a little threatening, we gesture towards our fist, which remains – for the moment at least – clenched in our pocket. When will I find in the language of this regime a single, truly honest word?

– Yesterday evening Gusti W. visited us, back after four months from Turö, where she and her sister Maria Strindberg had stayed with Karin Michaelis. Apparently a small group of communist émigrés had come together there. Gusti related the dreadful details. 'Horror stories' of course, which may only be whispered secretly into each other's ears. In particular the misery experienced by the now 60-year-old Erich Mühsam in an especially evil concentration camp. You could vary the proverb and say: something worse is a friend of something bad;[2] I really

---

[2]The original proverb is *'Das Bessere ist der Feind des Guten'* (Something better is the enemy of something good).

am beginning to see Mussolini's government as an almost humane and
European one.

I ask myself whether the words 'émigrés {*Emiganten*}' and
'concentration camp {*Konzentrationslager*}' should be included in
a dictionary of Hitler's language. Emigrés: that is an international
designation for those who fled from the Great French Revolution.
Brandes entitled one volume of his history of European literature 'The
Literature of the Emigrés'. Then there was talk of the émigrés from the
Russian revolution. And now there is a group of German émigrés –
Germany is in their camp! – and the 'émigré mentality' is a popular
mot savant. Thus in future this word will not necessarily have the Third
Reich's stench of putrefaction clinging to it. Things are quite different
in the case of 'concentration camp'. I only heard the word as a boy,
and at the time it had for me a thoroughly exotic, colonial and quite
un-German ring to it: during the Boar War there was much talk of
compounds or concentration camps in which the captured Boars
were guarded by the English. The word then disappeared entirely from
common German usage. And now it suddenly reappears, describing a
German institution, a peacetime establishment set up on European soil
and directed against Germans, a permanent establishment and not a
temporary measure against the enemy in time of war. I think that when
in future people say 'concentration camp' everyone will think of Hitler's
Germany and only of Hitler's Germany . . . Is it cold-heartedness and
petty schoolmasterishness on my part which makes me focus my mind
repeatedly and increasingly on the philology of this misery? I genuinely
examine my conscience. No! It is self-preservation.

9 November. Today in my Corneille seminar there were all of two
participants: Lore Isakowitz with the yellow Jewish card; Hirschowicz,
a non-Aryan student, father Turkish, with the blue card for stateless
people – the real German students have brown cards. (Once again
the question of delimitation: is this an aspect of language in the Third
Reich?) . . . Why do I have so worryingly few students attending my
lectures? French is no longer a popular option for students training for
the teaching profession; it is considered unpatriotic, and, to crown it all,
lectures on French literature delivered by a Jew! You really do have to
have a little courage to attend my lectures. But it is also the case that all
subjects are now poorly attended: the students are having far too much
of their time taken up by '*Wehrsport*' and a dozen other similar activities.

And to cap it all: now, of all times, every single one of them has to help almost incessantly with election propaganda, take part in parades, meetings, and so on.

This is certainly the most preposterous piece of humbug I have yet experienced from Goebbels, and I can hardly believe it will be possible to better it. The plebiscite for the Führer's policies and the 'unified list of candidates {*Einheitsliste*}' for the Reichstag. For my part I find the whole business staggeringly crude and clumsy. Plebiscite – for anyone who knows the word (and anyone who doesn't will have it explained to them), plebiscite is after all invariably associated with Napoleon III, someone with whom Hitler really ought not to associate himself. And the 'unified list of candidates' shows all too clearly that the Reichstag is no longer a parliament. And the entire propaganda is truly such consummate humbug – people wear little badges on their coat lapels bearing the word 'Yes', you can't say no to the people selling these emblems without appearing suspicious – it is such a rape of the general public that it ought to bring about the very opposite of its intended effect. . .

Ought to – but I have been mistaken on every occasion so far. I make intellectual judgements, and Herr Goebbels banks on the intoxication of the masses. And, what's more, on the anxiety of the intellectuals. Particularly given that nobody believes that the secrecy of the ballot will be observed.

He has already won a massive victory over the Jews. On Sunday there was a repulsive scene with Herr and Frau K., whom we had had to invite for coffee. I say had to, because the snobbery of this woman, who without so much as a thought repeats parrot-fashion the latest tittle-tattle or current opinion, has been getting on our nerves for a long time now; but her husband, although he likes to play the role of the wise Nathan,[3] always seemed to me to be tolerably sensible. So it was that on Sunday he explained that with 'a heavy heart' he had decided, just like the Central Organization of Jewish Citizens, to vote 'Yes' in the plebiscite, and his wife added that the Weimar system had finally proved itself to be unworkable and that one had to 'see things for what they really are'. I lost my composure entirely, banged my fist on the table so that the cups rattled and repeatedly shouted the same question at the

---

[3]The protagonist of Lessing's play *Nathan der Weise,* Nathan the Wise.

husband: did he believe the policies of this government to be criminal
or not. He answered in a most dignified manner that I was not entitled
to ask this question, and then inquired sarcastically for his part, as to
why, in that case, I was remaining in office. I said that I had not been
appointed by Hitler's government, didn't serve it and hoped to outlive
it. Frau K. continued to maintain that the Führer – she really did say 'the
Führer' – was undeniably a brilliant man, whose extraordinary influence
couldn't be denied and from whom one could not pull back . . . Today
I almost want to offer my apologies to the K.s for the extent of my
ferocity. In the meantime I have heard very similar opinions expressed
by all kinds of Jewish people in our circle of friends. People who, without
a doubt, must be regarded as intellectuals and who would generally be
numbered amongst the quiet and independent thinkers . . . Some kind
of fog has descended which is enveloping everybody.

10 November, evening. I heard the apogee of propaganda this
afternoon on Dember's radio (our Jewish physicist, already dismissed,
but also already negotiating for a professorship in Turkey). On this
occasion the organization by Goebbels, who also served as the
compère of his own show, amounted to a masterpiece. The emphasis
is on work and peace in the service of peaceful work. First the sound of
sirens wailing across the whole of Germany and then a minute of silence
across the whole of Germany – they have picked this up from America
of course, and from the peace celebrations at the end of the Great War.
This is followed by the framework around Hitler's speech, perhaps not
a great deal more original either (cf. Italy), but executed to absolute
perfection. A factory floor in Siemensstadt. For a few minutes the noise
of all the machines at work, the hammering, rattling, rumbling, whistling,
grinding. Then the sirens and singing and the gradual falling silent of the
wheels as they are brought to a standstill. Then quietly, out of the silence,
Goebbels's deep voice with the messenger's report. And only after all of
this: Hitler himself, HE speaks for three quarters of an hour. It was the
first time that I had heard one of his speeches from beginning to end,
and my impression was essentially the same as before. For the most
part an excessively agitated, hectoring, often rasping voice. The only
difference was that on this occasion many passages were declaimed
in the whining tone of an evangelizing sectarian. HE advocates peace,
HE proclaims peace, he wants the unanimous support of Germany
not out of personal ambition, but only in order to be able to defend

peace against the attacks of a rootless international clique of profiteers, who for the sake of their own profit unscrupulously set populations of countless millions against each other . . .

All of this, together with the well-rehearsed heckling ('The Jews!'), I had of course been conversant with for a long time. But in all its hackneyed overfamiliarity, its deafening mendacity – audible surely to the deafest of ears – it acquired a special and novel authority from a peculiarity of the foregoing propaganda, an aspect which I consider to be the most outstanding and ultimately decisive amongst its successful individual ingredients. The advance notice and radio announcement stated: 'Ceremony between 13.00 and 14.00. In the thirteenth hour Adolf Hitler will visit the workers.' This is, as everyone knows, the language of the Gospel. The Lord, the Saviour visits the poor and the prodigal. Ingenious, right down to the timing. Thirteen hundred hours – no, 'the thirteenth hour' – sounds too late, but HE will work miracles, for him there is no such thing as too late. The Blood Banner at the rally was of the same order. But this time the dividing line separating it from ecclesiastical ceremony has been broken down, the antiquated costume has been shed and the legend of Christ has been transported into the here and now: Adolf Hitler, the Redeemer, visits the workers in Siemensstadt.

14 November. Why do I reproach K. S. and the others? When the government's triumphal victory was announced yesterday – 93 per cent of votes for Hitler, 40 million Yes, 2 million No; 39 million in favour of the Reichstag (that splendid unified list of candidates), 3 million 'spoilt' ballot papers – I was just as overwhelmed as everyone else. I could keep telling myself, first, that the result was rigged, and second, in the absence of any controls, also undoubtedly doctored, just as a mixture of sham and intimidation must be at the root of the news from London that people there are particularly surprised that there was even a majority of Yes votes in the concentration camps – and yet I was, and indeed remain, at the mercy of the results of this triumph for Hitler.

I am reminded of the crossing we made twenty-five years ago from Bornholm to Copenhagen. In the night a storm had raged accompanied by terrible seasickness; but soon one was sitting on deck under the beautiful morning sun, protected by the nearby coast, in a calm sea, looking forward to breakfast. At the end of the long bench a little girl stood up, ran to the deck rail, and threw up. A second later her mother, who was sitting next to her, stood up and did the same. Almost at once the gentleman next to the lady followed suit. And then a young boy, and then . . . the movement worked its way steadily and swiftly along the bench. No one was passed over. At our end we were still far away from the blast: it was observed with interest, there was laughter, there were mocking expressions. And then the vomiting got closer and the laughter subsided, and then people were running towards the rail from our end. I looked on attentively and observed myself closely. I told myself that there is such a thing as objective observation, and that I had been trained in it, and that there was such a thing as a firm resolve, and I looked forward to breakfast – and at that point it was my turn and I was forced to the rail just like all the others.

*

I have scribbled down the raw material from my diary relating to the new conditions and the new language for the first few months of Nazism. At that time I was incomparably better off than later; I was still in post and in my own house, I was still the observer left almost entirely unmolested. On the other hand I was not yet at all dulled, I was still so used to living in a state governed by the rule of law that I considered many things at the time to be the depths of hell which I would later deem to be at most its vestibule – Dante's Limbo. At any rate, regardless of how much worse it was going to get, everything which was later to emerge in terms of National Socialist attitudes, actions and language was already apparent in embryonic form in these first months.

Chapter 6
The First Three Words of the Nazi Language

The very first word which struck me as specifically Nazi – not in its formation but in its usage – is associated in my mind with the bitterness surrounding the first loss of a friend brought about by the Third Reich. Thirteen years previously, we and T. had all moved to Dresden and the Institute of Science and Technology at the same time, I as a professor, he as a new student. He was almost what you would call a child prodigy. Child prodigies often go on to disappoint, but he seemed already to have passed through the perilous years of juvenile prodigiousness unscathed. From the most petty bourgeois background imaginable and very poor, he had been discovered during the war in a manner worthy of a novel. A famous visiting professor wanted to have a new machine demonstrated to him in the test bay of a Leipzig factory; as a result of conscription to military service there was a severe shortage of engineers, the only mechanic on duty at the time knew nothing about it, the professor got annoyed – at that moment a greasy young apprentice crawled out from under the machine and provided the necessary explanation. He had acquired the relevant information by paying attention to things that were none of his business and through independent studies at night. The professor promptly stepped in with a helping hand, the boy's remarkable energy was reinforced by his success, and a short time later, almost on one and the same day, this young man, whose formal education had not proceeded beyond elementary school level, passed both his exam as a journeyman fitter and his university entrance qualification. As a result the opportunity of earning a living through a career in technology whilst studying at the same time offered itself to him. His mathematical and technological gifts stood the test of time: at a very young age, and without having taken the normal examination to qualify as an engineer, he was appointed to a high-ranking post.

But what I found attractive about him – despite the fact that I am unfortunately someone for whom nothing could be more alien than the mysteries of mathematics and technology – was the all-round character of his educational aspirations and reflections. He came and stayed in our house, and from being a lodger he became almost a foster son, calling us, half jokingly but also very much in earnest, mother and father; we also contributed to some extent to his education. He married young and the warm, close relationship between us remained unaffected. That it could be destroyed by differences of political opinion never entered the mind of any of the four of us.

And then National Socialism penetrated Saxony. I noticed in T. the first signs of a change in attitude. I asked him how he could sympathize with these people. 'They don't want anything different from the Socialists,' he said, 'they are also a workers' party after all.' – 'Can't you see that they have set their sights on war?' – 'At most a war of liberation which would benefit the entire national community, thereby helping the workers and the ordinary people as well. . .'

I began to have serious doubts about the extent and strength of his common sense. I tried a different tack in my attempt to make him more sceptical. 'You have lived in my house for a number of years, you know the way I think, and you have often said yourself that you have learned something from us and that your moral values accord with ours – how, in the light of all this, can you possibly support a party which, on account of my origin, denies me any right to be a German or even a human being?' – 'You're taking it all much too seriously, Babba.' – (The Saxon term of address was presumably meant to give his remark, and indeed the whole discussion, a lighter tone.) – 'The fuss and bother about the Jews is only there for propaganda purposes. You wait, when Hitler is at the helm he'll be far too busy to insult the Jews . . .'

But the fuss and bother did have an effect – on our foster son as well. Some time later I asked him about a young man he knew. He shrugged his shoulders: 'He's working at AEG, you know what that means? . . . You don't? . . . "Alles echte Germanen {All Teutons through and through}?" 'And he laughed and was surprised that I didn't join in.

And then, when we hadn't seen one another for some time, he rang us up and invited us out for a meal, it was shortly after Hitler came to power. 'How are things with you at work?' I asked. 'Very good!' he answered. 'Yesterday we had a great day. There were a few shameless communists in Okrilla, so we organized a punitive expedition.' – 'What did you do?' – 'You know, we made them run the gauntlet of rubber truncheons, a mild dose of castor-oil, no bloodshed but very effective all the same, a proper punitive expedition in fact.'

Strafexpedition {punitive expedition} is the first term which I recognized as being specifically National Socialist, it was the very first of my LTI and is the very last word I heard from T.; I hung up without even bothering to refuse the invitation.

For me the word *Strafexpedition* was the embodiment of brutal arrogance and contempt for people who are in any way different, it sounded so colonial, you could see the encircled Negro village, you could hear the cracking of the hippopotamus whip. Later, but unfortunately not for very long, this memory had something comforting about it despite all the bitterness. 'A mild dose of castor-oil': it was so obvious that this operation was imitating the fascist customs of the Italians: the whole of Nazism seemed to me to be nothing more than an Italian infection. This comforting thought dissolved into thin air like early morning mist when confronted with the increasingly inescapable truth: the fundamental, mortal sin of Nazism was German and not Italian.

In fact the memory of the National Socialist (or fascist) term *Strafexpedition* itself would have faded for me as it did for millions of others had it not had the personal association, because it was only used in the early stage of the Third Reich, indeed it was overtaken by the very founding of the regime, made obsolete like the flechette by the aerial bomb. The semi-private, recreational sport of the punitive expedition was immediately replaced by the routine, official police operation, and castor-oil by the concentration camp. And six years after the beginning of the Third Reich the domestic expedition-turned-police-operation was drowned out by the pandemonium of world war, conceived by those who unleashed it as a kind of punitive expedition against all kinds of despised peoples. That's how words fade away. – With the other two, which signified the very opposite, it is an entirely different matter – You are naught, but I am everything! – they require no personal reminiscence in order to remain firmly in the memory, they will be there until the very last and will not be left out of any history of the LTI. The next linguistic note in my diary reads: *Staatsakt* {state occasion}. Goebbels staged it, the first in an almost incalculably long series, on 21 March 1933 in the Garrison Church in Potsdam. (A strange insensitivity of the Nazis to the potential for satirical comedy to which they lay themselves open; one is almost tempted at times to believe in their subjective innocence! They used the glockenspiel of the Garrison Church, 'Be Forever Honest and True', as the jingle for Berlin Radio, and installed their farcical, non-existent parliamentary sessions in a theatre, the auditorium of the Krolloper.)

If the LTI verb *aufziehen* {to mount, set up} can legitimately be applied anywhere, then it is undoubtedly here; the fabric of these state occasions was always set up according to the same pattern, albeit in two different manifestations – one with and one without a coffin in the middle. The splendour of the banners, parades, garlands, fanfares and choruses, the all-embracing framework of speeches, these all remained constant features and were undoubtedly modelled on the example of Mussolini. During the war the coffin increasingly took centre stage and the already somewhat diminished impact of this advertising ploy was revitalized by the whiff of scandal. Whenever a state funeral was held for a general who had died in action or had had a fatal accident, the rumour went round that he had fallen out of grace with the Führer and had been removed on his orders. The fact that rumours of this kind could spread is – regardless of whether they corresponded to the truth or not – valid evidence both for the truth content attributed to the LTI and for the fact that people believed it could spread lies. The greatest lie which any state occasion ever voiced, however, and a lie which has since been proved as such, was the funeral ceremony for the Sixth Army and its Field Marshal. Ammunition for future acts of heroism was to be beaten out of defeat by claiming that many had loyally stuck it out until the bitter end, when in fact they had given themselves up in order not to be slaughtered like thousands of their comrades for a pointless and criminal cause. In his Stalingrad book Plievier contrived to make much shocking satirical mileage out of this state occasion.

In purely linguistic terms this word is doubly conceited. On the one hand it indicates that honours bestowed by National Socialism amount to recognition by the state, which indeed corresponds with the facts. It thus embodies the *L'Etatc'est moi* of absolutism. But to this statement it immediately adds a demand. A state ceremony is an integral part of the history of the state, consequently something that must be continually kept alive in the minds of the people. A state ceremony has a particularly grand historical significance.

Which brings us to the word that National Socialism used from beginning to end with inordinate profligacy. It takes itself so seriously, it is so convinced of the permanence of its institutions, or at least is so keen to persuade others of that permanence, that every trifle, however insignificant, and everything that it comes into contact with, has a historical significance. Every speech delivered by the Führer is historical {*historisch*}, even if he says the same thing a hundred times over, every meeting the Führer has with the Duce is historical, even if it doesn't make the slightest difference to the existing state of things; the victory of a German racing car is historical, as is the official opening of a new motorway, and every single road, and every single section of every single road, is officially inaugurated; every harvest festival is historical, every Party Rally, every feast day of any kind; and since the Third Reich seems to know nothing but feast days – you could say that it suffered, indeed was mortally ill, from a lack of the everyday, just as the human body can be mortally ill from a lack of salt – it views every single day of its life as historical.

Over and over again the word was used in headlines, editorials and speeches and robbed of its venerable ring! If it is to recover it will have to be afforded infinite protection.

It is not necessary, however, to deliver a similar warning against the excessive use of the word *Staatsakt,* given that we don't have a state any more.

Chapter 7
Aufziehen

I wind up a clock {*aufziehen*}, I mount the warp on a loom {*aufziehen*}, I wind up a mechanical toy {*aufziehen*}: what we are dealing with in each case is a mechanical activity executed on an inanimate object which offers no resistance.

The automaton, the humming top, the walking, nodding animal all point towards the metaphorical use of the term: I wind someone up {*aufziehen*}. Which means that I tease him, I make a fool of him, I walk all over him; Bergson's definition of comedy as the process whereby something living is turned into something inanimate is here reinforced by common usage.

The term '*Aufziehen* {a wind-up}' is undoubtedly harmless in this context, but nevertheless a pejorative. (This is the word used by philologists to designate an 'impaired' or diminished meaning; from the Imperial name Augustus, the Exalted One, derives the pejorative 'stupid old Auguste' the circus clown.)[1]

In the modern age '*aufziehen*' acquired a well-defined new meaning, both positive and, at the same time, decidedly pejorative. It was said of an advert that it had been impressively set up {*aufgezogen*}. This constituted an acknowledgement of the commercial efficacy of the advertising campaign, but it also indicated that there was an element of excess, of sales patter which did not precisely match the real value of the thing on offer. The verb cropped up as an unequivocal and

---

[1]'*Der dumme August*' is proverbial in German for someone who plays the fool.

unmistakable pejorative when a theatre critic judged that an author had carried off this or that scene on a grand scale {*groß aufgezogen*}. This meant that the man was more an unscrupulous technician (and seducer of the audience) than a genuine writer.

Right at the beginning of the Third Reich it looked for a moment as if the LTI would adopt this metaphorical connotation of censure. The Nazi newspapers celebrated as an act of patriotism the fact that 'decent students' had 'destroyed Professor Magnus Hirschfeld's Institute for Sexual Research that paraded as science {*wissenschaftlich aufgezogen*}'. Hirschfeld was a Jew and thus his Institute 'paraded as science' and was not truly scientific.

But a few days later it became apparent that the verb *per se* no longer had any pejorative associations. On 30 June 1933 Goebbels stated in the University of Political Science that the NSDAP had 'set up {*aufgezogen*} a massive organization involving millions of people and bringing together all kinds of activities including folk theatre, popular games, tourism and sport, hiking, singing and all supported financially by the state'. Here '*aufziehen* {to set up}' is nothing but honest, and when the government renders account for the success of the propaganda leading up to the vote in the Saarland it talks of 'an action set up {*aufgezogen*} on a grand scale'. It doesn't enter anyone's mind to associate the word with advertising. In 1935 Holle & Co. publishes a translation from the English of *The Autobiography of a Japanese Publisher. Seiji Noma*. In it appears the highly appreciative statement: 'I now decided to construct {*aufziehen*} an exemplary organization for the training of student orators.'

The total indifference towards the mechanistic meaning of the verb has its origins in the fact that it is repeatedly uttered by an organization. This reveals one of the foremost tensions within the LTI: whilst stressing the organic and natural growth it is at the same time swamped by mechanistic expressions and insensitive to the stylistic incongruities and lack of dignity in such combinations as 'a constructed organization {*aufgezogene Organisation*}'.

'The only question is whether the Nazis can actually be held responsible for '*aufziehen*'', F. interjected. We were working at the same mixing drum for German teas during a nightshift in Summer 1943, it was extremely exhausting work, especially given the heat, as we had to keep our heads and faces covered like surgeons because of the terrible dust;

during the breaks we took off our glasses, protective handkerchiefs and caps – F. wore an old judge's biretta, he had been a senior official at a district court – sat on a box and debated national psychology, if we weren't discussing the progress of the war, that is. Like everyone else who lived in the Jews' House in the narrow Sporergasse, he perished during the night of 13 to 14 February 1945.

He claimed to have heard and read the word *'aufziehen'* in an entirely neutral sense in around 1920. 'Contemporary with and similar to the verb *plakatieren* {to placard or broadcast}', he said. I replied that I had no knowledge of *'aufziehen'* being used in a neutral sense at that time, and that the combination he remembered with *'plakatieren'* must inevitably imply a pejorative tone. Above all, however – and this is a principle I adhere to in relation to all significant observations of this kind – I never try to ascertain the first occurrence of an expression or a particular connotation of a given word, not only because this is completely impossible in most cases, but also because every time you believe you have found the first person who used the word there will always be some antecedent or other. F. need look no further than in Büchmann under *'Übermensch* {Superman}': the word can be traced right back to antiquity.

And I too have recently discovered an *'Untermensch* {subhuman}' in our old friend Fontane, in *Der Stechlin,* and that despite the fact that the Nazis are so proud of their Jewish and communist subhumans and all the associated notions of inferior humanity.

Let them be proud of it, just as Nietzsche was proud of his Superman despite his famous predecessors. For a word, or the particular nuance or connotation of a word, only takes on a linguistic life of its own and becomes truly alive within a language, where it enters into common usage within a particular group, or the public at large, and is able to assert its presence over a period of time. Seen this way, the *'Übermensch'* is undoubtedly Nietzsche's creation, whilst the *'Untermensch'* and non-derisory, neutral use of *'aufziehen'* can be laid solely to the credit of the Third Reich. –

Will their time run out with that of Nazism?

I am doing my best to see to it that it will, but I am doubtful.

I elaborated on this note in January 1946. On the day after I had finished it we had a meeting of the Dresden Cultural Association. A dozen people, whose special cultural credentials have been established by the very fact of their having been voted into office, and who thus now have to set an example to others. The matter in hand was the organization of one of those weeks of culture that are held everywhere these days, and in particular the arrangements for an art exhibition. One of the gentlemen said that quite a few of the pictures donated to the cause of '*Volkssolidarität* {people's solidarity}', and now intended for the exhibition, were daubs. The reply came without delay: 'Impossible! If we organize an art exhibition here in Dresden then we must set it up {*aufziehen*} on a grand scale, and in such a way that it is unimpeachable.'

Chapter 8
Ten Years of Fascism

Invitation from the Italian Consulate in Dresden to a screening on Sunday morning 23 October 1932 of the film – *a film sonoro* to be precise, because there are still silent ones at the moment – *Ten Years of Fascism*.

(It is worth noting here in parentheses that the word *Faschismus* {fascism}, is already spelled with *sch* rather than *sc,* which means that the word has already entered the language. But fourteen years later, in my capacity as state commissioner, I ask a pupil taking his university entrance examination about the meaning of the word, and he answers without hesitation: 'It comes from the word *fax,* meaning a torch.' He is not unintelligent, was doubtless a *Pimpf*[1] and a member of the Hitler Youth, presumably collects stamps and knows the lictor's fasces on the Italian stamps of the Mussolini period, and, what's more, he of course knows it perfectly well from many years spent reading Latin, but nevertheless doesn't realize what the word 'fascism' means. His peers correct him: 'from *fascis*'. But how many other people must there be who are in the dark about the derivation of this word and concept if a grammar schoolboy with a National Socialist education doesn't know it? . . . Continually and from all directions I am assailed by the same nagging doubt: how much can be said with certainty about the knowledge and thinking of a nation, about its intellectual and spiritual health?)

For the first time I hear and see the Duce talking. The film is a great artistic achievement. Mussolini speaks to the crowd from the balcony of

---

[1] A member of the *Jungvolk,* the branch of the Hitler Youth for boys aged 10 to 14.

the palace in Naples; shots of the masses and close-ups of the speaker, the words of Mussolini alternate with the responses of those he is addressing. You can see clearly how the Duce literally pumps himself up for each sentence, how, following brief moments of deflation, he repeatedly generates the impression of utmost energy and tautness, you hear the passionately sermonizing, ritualistic and ecclesiastical intonation of his terse outbursts, each consisting of only the shortest of sentences, like fragments of a liturgy to which everyone can react emotionally without the least bit of intellectual effort, even if they don't understand the meaning – indeed all the more so if they don't. His mouth is gigantic. Now and then he gesticulates with his fingers in a typically Italian manner. And the howling of the masses, ecstatic interjections or, when an enemy is invoked, shrill whistling. And again and again, accompanying all this, the raised arm of the Fascist salute.

Since then we have seen and heard all of this so many thousands of times, endlessly repeated with only the slightest of variations, in recordings of the Nuremberg Rallies, from the Berlin Lustgarten or the Munich Feldherrnhalle, and so on, so that the Mussolini film appears to us to be a very ordinary achievement, and in no way exceptional. But just as the term 'Führer' is only a translation into German of 'Duce', the brown-shirt a variation of the Italian black-shirt, and the German salute only an imitation of the Fascist salute, so the whole style of filming such scenes in Germany for propaganda purposes, indeed the very scene itself, the speech of the Führer to his assembled peoples, is based on the Italian model. In both cases the aim is to bring the leader into direct contact with the people themselves, all the people and not just their representatives.

It you trace this idea back you inevitably end up with Rousseau, and in particular his *Contrat social.* In writing as a citizen of Geneva, and thus being faced with the special case of a city state, it is almost inevitable that his imagination would give coherent shape to politics in an antique mould, confine it to municipal boundaries – politics is after all the art of leading a *polis,* a city. According to Rousseau the statesman is the orator who speaks to the people assembled on the marketplace, and according to Rousseau, sporting and cultural events in which the national community takes part are political institutions and means of advertising. It was the great idea of Soviet Russia to use the new technical innovations, in particular film and radio, to extend infinitely the limited scope of the method set out both in antiquity and by Rousseau for having the statesman turn 'to everyone' in person, even if 'everyone' amounts to millions, and even if thousands of kilometres separate their individual groups. In this way the speech, as one of the tools and duties of the statesman, was reinvested with the status that it had enjoyed in Athens, indeed an even greater status given that instead of Athens the orator now addressed an entire country, and indeed more than just one country.

But a speech was not only more important than it had been previously, it was also, of necessity, different in nature. In addressing itself to everyone rather than just select representatives of the people it had to make itself comprehensible to everyone and thus become more populist. Populist {*volkstümlich*} means more concrete; the more emotional a speech is, the less it addresses itself to the intellect, the more populist it will be. And it will cross the boundary separating populism from demagogy and mass seduction as soon as it moves from ceasing to challenge the intellect to deliberately shutting it off and stupefying it.

The ceremonially decorated marketplace in which the crowd is addressed, or the hall or arena adorned with standards and banners, can, to some extent, be seen as an integral part of the speech itself, as its body; the speech is embedded and stage-managed in a frame of this kind, it is a total work of art simultaneously addressing itself to the ears and the eyes, the ears indeed twice over, since the roaring of the crowd, its applause and its disapproval have at least as powerful an effect on the individual member of the audience as the speech itself. What is more, the tone of the speech is itself undoubtedly influenced by this staging, becoming increasingly emotional. The sound film communicates this total work of art in its entirety; the radio replaces the visible spectacle with a commentary which corresponds to the messenger's report of the ancient world, whilst faithfully reproducing the exhilarating duplication of auditory stimuli, the spontaneous responses of the masses. ('Spontaneous {*spontan*}' is one of the favourite words of the LTI, of which more later.)

The German language only has one adjective corresponding to *Rede* {speech} and *reden* {to speak} – *rednerisch* {rhetorical}, an adjective which does not have a particularly good ring to it, a rhetorical achievement is always open to accusations of being merely hot air.

One could almost speak here of a distrust of public speakers intrinsic to the German national character.

Peoples who speak Romance languages, on the other hand, who have no such distrust, but rather a high regard for public speakers, distinguish clearly between oratory and rhetoric. For them an orator is an honourable man, someone who tries to convince through words, someone who in all sincerity strives for clarity and appeals to both the hearts and minds of his listeners. The term 'oratorical' is a tribute extended by the French to classic voices of pulpit and stage such as Bossuet and Corneille. The German language has also seen orators of comparable stature, one need only think of Luther and Schiller. In the West we have the special term 'rhetorical {*rhetorisch*}' for all that is notoriously prolix {*das Rednerische*}; the rhetor – this can be traced back to Greek sophistry and the age of its decline – is the patter-merchant, the one who throws up a smoke-screen around common sense. Is Mussolini one of the orators or the rhetors of his people? Certainly he was always closer to the rhetor than the orator, and during the course of his disastrous career he ultimately succumbed entirely to the temptation of rhetoric. Yet much of what sounds so extravagant {*rednerisch*} to the German ear in his speeches is in fact not so at all, as it rarely exceeds the kind of colour which is entirely natural to the Italian language. *Popolo di Napoli!* People of Naples! was the address used at that anniversary celebration. To a German it all sounds rather bombastic and antiquated. But I was reminded of an advertising flier handed to me shortly before the First World War in Scanno. Scanno is a small town in the Abruzzi, and the people of the region are proud of their physical strength and audacity. A newly opened department store was extolling its virtues and the term of address read: *Forte e gentile Popolazione di Scanno!* Strong and noble people! How modest Mussolini's 'People of Naples!' sounded in comparison.

Four months after hearing Mussolini, I heard Hitler's voice for the first time. (I never saw him, never heard him speak directly, that was forbidden for Jews; at the outset I sometimes encountered him in sound films, later, after it was forbidden for me to go to the cinema and I was also not allowed to own a radio, I heard his speeches or snatches of them from loudspeakers on the street and at the factory.) He had become Chancellor on 30 January 1933, the elections to confirm his selection and provide him with a willing Reichstag were to take place on 5 March.

The preparations for the election, part of which – also a piece of LTI! – was the burning of the Reichstag, were carried out in the grandest of scales and the man himself was not open to even the slightest doubt as to his success; in Königsberg he gave a speech in anticipation of certain triumph. That the setting of his speech was comparable with that of Mussolini's in Naples was obvious to me despite the invisibility and remoteness of the Führer. For a huge animated crowd jostled in front of the illuminated hotel façade next to the main railway station in Dresden from which a loudspeaker relayed the speech, storm-troopers stood on the balconies with large flags bearing swastikas and a torch-light procession approached from the Bismarckplatz. I only caught scraps of the speech itself, in truth more sounds than sentences. But already at that point I had the same impression which was subsequently to be repeated again and again until the very end. What a contrast with his prototype Mussolini!

The Duce, regardless of how much one sensed the physical exertion with which he galvanized his sentences, and with which he strove to control the crowd at his feet, the Duce always swam with the resonant flow of his native language, gave himself up to it despite his claim to power, was, even when he slipped from oratory into rhetoric, a public speaker free of strains and cramps. Hitler on the other hand, regardless of whether he was playing up the unctuousness or the sarcasm – the two tones between which he always liked to alternate – Hitler always spoke, or rather screamed, convulsively. It is possible to maintain a certain dignity and inner calm even at moments of extreme agitation, a degree of self-assurance, a sense of accord with oneself and one's following. Hitler, the studied, all-out man of rhetoric, the rhetor as a matter of principle, lacked this from the outset. Even when triumphant he was insecure and would shout down opponents and opposing ideas. Composure and musicality were never to be heard in his voice, in the rhythm of his sentences, always just a crude scourging of others and of himself. The stages in his development, especially during the war years, entailed little more than a progression from malicious agitator to agitated quarry, from convulsive condemnation through rage and impotent rage to despair. For my own part I have never been able to understand how he was capable, with his unmelodious and raucous voice, with his crude, often un-Germanically constructed sentences, and with a conspicuous rhetoric entirely at odds with the character of the German language, of winning over the masses with his speeches, of holding their attention and subjugating them for such appalling lengths of time. Because regardless of how much blame can be assigned to the after-effects of a suggestion once planted in somebody's mind, to unscrupulous tyranny and acute fear – ('Rather than get me'self strung up I'll believe in that there victory' was a Berlin joke later on) – the terrifying fact remains that the suggestion was able to take root, and, despite all the horrors, was able to live on in millions of people right up to the last moment.

Christmas 1944, when the last German offensive on the western front had already failed, and when there was not the slightest room for doubt as to the outcome of the war, when workers I met in the street on my way to the factory or on the way home would regularly whisper in my ear, 'Chin up, comrade! It won't be much longer now . . .', it was at this point that I spoke to a companion in misfortune about the supposed atmosphere in the country. He was a Munich businessman, with much more of a Munich disposition than a Jewish one, a thoughtful, sceptical and entirely unromantic man. I told him about the frequent words of comfort that I had received. He said he had heard them too but didn't set much store by them. The masses still swore by the Führer. 'And even if a few per cent are against him now: let him deliver a single speech here and they will all follow him again, every single one of them! In the early days I heard him speak in Munich on numerous occasions before anyone had even heard of him in North Germany. No one resisted him. Myself included. You can't resist him.' I asked him what it was that made him so irresistible. – 'I have no idea, but you simply can't resist him' was the immediate and obstinate reply.

And in April 1945, when even the most blinkered knew it was all over, when everyone in the Bavarian village to which we had fled was cursing the Führer, and when the procession of fugitive soldiers had become an unbroken chain, you could still find the odd person amongst the war-weary, the disappointed and the embittered who, with staring eyes and pious lips, would swear that on 20 April, the Führer's birthday, the 'turning point {Wende}', the victorious German offensive, would come: the Führer said so and the Führer doesn't lie, he should be believed over and above any rational arguments.

What is the key to this undeniable miracle? There is a widely held psychiatric explanation with which I am in total agreement, and to which I wish merely to add a philological one.

On the evening of the Führer's speech in Königsberg, a colleague who had seen and heard Hitler on numerous occasions told me he was convinced that the man would end up in a state of religious mania. I also believe that he really did strive to see himself as a new German saviour, that within him there was a never-ending conflict between excessive megalomania and delusions of persecution, whereby the two illnesses aggravated each other, and I believe that it was this disease which infected the body of a German nation already weakened and spiritually shattered by the First World War.

But from the point of view of the philologist I also believe that Hitler's shamelessly blatant rhetoric was able to make such an enormous impact because it penetrated a language which had hitherto been protected from it with the virulence which accompanies the outbreak of a new epidemic, because this rhetoric was in essence as un-German as the salute and uniform copied from the Fascists – replacing a black-shirt with a brown-shirt is not a particularly original idea – and as un-German as the whole decorative embellishment of the public occasions.

But regardless of how much National Socialism learned from the preceding ten years of Fascism, and how much of the infection was caused by foreign bodies, it was, or rather became, in the end, a specifically German disease, a rampant degeneration of German flesh which, through a process of reinfection from Germany, destroyed not only Nazism, but also Italian Fascism, which was undoubtedly criminal, but not quite so bestial.

Chapter 9
Fanatical

As a student I once got annoyed with an English specialist who counted how many times drumming, piping and other war-like music occurred in the works of Shakespeare. In my foolishness I called this activity dry pedantry . . . And in my diaries of the Hitler period there appears as early as 1940 the note: 'Topic for a university seminar: ascertain how often the words *fanatisch* {fanatical} and *Fanatismus* {fanaticism} are used in official communications, how often they occur in publications which have nothing directly to do with politics, in the latest novels for example, or in translations from other languages.' Three years later I come back to this question with the unequivocal answer: impossible! 'Their use is legion, fanatical is used as frequently "as there as notes on a violin or grains of sand on the beach". More important, however, than the frequency of the word is its change in meaning. I have already spoken about this in my *18ième,* in which I quoted a very strange passage from Rousseau, one which probably very few people have noticed. If only the manuscript had survived . . .'

It has survived.

Fanatique and *fanatisme* are words which the French Enlightenment uses as terms of the utmost censure. There are two reasons for this. Originally – the root of the word is *fanum,* the shrine, the temple – a fanatic was someone in a state of religious rapture racked by ecstatic convulsions. Because the Enlightenment thinkers oppose anything which leads to the dulling or suppression of thinking, and because, as enemies of the Church, they attack religious mania with particular ferocity, the fanatic is the natural adversary of their rationalism. For them the personification of the *fanatique* is Ravaillac who murdered good

King Henri IV out of a religious fanaticism of this kind. If, on the other hand, you accuse the Enlightenment thinkers themselves of fanaticism, they will deny it, claiming that their own zeal is simply a battle against the enemies of reason fought with the weapons of reason. Wherever Enlightenment thinking is to be found, the notion of fanaticism always evokes a feeling of antipathy and censure.

Like all other Enlightenment thinkers – the 'philosophers' and 'encyclopaedists' who were his allies before, on becoming an outsider, he began to hate them – Rousseau also used the term 'fanatical' in a pejorative sense. In the *Confessions* of the Savoyard curate we read the following concerning Christ's encounter with the Jewish zealots: 'In the midst of raging fanaticism the voice of sovereign wisdom rang out.' But immediately afterwards, when, as the mouthpiece of Jean-Jacques, the curate vilifies the chauvinism of the encyclopaedists with, if anything, greater vehemence than he had previously censured ecclesiastical intolerance, we read in a lengthy note: 'Bayle has proved conclusively that fanaticism is more pernicious than godlessness, a fact which is indisputable; but he also kept to himself a no-less-significant truth: namely that in all its bloodlust and cruelty, fanaticism is a great and powerful passion which inflames the hearts of men, enables them to scorn death, gives them abundant vitality, and should be better directed to bring forth exalted virtues; a lack of faith, on the other hand, along with sagacious Enlightenment thinking in general, leads to an excessive desire to cling onto life, to debility and to abasement of the soul, it channels all passions into the service of vulgar private interests and reprehensible egotism, thereby stealthily undermining the true principles on which every society is based.'

Here already is the complete transformation of fanaticism into a virtue. Yet, despite Rousseau's international reputation, it remained unproductively hidden in this note. What Romanticism gained from Rousseau was the glorification not of fanaticism but of passion in all its guises and for whatever cause. In Paris, near to the Louvre, there is a beautifully slender little monument: a fresh young drummer-boy storming round the corner. He is raising the alarm, drumming up enthusiasm, he represents the enthusiasm of the French Revolution and of the century which followed it. It was not until 1932 that the tortuous figure of his brother, fanaticism, marched through the Brandenburg Gate. Up until then fanaticism remained, despite Rousseau's clandestine praise, a disparaged quality, something which stood somewhere between sickness and criminality.

In German there is no adequate substitute for this word, not even if one isolates it from its original, restricted application to the domain of ritual. *Eifern* {zealousness} is a more harmless expression, when you hear the word 'zealot' you imagine a passionate preacher rather than a violent criminal pure and simple. *Besessenheit* {obsession} denotes a morbid and thus excusable or pitiable condition rather than one which might give rise to actions constituting a public danger. The word *Schwärmer* {enthusiast} is incomparably lighter in tone. It is true that in his struggle to achieve clarity Lessing became notorious for his enthusiasm. 'Do not relinquish him' (he writes in *Nathan*) 'to the enthusiasts amongst that rabble of yours.' But one has to ask oneself whether in the hackneyed combinations '*düsterer Fanatiker* {grim fanaticism}' and '*liebenswürdiger Schwärmer* {lovable enthusiast}' the epithets are interchangeable, i.e. whether it would thus be possible to speak of a *düsterer Schwärmer* {grim enthusiast} and a *liebenswürdiger Fanatiker* {lovable fanatic}. One's linguistic hackles rise at the mere thought. An enthusiast does not become narrow-mindedly obsessed with something, instead he takes to the air, ignores the actual state of things on the ground and allows his enthusiasm to soar upwards to take up residence in castles in the sky. Deeply moved, King Philipp held Posa to be a '*sonderbarer Schwärmer* {a man of singular enthusiasms}'.

Thus the German word *fanatisch* {fanatical} stands alone, untranslatable and irreplaceable, and as a value judgement it is invariably very negatively loaded, it denotes a threatening and repulsive quality. Even when one occasionally comes across the expression in an obituary for a research scientist or an artist – he was fanatical about his discipline or his art – the tribute always conjures up associations of petulant introvertedness and embarrassing remoteness. Prior to the Third Reich no one would have thought of using the word 'fanatical' in a positive sense. And indeed it is so indelibly stamped with these negative connotations that even the LTI itself sometimes used it negatively. In *Mein Kampf* Hitler speaks dismissively of '*Objektivitätsfanatiker* {fanatical objectivists}'. In a work which appeared during the heyday of the Third Reich, and the style of which amounts to an unremitting sequence of National Socialist linguistic clichés, in Erich Gritzbach's monographic paean *Hermann Göring, Werk und Mensch* (Hermann Göring, The Man and his Works), there is an assertion that the false doctrine of that most despicable of heresies, communism, has proved itself capable of training people to become fanatics. But what we have here is an almost comic *faux pas,* a totally inadmissible relapse into linguistic habits of an earlier age, a relapse moreover which even the master of LTI himself occasionally suffered; indeed as late as December 1944 (presumably with the passage of Hitler's quoted above in mind) Goebbels refers to the 'muddle-headed fanaticism {*Fanatismus*} of certain incorrigible Germans'.

I refer to these sort of things as a comic relapse, the reason being that since National Socialism is founded on fanaticism, and trains people to be fanatical by all possible means, the word 'fanatical' was, throughout the entire era of the Third Reich, an inordinately complimentary epithet. It represents an inflation of the terms 'courageous', 'devoted' and 'persistent'; to be more precise, it is a gloriously eloquent fusion of all of these virtues, and even the most innocuous pejorative connotation of the word was dropped from general LTI usage. On public holidays, on Hitler's birthday or, for example, on the anniversary of the day the Nazis came to power, there wasn't a single newspaper article, message of congratulation, or address to some army unit or other organization, which didn't include a 'fanatical vow {*fanatisches Gelöbnis*}' or 'fanatical declaration {*fanatisches Bekenntnis*}', or which didn't affirm its 'fanatical belief {*fanatischen Glauben*}' in the everlasting life of Hitler's Reich. And even more so during the war, and most of all at the point where the defeats could no longer be hushed up! The more hopeless the situation became, the more frequent were the assertions of 'fanatical faith {*fanatische Glaube*} in the final victory', in the Führer, in the people or in the fanaticism of the people as a fundamental German virtue. Quantitatively the word was used most in the immediate wake of the attempt on Hitler's life on 20 July 1944: the word appears in literally every single one of the countless pledges of allegiance to the Führer.

The use of the word in other fields, in narrative fiction and in everyday conversation, went hand in hand with its prevalence in the world of politics. Where, in times gone by, one might have said or written something passionately {*leidenschaftlich*}, one now did so fanatically. This was inevitably accompanied by a certain attrition, a kind of debasement of the concept. In the Göring monograph mentioned above, the Reich Marshal is extolled for being, amongst other things, a 'fanatical animal lover {*fanatischer Tierfreund*}'. (The reproachful subsidiary meaning associated with the fanatical artist is entirely absent here, given that Göring is repeatedly portrayed as the most devoted and companionable of men.)

The question simply remains as to whether this attrition also implied that the word had the sting taken out of it. You could answer in the affirmative on the grounds that the word 'fanatical' has now simply been invested with a new meaning and refers to a happy mix of courage and fervent devotion. But that is not the case. 'Language which writes and thinks for you . . .' Poison which you drink unawares and which has its effect – this can't be said often enough.

However, to the leading spokesman of the Third Reich, determined to maximize the effect of this inflammatory poison, the overuse of the word must have looked like a growing weakness. And so Goebbels was forced to come up with the nonsensical notion of trying to exceed the already excessive. In the *Reich* of 13 November 1944 he writes that the situation can be saved 'only by fierce fanaticism {*wilden Fanatismus*}'. As if fierceness was not already the essential condition of the fanatic, as if there could be such a thing as tame fanaticism.

This point marks the decline of the word.

Four months previously it had celebrated its greatest triumph, had so-to-speak been blessed with the greatest honour that the Third Reich had in its power to bestow – the military honour. It is a special task unto itself to trace the way in which the customary detachment and almost coquettish sobriety of official military language, above all in the daily news bulletins during the war, were gradually engulfed by the bombast of Goebbels's style of propaganda. On 26 July 1944 the adjective 'fanatical' was used, for the first time in a military despatch, as an accolade applied to German regiments. Our 'troops fighting fanatically' in Normandy. Nowhere else is the colossal difference in military ethos between the First and Second World Wars as terrifyingly apparent as here.

Only a year after the collapse of the Third Reich a strangely conclusive piece of evidence can be advanced to support the claim that 'fanatical', this key National Socialist term, never really had the sting taken out of it by excessive use. For although scraps of the LTI surface all over the place in contemporary language, 'fanatical' has disappeared. From this one can safely conclude that either consciously or subconsciously people remained aware of the real facts of the case all through those twelve years, namely, that a confused state of mind, equally close to sickness and criminality, was for twelve years held to be the greatest virtue.

Chapter 10
Autochthonous Writing

Although matters relating to my field of expertise were not uppermost in my mind during those terrible years, I did on occasion see before me the intelligent mocking face of Joseph Bédier. It is part of the job of the literary historian to discover the origins of motifs, fables and legends, and sometimes this branch of the discipline can develop into an occupational disease, a mania: everything must have an origin which is remote both geographically and historically – the more remote, the more erudite the researcher who locates the distant source – nothing is allowed to have its roots in the very place where one runs across it. I can still hear the irony in Bédier's voice as he elucidated *ex cathedra* in the *Collège de France* the supposedly oriental or supposedly 'druidic' origin of some comic or pious fairy-tale or of some literary curiosity. Bédier repeatedly demonstrated how certain situations and impressions can, at different times and in different places, provoke the same responses, because in certain things human nature proves itself to be extremely consistent over time and space.

The first time I was reminded of him, albeit indistinctly, was in December 1936. It was at the time of the trial of the murderer of Gustloff, the Nazi foreign agent. Ponsard's *Charlotte Corday,* a French tragedy written almost a hundred years ago, for many years a work of world renown and regularly on the curriculum of German schools until it (unfairly) fell out of favour and was forgotten, has the assassination of Marat as its subject matter. The assassin rings his doorbell, she is determined to murder the man she believes to be an unscrupulous bloodhound and a monster devoid of any human qualities. A woman opens the door and

Charlotte Corday recoils in horror: dear God, he has a wife, somebody loves him – *grand Dieu, sa femme, on l'aime!* But then she hears him name a loved one as a victim 'for the guillotine', whereupon she stabs him. The testimony of Frankfurter, the Jewish defendant, at the court in Chur sounded like a modern rendering of the salient points of this scene. He had been determined to kill the butcher, Frau Gustloff had opened the door and he had wavered – a married man, *grand Dieu, on l'aime.* Then he heard Gustloff on the telephone refer to 'these Jewish pigs', at which point he pulled the trigger . . . Should I surmise from this that Frankfurter had read *Charlotte Corday?* I would rather take the scene from the trial in Chur in my next lecture on Ponsard as belated proof of the authenticity of the actions in this French play.

Bédier's observations were more in the primitive domain of folklore than of the purely literary, and it is to this realm that the other facts belong that made me recall him.

In Autumn 1941, at the point when it was no longer possible to speak of a speedy end to the war, I heard many reports of Hitler's fits of rage. First they were tantrums, then outbursts of blind rage, the Führer was said to have bitten into his handkerchief, then a cushion, thrown himself to the ground and chewed the carpet. And then – these stories were always spread by ordinary people, workers, hawkers, recklessly trusting postmen – he 'gnashed the fringe of the carpet', gnashed it regularly and bore the nickname 'carpet gnasher'. Is it really necessary to point to biblical sources, to the grass-gnashing Nebuchadnezzar?

The epithet 'carpet gnasher {*Teppichfresser*}' is what you might call the germ of a legend. However, the Third Reich also brought forth real, full-grown legends. One of these was related to us by a very sober individual shortly after the outbreak of war, when Hitler was at the height of his power.

At the time we still had the small house high above the city, but were already extremely isolated and under constant surveillance – by then it demanded a degree of courage to visit us at all. A trader from down in the city, who used to deliver things to our door in better times, had remained faithful to us, and once a week he brought up everything we needed; on each occasion he reported anything encouraging he had heard, and which he believed might keep our spirits up. He was no politician, but was incensed by the obvious mismanagement, injustice and tyranny of National Socialism. At the same time he saw everything from a down-to-earth and practical point of view; he was not very educated, had no erudite interests, philosophy was not his thing and religion appeared not to be either. Before the encounter I am about to relate I had never heard him speak of religious matters or those relating to the life hereafter, and was never to again. All in all he was a petty-bourgeois grocer who only differed from hundreds of thousands of his kind in not allowing himself to be intoxicated by the perfidious phrases of the government. Generally he entertained us with some scandal or other relating to the Party which had come to light only to be promptly covered up again, a case of fraudulent bankruptcy, or of someone buying himself into power, or of flagrant blackmail. Following the suicide of our mayor, a man who had hopelessly compromised himself – he was first forced to commit suicide and then given an honourable burial in what almost amounted to a state occasion *en miniature* – V. repeatedly told us, 'You mark my words, you've outlived Kalix, now you'll outlive Mutschmann and Adolf!' This sober man, a Protestant moreover, and therefore not imbued from childhood with stories of saints and martyrs, told us the following story with the same unhesitating trust that had characterized his tales of Kalix's small-scale spite and Mutschmann's large-scale malice.

A lieutenant-colonel of the SS in Halle or Jena – he always gave precise details of people and places, everything he told us was 'vouched for' by 'absolutely reliable sources' – a high-ranking SS officer had taken his wife to a private clinic to give birth. He checked her room, above the bed was a picture of Jesus. 'Take down that picture', he told the nurse, 'I don't want a Jewish boy to be the first thing my son sees.' The timid nurse evaded the command by saying she would inform the matron, and the SS man left having repeated his injunction. First thing the next morning the matron telephoned him: 'You have a son, Lieutenant Colonel, your wife is well and so is your child. Except that your wish has been granted: the child has been born blind . . .'

How often during the Third Reich people railed at the sceptical intelligence of the Jews and their incapacity for faith! But the Jews also produced their own legends and believed them. At the end of 1943, following the first major bombing raid on Leipzig, I repeatedly heard people in the Jews' House say that in 1938 the Jews had been dragged from their beds at 4.15 in the morning to be deported to the concentration camps, and that recently all the clocks in the town had stopped during the bombing raid at 4.15.

Seven months previously, Aryans and Non-Aryans had been united in their belief in a common legend. The Babisnau poplar. The tree stands on the range of hills to the south east of the city, strangely isolated, conspicuous and pre-eminent, visible from a surprisingly large number of different locations. It was at the beginning of May that my wife told me for the first time that in the tram she had heard people talking about the Babisnau poplar, but didn't know what it was all about. A few days later I also heard people at the factory uttering the words 'the Babisnau poplar!' I asked why they were talking about it. They replied, 'Because it's in blossom.' This was a rare occurrence; it had happened in 1918, and 1918 was the year in which peace was declared. A female worker immediately corrected him, saying that this had not only happened in 1918, but also in 1871. 'And in other wars during the last century,' a forewoman added, and the porter concluded that 'every time it has blossomed peace has been made'.

The following Monday Feder said, 'There was a real exodus yesterday to the Babisnau poplar. It really is blossoming magnificently. Perhaps there will be peace – you can never dismiss popular belief out of hand.' Feder, with his Star of David, and the cap to protect him from the dust, which he had fashioned from his old judge's biretta.

Chapter 11
Blurring Boundaries

Every elementary school pupil learns that there are no fixed boundaries separating the different kingdoms of nature. Generally less well-known and acknowledged is the fact that there are also no hard and fast boundaries in the realm of aesthetics.

Modern painting and literature – this is the correct order, because painting was there before literature – are generally subdivided into two categories, Impressionism and Expressionism; the terminological scissors have to be able to cut and divide cleanly, since we are dealing here with absolute opposites. The Impressionist is entirely at the mercy of the impression of things, he reproduces what he has taken in: he is passive, he allows himself to be influenced by his experiences at every moment, is a different person at every moment, has no fixed, uniform and unchanging soul, no immutable self. The Expressionist starts with himself, he doesn't acknowledge the power of material objects but rather stamps them with his own signature, with his own will, expresses himself through them and in them, moulds them according to his own nature: he is active and his actions are determined by a resolute self-assurance in his constant and immutable self.

So far so good. However, the artist of impressions deliberately reproduces what he himself actually saw, and how he saw it, rather than an objective image of the real world; he doesn't reproduce the tree with all its leaves, the individual leaf with its unique shape, the actual green or yellow hues, the actual light of a particular time of day or year, under particular weather conditions, but rather the way his eyes perceive the leaves merge into a single mass, colour and light corresponding to his disposition at that particular moment, in other words the mood which he imposes onto the reality of material objects. Is there anything passive about his behaviour? He is just as aesthetically active and just as much an expressive artist as his counterpart, the Expressionist. The distinction only survives on an ethical level: the self-confident Expressionist prescribes fixed rules for himself and the world around him, he has a sense of responsibility. The vacillating Impressionist, who changes from one hour to the next, claims amoral behaviour as an excuse for his own irresponsibility and that of others.

Yet here too the boundaries inevitably become blurred. Conscious of the helplessness of the individual, the Impressionist becomes socially compassionate and actively engages in supporting oppressed and bewildered creatures; there is no difference here between Impressionists such as Zola or the Goncourt brothers, and Expressionists like Toller, Unruh or Becher.

No, I have no faith in purely aesthetic observations in the context of the history of ideas, literature, art and language. The starting point has to be fundamental human attitudes; the sensual means of expression can from time to time be identical despite entirely contradictory goals.

This is particularly true of Expressionism: Toller, who was killed by National Socialism, and Johst, who became president of an academy in the Third Reich, both belong to the Expressionist movement.

The LTI either inherits from the Expressionists, or shares with them, certain ways of expressing the importance of the will and a fervently thrusting forward momentum. *Die Aktion* and *Der Sturm*[1] were the titles of the periodicals published by the young Expressionists still trying at the time to make a name for themselves. In Berlin they were the most left-wing and the hungriest bohemians amongst the artistic clientele of the Café Austria by the Potsdamer Brücke (some also frequented the more famous and elegant Café des Westens, but these were the ones who had already made it, and here there were also other 'trends'), in Munich it was the Café Stephanie. That was during the years before the First World War. In the Café Austria we waited during the night of the elections in 1912 for the press telegrams and rejoiced as the hundredth victory for the Social Democrats was announced; we thought that the

[1] *Die Aktion* (The Action) and *Der Sturm* (The Storm) were pre-eminent Expressionist periodicals.

gateway to freedom and peace had now been opened wide once and for all . . .

The words *Aktion* {action} and *Sturm* {storm} migrated around 1920 from the ladylike café to the manly beer-house. From beginning to end the word *Aktion* was one of those indispensable foreign words in the LTI which was not germanized, it was bound up with memories of the heroic early period and evoked the image of the pub brawl; *Sturm* became a hierarchical military term for diverse groupings: the hundredth *Sturm*,[2] the mounted cavalry storm of the SS, although here the tendency to translate the term into German and establish connections with existing traditions also played a part.

The most widespread use of the term *Sturm* is also the most elusive: who now remembers – and indeed who actually knew during the years of Nazi rule – that SA stood for *Sturmabteilung* {Storm Detachment}?

SA and SS, the *Schutzstaffel* {Elite Guard} or praetorian guard, are abbreviations which became so satisfied with themselves that they were no longer really abbreviations at all; they took on independent meanings which entirely obscured their original signification.

I am forced here to write SS with the sinuous lines of a normal typeface. During the Hitler period printers' cases and keyboards of official typewriters included the special angular SS character. It was in keeping with the Germanic rune of victory and was created in honour of this symbol. However, it was also connected with Expressionism.

Amongst the expressions used by soldiers during the First World War was the adjective *zackig* {smart}.[3] A strict military salute is *zackig,* a command or an address can be given in a *zackig* manner, anything that conveys a taut and disciplined expenditure of energy is *zackig.* It designates a form of expression quintessential to Expressionist painting and Expressionist literary language. On seeing a National Socialist SS symbol, the first thing to spring to mind for someone without a philological education was undoubtedly the concept of '*zackig*'. But there was more.

Long before the Nazi SS even existed, its symbol was to be seen painted in red on electricity substations, and below it the warning

---

[2]The *Hundertschaften* (Hundreds) were action squads of Storm Troopers which existed until 1923.
[3]*Zackig* literally means jagged, pointed or angular (*Zickzack* being the German for zigzag). Figuratively it can mean smart, brisk, dynamic or zippy.

'Danger – High Voltage!' In this case the jagged S was obviously a stylized representation of a flash of lightning. That thunderbolt, whose velocity and capacity for storing energy made it such a popular symbol for the Nazis! Thus the SS character was also a direct embodiment, a painterly expression of lightning. Here the double line may well suggest increased energy, because the little black flags of the children's formations only bore one jagged bolt, what you might call a half-SS.

Although someone who comes up with a particular symbol may not be aware of it, there are often many reasons for it; this seems to me to be the case here: SS is two different things at once, an image and an abstract character, it encroaches on the realm of painting, it is a pictogramme, a return to the physicality of the hieroglyph.

In fact, the first artists to use their means of expression to blur boundaries in this way in the modern age were the very opposite of the self-confident Expressionists and National Socialists, they were the sceptics, those who undermined the idea of a unified self and of morality, the decadents. Guillaume Apollinaire, a Pole born in Rome who adored France, his country of adoption, was a writer and literary experimenter who painted by arranging letters into shapes: the words of the sentence 'a lighted cigar, smoking' (*un cigare allumé qui fume*) are printed in such a way that the curve of the rising smoke is made up of the corresponding letters following the straight line of the word 'cigar'.

Within the LTI itself, the special jagged form of the letters SS represents for me the link between the visual language of the poster and language in the narrower sense. There is also another link of this kind: a similarly jagged torch, either erect or turned towards the ground – the rune of blossoming and wilting. As a symbol of passing away it was only used as a replacement for the Christian cross on death announcements, whilst in its other form, pointing upwards, it not only served as a replacement for the star on birth announcements, but also appeared on stamps used by chemists and bakers. One would assume of course that these two runes would become as established as the SS symbol, given that they too were encouraged on account of their physicality and Germanness. This was not the case however.

On a number of occasions I made a statistical record over a couple of weeks of the relationship between the use of the runes and the use of the star and cross motifs. I regularly checked one of the neutral Dresden newspapers (despite the fact that we were not allowed to have them, or keep them in our rooms, they somehow always made their way into the Jews' House) – neutral at least insofar as a newspaper could be, i.e. only neutral in comparison with a dedicated Party paper – and I fairly often saw the *Freiheitskampf,* the Dresden Party newspaper, and the *DAZ,*[4] which had to maintain a slightly higher standard, particularly given that following the silencing of the *Frankfurter Zeitung* it had to represent Germany abroad. It was necessary to take into account the fact that the runes would appear more frequently in the official Party paper than in the others, and also that the *DAZ* frequently served as an advertiser for specifically Christian circles. Despite this, the number of runes appearing in the *Freiheitskampf was* not significantly greater than in the other papers. The largest number of runes appeared in the wake of the first serious defeats, especially after Stalingrad, because at the time the Party exerted increased control over public opinion. Yet, even at that point, only at most a half, and sometimes barely one third of the two dozen announcements of soldiers who had died in action, bore a rune. I was also repeatedly struck by the fact that it was precisely those announcements which were most trenchantly National Socialist in tone which continued to use the star and cross. The same was true of the birth announcements: barely half, and often far fewer, bore the rune, and the most National Socialist of them – in that personal announcements had an LTI style all of their own – often lacked the rune. It is easy to explain why the positive and negative runes of life did not catch on and become accepted, whilst the SS image became entirely ubiquitous. SS was an entirely new term for an entirely new institution, SS didn't have to replace anything. However, in the case of birth and death, the oldest and most immutable of human institutions, the star and cross have been the customary symbols for almost two thousand years. Thus they were rooted too deep in the imagination of the people to be dug up and entirely eradicated. –

But what if these runes of life had in fact caught on and become all-powerful during the Hitler period – would I have had trouble finding an explanation for this phenomenon? Not for a minute! Because in that

---

[4]Abbreviation of *Deutsche Allgemeine Zeitung.*

case I would simply have written, with an equally good conscience, that it was obvious that this would happen.

The reason being that the entire thrust of the LTI was towards visualization, and if this process of visualizing could be achieved with recourse to Germanic traditions, by means of a runic sign, then so much the better. And as a jagged character the rune of life was related to the SS symbol, and as an ideological symbol also related to the spokes of the wheel of the sun, the swastika. And thus, as a result of all this, it was the most obvious thing on earth that the cross and star would be entirely displaced by the runes of life.

But if it really is the case that I can provide equally good reasons for what did happen and what didn't, but should have, what have I actually proved or explained? Here too – the blurring of boundaries, uncertainty, vacillation and doubt. Montaigne's position: *Que saisje,* what do I know? Renan's position: the question mark – the most important of all punctuation marks. A position in direct opposition to National Socialist intransigence and self-confidence.

Mankind's pendulum swings between these two extremes and tries to find a happy medium. It was endlessly claimed by Hitler and others during the period that all progress was thanks to the intransigent, that all inhibitions stemmed from the supporters of the question mark. This is not necessarily true, but it is certainly the case that only the intransigent have blood on their hands.

Chapter 12
Punctuation

From time to time it is possible to detect, both amongst individuals and groups, a characteristic preference for one particular punctuation mark. Academics love the semicolon; their hankering after logic demands a division which is more emphatic than a comma, but not quite as absolute a demarcation as a full stop. Renan the sceptic declares that it is impossible to overuse the question mark. The *Sturm und Drang* needed an unusually large number of exclamation marks. The early Naturalists in Germany were fond of the dash: the sentences and lines of argument are not set down with bureaucratic precision, instead they break off, go off at tangents, remain incomplete and are, in keeping with the spirit of their inception, intrinsically fleeting, unstable and associative, akin both to an inner monologue and the kind of heated discussion that often takes place between people who are not used to systematic thinking.

One would naturally assume that the LTI, given its fundamentally rhetorical nature and constant appeal to the emotions, would be devoted to exclamation marks like the *Sturm und Drang*. In fact they are not at all conspicuous; on the contrary, the LTI appears to me only to have used this sign very sparingly. It is as if it turns everything into a command or proclamation as a matter of course and therefore has no need of a special punctuation mark to highlight the fact – where after all are the sober utterances against which the proclamation would need to stand out?

Instead the LTI makes exhaustive use of what I would call ironic inverted commas.

The simple, primary inverted comma merely denotes the exact words spoken or written by someone else. The ironic inverted comma is not restricted to this neutral form of quotation, instead it questions the truth of that which is quoted, declares that the reported remark is untrue. In rendering that which in spoken language would be expressed by the mere adoption of a sarcastic tone, the ironic inverted comma is closely allied to the rhetorical character of the LTI.

It certainly wasn't invented by it. During the First World War, when the Germans were extolling the virtues of their superior culture and looking down on Western civilization as if it were an inferior, entirely superficial achievement, the French never failed to include the ironic sixty-sixes and ninety-nines when referring to the '*culture allemande*', and it is likely that there was an ironic use of the inverted comma alongside the neutral one right from the outset.

But in the case of the LTI the ironic use outweighs the neutral one many times over. Because the LTI particularly loathes neutrality, because it always has to have an adversary and always has to drag this adversary down. If the Spanish revolutionaries gain a victory, if they have officers or a general staff, then they are invariably 'red "victories"', 'red "officers"', 'a red "general staff"'. Later the same was true of the Russian '"strategy"' and of Yugoslavia's '"Marschal" Tito'. Chamberlain and Churchill and Roosevelt are always only 'statesmen' in ironic inverted commas, Einstein is a 'research scientist', Rathenau a 'German' and Heine a '"German" writer'. There is not a single newspaper article or imprint of a speech which is not crawling with these ironic inverted commas, and they are also to be found in more temperate and expansive studies. They belong to both the printed LTI and the intonation of Hitler and Goebbels, they are intrinsic to them.

As a sixth-former in 1900 I had to write an essay about monuments. One of the sentences in the essay read: 'After the war of 1870 there was a victorious Germania bearing a flag and sword on almost every German marketplace; I could give hundreds of examples.' My sceptical Latin master wrote in the margin in red ink: 'Provide a dozen examples by the next class.' I could only find nine, and was cured once and for all of biting off more numbers than I could chew. Nevertheless, and despite the fact that I have a good deal to say in my LTI observations concerning precisely the misuse of numbers, I can declare with a clear conscience regarding the use of ironic inverted commas that 'thousands of examples can be given.' One of these otherwise thoroughly uniform thousand examples reads: 'there is a difference between German cats and "pedigree" cats'.

Chapter 13
Names

There was an old grammar school joke which was handed down from generation to generation; now that Greek is taught in only a handful of secondary schools it has probably died out. The joke ran as follows: how did the German word *Fuchs* {fox} evolve from the Greek word for fox, alopex (ἀλώπηξ)? Through the sequence alopex, lopex, pex, pix, pax, pucks, Fuchs. I hadn't thought of this again since my Matura some thirty years ago. On 13 January 1934 it suddenly sprang into my mind with such clarity that it was as if I had last quoted it only the day before. This happened whilst I was reading the 72nd issue of our termly bulletin. In it his Magnificence[1] informed us that our colleague Israel, professor extraordinarius and National Socialist city councillor, had reverted to using his old family name 'with the permission of the Ministry'. 'In the sixteenth century it was called Oesterhelt, which is in Lusatia, and was corrupted to Israel via, amongst others, the names Uesterhelt, Isterhal (also Isterheil and Osterheil), Istrael and Isserel.'

This was the first time that I was made aware of the question of names in the LTI. Later, every time I passed the shiny new Oesterhelt nameplate – it was attached to some garden gate or other in the Swiss quarter – I reproached myself for considering even this particular question as *sub specie Judaeorum*. It was by no means restricted to specifically Jewish matters, and is also not a question that only relates to the LTI.

In every revolution, be it political, social, artistic or literary in nature, there are always two principles at work: on the one hand the appetite

---

[1] '*Seine Magnifizenz*' is the title given to German university rectors.

for the new, whereby the total contrast with what was previously valid is swiftly stressed, and on the other the need to connect with the past, to use tradition as a defence. What one is doing isn't absolutely new, rather it is a return to those things which the foregoing age had shamefully rejected, a return to humanity, the nation, morality or the true nature of art, and so on. Both tendencies are manifest in naming and renaming.

The custom of taking both the forenames and surname of a pioneer of the new order to name a newly born child, or to rename someone, is probably almost exclusive to America, and in particular black America. The great English revolution professes its faith in puritanism and revels in Old Testament names, often reinforced by a biblical quotation (Joshua – my soul gives praise to the Lord). The great French Revolution seeks its role models in classical, and in particular Roman, antiquity, and every tribune adopts for himself and his children names recalling Cicero and Tacitus. And in just the same way a good National Socialist underlines his blood relationship and spiritual affinity with the Teutons {*Germanen*}, with the people and gods of the north. The popularity of Wagner and a well-established tradition of nationalism had prepared the ground, names like Horst and Sieglinde were already very widespread when Hitler emerged; alongside the Wagner cult and after it, and perhaps of greater importance, there was also the obvious influence of the youth movement, the songs of the *Wandervögel.*[2]

But the Third Reich makes a duty and a uniform out of what before was just a fashion or one custom amongst many others. If the National Socialist youth leader is called Baldur, how could one possibly hold back?[3] As late as 1944 I notice that of nine births announced in a Dresden newspaper six have explicitly Teutonic {*germanisch*} names: Dieter, Detlev, Uwe, Margit, Ingrid, Uta. Double-barrelled names, linked by a hyphen, are particularly popular owing to their rich sonority and two-fold profession of faith, i.e. their rhetorical character (and thus also their rightful place within the LTI): Bernd-Dietmar, Bernd-Walter, Dietmar-Gerhard . . . Also typical of the LTI is the recurrent use of the diminutive form: Little Karin {*Klein Karin*}, Little Harald {*Klein Harald*}; the idea is to

[2]The *Wandervögel* (sometimes translated as the 'Birds of Passage') was a youth group founded in 1901. It launched the German youth movement.
[3]Baldur von Schirach (1907–74), who became Reich Youth Leader in 1931.

add a little sweetness and light to the heroic ballad-like name, the result is delightfully seductive.

Am I really exaggerating so terribly when I talk of standardization? Perhaps not if one considers that a string of established forenames either fell into disrepute or were as good as banned. Christian forenames are particularly unwelcome; their owners are all too easily suspected of belonging to the opposition. Shortly before the catastrophe in Dresden a copy of the *Illustrierter Beobachter* fell into my hands in the form of wrapping paper, I think it was dated 5 February 1945. It contained an extraordinary article: 'Heidrun'. Extraordinary that it should appear in this most official of Nazi newspapers (the supplement to the *Völkischer Beobachter*).

On a number of occasions during these years I was reminded of a strange scene in a play by Grillparzer. *Der Traum ein Leben* (A Dream Is Life), the final act. The young hero has become hopelessly tangled up in a crime involving bloodshed, and punishment is inevitable. Suddenly a clock sounds and he murmurs: 'Hark! The clock strikes! Three hours till dawn / In a short time it will all be over.' For a moment he is half awake, he suspects that what has tortured him is but an edifying dream, nothing more than an unrealized aspect of his own self. 'Delusions, phantoms of the night; / Folly born of sickness, if you will, / And we must see them, for we are ill.'

On a number of occasions, but never more transparently than in this late Heidrun article, the 'Three hours till dawn', the partial recognition of guilt, can be overheard in texts published by Hitler's supporters; the only problem is that when they finally awoke, far too late, their folly born of sickness had not simply vanished into thin air like a ghost; they really had murdered . . . In the Heidrun article the author makes fun of his Pgs[4] twice over. He writes that if, before leaving the Church (which was an essential step for members of the SS and highly orthodox Nazis), during what was thus a more un-German period in their life, if, during those years, parents had made the mistake of christening their first-born daughter Christa, they would later attempt to improve the poor creature's lot with a little spelling change, electing to begin her half-oriental name with a German 'K', Krista. And to complete the atonement the second daughter was given the thoroughly Teutonic and pagan name 'Heidrun',

[4]See note on p. 13.

which Müller and Schulze believed to be a German rendering of Erika. However, Heidrun is in fact the *Edda's* 'Goat Star', who has mead in her udders and lasciviously pursues the Ram. Thus an altogether unsuitable Nordic name for a young girl . . . I wonder whether any child has heeded the article's warning? It was published late, not even three months before the capitulation. A few days ago I came across a Silesian Heidrun in a missing persons' broadcast on the radio . . .

Whilst Christa and her kin can still make it into the registry of births, deaths and marriages, despite the whiff of notoriety, names derived from the Old Testament are prohibited: no German child can be called Lea or Sara; if an unworldly priest were one day to come up with the idea of registering such a name, the registrar would refuse to enter it and the priest's complaint would be dismissed from on high.

Every possible attempt was made to protect German national comrades {*Volksgenossen*} entirely from names of this kind. In September 1940 I saw a church advertisement on poster columns: 'A Hero of the People: Oratorio by Handel'. Below was printed in timorously small type and in brackets 'Judas Makkabaeus; new edition.' At around this time I read a historico-cultural novel translated from English: *The Chronicle of Aaron Kane.* Rütting & Loening, the same publishing house that had produced the great Beaumarchais biography by the Viennese Jew Anton Bettelheim! – the publisher apologized on the first page for the fact that the biblical names of the characters stemmed from the puritanism current at that particular time and in that particular country, for which reason it was not possible to change them. Another English novel – I can't remember the author any more – bore the German title *Geliebte Söhne* (Beloved Sons). The original title, printed inside in tiny letters, was *O Absalom!* In the Physics Department the name Einstein had to be hushed up and the 'Hertz' unit of frequency could also not be referred by its Jewish name.

However, since the idea is not only to protect the German national comrades from Jewish names, but also, more importantly, to safeguard them from any contact with the Jews themselves, the latter are most carefully segregated. And one of the principal means of this kind of segregation is to point to their names. Anyone who does not have an unmistakably Hebraic name, one which has not established itself in German, such as Baruch or Recha, has to add 'Israel' or 'Sara' to his forename. He has to inform his local registry office and his bank, he must not forget to include it in every signature, and all business associates have to be reminded not to forget it when sending post. If he is not currently married to an Aryan woman and in addition has not had children with her – an Aryan wife is not enough – he must wear the yellow Jewish star. The word 'Jew' on the star, the letters of which resemble Hebraic script, serves as a forename worn on the chest. Our name appeared twice on the door in the corridor, above my name there is a Star of David, below my wife's the word 'Aryan'. Initially my food ration-cards bore a single J, later the word 'Jew' was printed diagonally across the card and in the end every tiny section bore the full word 'Jew', around sixty times on one and the same card. When I am referred to officially it is always 'the Jew Klemperer'; when I have to report to the Gestapo there are blows if I don't announce sufficiently 'smartish {*zackig*}': 'The Jew Klemperer is here.' The use of an apostrophe can heighten the humiliation, substituting a peremptory command for the direct address: one day I read the following about my cousin the musician, who had emigrated to Los Angeles in good time: '*Jud*' {Jew} Klemperer escaped from the lunatic asylum and recaptured.' When the hated 'Kremlin Jews' Trotsky and Litvinov are referred to, it is always as Trotsky-Braunstein and Litvinov-Finkelstein. When Laguardia, the hated mayor of New York, is referred to, it is always as 'the Jew Laguardia' or at least 'the half-Jew Laguardia'.

And if, despite all the torment, a Jewish couple should come up with the idea of having children, they are not allowed to give their litter – I can still hear the Spitter screaming at a genteel old lady: 'Your litter got away but we'll finish you off you Jewish swine!', and they did finish her off; the following day she didn't wake up from her veronal-induced sleep – these parents were forbidden from giving their offspring a misleadingly German forename; the National Socialist government provided them with a whole series of Jewish names from which to choose. They are a strange collection, only a very few have the full dignity of the Old Testament.

In his studies from 'Semi-Asia {*Halbasien*}', Karl Emil Franzos recounts how the Galician Jews in the eighteenth century came by their names. It was a step taken by Joseph II in the spirit of enlightenment and humanitarianism; but many Jews objected vociferously for reasons of orthodoxy, and scornful, subordinate officials forced the recalcitrants to adopt ridiculous and embarrassing surnames. This scorn which arose despite the best of intentions on the part of the legislator was consciously endorsed by the National Socialist government; they wanted not only to segregate the Jews, but also to 'defame {*diffamieren*}' them.

One method at hand was the use of jargon, which on account of its word formations seemed to the Germans to represent a distortion of the German language and to sound coarse and ugly. The fact that it is precisely jargon which testifies to the centuries-old devotion of the Jews to Germany, and that their pronunciation is by and large similar to that of Walter von der Vogelweide and Wolfram von Eschenbach, is, of course, something known only to a qualified Germanist, and I would like to meet the Professor of German Studies who during the Nazi period would have pointed these things out! To the list of forenames available to the Jews were thus added the Yiddish pet names Vögele, Mendele, and so on, which to a German ear sounded somewhat embarrassing and somewhat ridiculous.

In the last Jews' House we lived in I read a characteristic nameplate every day: it bore the names of a father and his son, Baruch Levin and Horst Levin. The father was not obliged to add the name Israel – Baruch was Jewish enough, it clearly came from Polish and orthodox Jewish territory. His son, on the other hand, could avoid using Israel because he was half-caste, his father having been won over to Germanness {*Deutschtum*} so successfully that he had entered into a mixed marriage. There was a whole generation of Jewish Horsts whose parents would stop at nothing to press home their near-Germanness. This generation of Horsts suffered less under the Nazis than their parents – spiritually, of course, because there was no generation gap when it came to the concentration camp and the gas oven, a Jew was a Jew. But the Baruchs felt they had been driven out of the land they loved. The Horsts on the other hand – there were many Horsts and Siegfrieds who, as full Jews, had to add the name Israel – the younger generation, didn't care about Germanness at all, and indeed in many cases felt almost hostile towards it. They had grown up in the same atmosphere of perverted Romanticism as the Nazis, they were Zionists . . .

But once again I have been forced into concentrating my attention exclusively on Jewish matters. Is it my fault or because of the nature of the theme? There must be non-Jewish aspects. There are indeed.

The compulsion to uphold tradition in the giving of names even influenced contemporaries who otherwise had no connection with

Nazism. A school headmaster who chose to retire rather than join the Party enjoyed telling me of the youthful heroic feats of his little grandson Isbrand Wilderich. I asked him how the boy had got his name. The answer was as follows, word for word: 'In the seventeenth century it was the name of one of our kin {*Sippe*}, which originally came from Holland.'

The simple use of the word *Sippe* testified to the extent to which even this headmaster, a man who defended Catholic piety against the blandishments of Hitler, had been infected by National Socialism. *Sippe,* a neutral word from an earlier age for relatives, for family in the broadest sense, subsequently degraded to a pejorative term – just like the clown August – is elevated to a noble status, genealogy becomes the bounden duty of every national comrade.

On the other hand, tradition is rapidly dispensed with if it is in any way opposed to the nationalist {*national*} principle. At this point a typical German trait often ridiculed as pedantry comes into play – thoroughness. A large part of Germany was settled by Slavs, and the place names reflect this historical fact. It is however contrary to the Third Reich's nationalist principles and sense of racial pride to tolerate place names which are not Teutonic. Accordingly the map is cleansed down to the last detail. I noted the following from an article in the *Dresdener Zeitung* of 15 November 1942 entitled 'German Place Names in the East': in Mecklenburg the prefix *'Wendisch* {Wendish}' was deleted from the names of many villages, 120 Slavonic place names were translated into German in Pomerania and around 175 in Brandenburg, the little villages in the Spreewald in particular were Germanized. In Silesia the number of German variations reached 2,700, and in the administrative district of Gumbinnen, where it was above all the 'racially inferior' Lithuanian endings which caused offence, and where, for example, Berninglauken was 'nordified {*aufnorden*}' to Berningen, here in Gumbinnen 1,146 out of a total of 1,851 districts were renamed.

The compulsion to uphold tradition crops up again when given the chance to rename streets in the spirit of Teutomania {*deutschtümelnd*}. The most ancient and obscure councillors and mayors are dug up and inscribed onto street signs with schoolmasterly accuracy. On the Südhöhe here in Dresden there is a newly laid road called the Tirmannstraße, and below the name they have added 'Magister Nikolaus Tirmann, Mayor, died 1437', and on other street signs in the suburbs you can also find 'Councillor in the 14th Century' or 'Author of a City Chronicle in the 15th Century' . . .

Was Joseph too Catholic a name, or did they simply want to make space for a Romantic painter, one who was thus more emphatically German? Be that as it may, the Josephstraße in Dresden became the Caspar-David-Friedrich-Straße, despite the fact that this led to a not insignificant postal conundrum; when we lived in a Jews' House in this street we repeatedly received letters addressed to 'Friedrichstraße c/o Mr Caspar David'.

Postmarks on which cities are given a special designation bear witness to a fondness for medieval guilds and professions as well as modern advertising. 'Leipzig, City of Fairs and Exhibitions' is neither new nor a National Socialist invention, the postmark 'Cleve, Workshop for Fine Quality Children's Shoes', on the other hand, is. In my diary I noted down the following: 'City of the Volkswagen Factory at Fallersleben', here the postmark incorporates not only information about the town's trade and a piece of industrial advertising, but also an openly political message: it highlights a particular industrial estate, a favourite of the Führer's and one set up dishonestly; the enticing Volkswagen which tempted the man on the street to part with his money was in fact planned from the outset as a military vehicle. The proud postmarks 'Munich, The Capital of the Movement' and 'Nuremberg, City of the Rallies' were overtly political and purely propagandistic.

Nuremberg was situated in a 'traditional Gau {Traditionsgau}', which was presumably meant to indicate that the glorious origins of National Socialism were to be found in this particular district. The use of the term 'Gau' to denote a province is another means of establishing a link with ancient Germanic customs {Teutschtum}, and the incorporation of exclusively Polish regions into the 'Warthegau' amounted to legalizing the theft of foreign lands by giving them German names. Similarly, the term Mark {march} was used for borderlands. Ostmark: this incorporated Austria into Greater Germany, Westmark: this annexed Holland. The will to conquer swaggered even more shamelessly when the Polish city of Lodz lost its own name and became Litzmannstadt after the man who defeated it in the First World War.

But when I write this name down I see a special stamp before me: Litzmannstadt-Ghetto. And then names emerge which have gone down in the infernal geography of world history: Theresienstadt and

Buchenwald and Auschwitz, etc. And then a name surfaces which hardly anyone knows – it was known only to us Dresdeners, and those who knew it best have all disappeared. The Jewish camp at Hellerberg: in Autumn 1942 the dwindling residue of Dresden Jews was lodged there in barracks more wretched than those intended for Russian prisoners of war, and from there they were sent to their death in the gas chambers of Auschwitz a few weeks later; only a handful of us who were in mixed marriages stayed behind.

Once again I have come back to the Jewish theme. Is it my fault? No, it is the fault of Nazism and Nazism alone.

But since I have now ended up again in the domain of local patriotism (so to speak), having had to satisfy myself with haphazard notes and suggestions on a topic so extensive that it warrants a doctoral thesis – perhaps there is a central post office which could provide the missing material – I want to mention a minor case of falsifying documents which concerns me personally and which helped save my life. I am sure that my case will not be the only one. The LTI was a prison language (of jailers and prisoners), and integral to the language of prisons (as acts of self-defence) are secret words, confusing ambiguities, forgeries, and so on.

Waldmann was better off than we were after we had been rescued from the destruction of Dresden and brought to the military airfield at Klotzsche. We had torn off our Stars of David, we had left the precincts of Dresden, we had sat together with Aryans inside a car, in short we had committed a whole bunch of deadly sins, each of which would have earned us the death penalty, a death by hanging, if we had fallen into the hands of the Gestapo. 'In the Dresden address book', said Waldmann, 'there are eight Waldmanns, and I am the only Jew amongst them – who is going to spot my name?' But with mine it was an entirely different matter. A common Jewish name beyond the border with Bohemia, Klemperer has nothing to do with the trade of the *Klempner* {plumber} but instead refers to someone who knocks, the beadle who knocks on the doors and windows of the pious in the morning and calls them to morning prayers, and there were only a small number of well-known specimens in Dresden, and after so many years of terror I was the only surviving one. The apparent loss of all my papers would only make me suspect, and it was impossible in the long run to avoid all encounters with officials: we needed ration cards, we needed tickets to travel – we were still very civilized and still believed such cards to be necessary . . . at almost the same instant we remembered a medicine bottle that had been prescribed for me. The prescription, in a doctor's illegible handwriting, had completely changed my name by two minor alterations. A single dot sufficed to turn an 'm' into 'in' and a millimetre-long line changed the first 'r' into a 't'. Thus Klemperer became Kleinpeter. There was unlikely to have been a post office which would have registered the total number of these Kleinpeters in the Third Reich.

Chapter 14
Kohlenklau

In spring 1943 the employment office sent me to work as an unskilled worker in the Willy Schlüter tea and medicinal bath factory, which had swelled to a great size thanks to the orders placed by the army. Initially I was engaged as a packer, with the task of filling cardboard boxes with the finished tea – an extremely monotonous job, but physically completely undemanding; this task was soon left exclusively to women, and I ended up in the factory buildings themselves with their mixing drums and cutting machines; when large supplies of raw materials showed up, the Jewish group also had to help with unloading and storage. The Schlüter tea – presumably like all other ersatz teas at that time – was somewhat like a regiment: the name remained the same, whilst the contents were always changing; anything that could be got hold of was thrown in.

One afternoon in May I was standing in the lofty, high-ceilinged cellar, a single space stretching beneath the full length of one wing of the building. Save but a few alcoves and narrow passageways, this substantial warehouse was piled high with stores, and there was only a small amount of space left just below the roof. Huge, bulging sacks full of hawthorn, lime blossom, heather, peppermint and savory were piled up on top of one another, new ones were constantly being thrown from the courtyard, through the window and onto the chute, where they slid down only to pile up faster than they could be dragged to their correct places. I helped pull the sacks out of the jumbled heap and sort them, and watched the carriers admiringly as they undertook the difficult ascent to the remaining storage spaces bearing their heavy and ungainly burdens on their backs. A female clerk next to me who had just come down with an order laughed: *'Kohlenklau* {Squander-Bug, literally: coal thief} is at it again, he really could get a job in any circus.' I asked a workmate whom she meant, and was given the rather patronizing answer that surely everyone who wasn't blind and deaf knew perfectly well who it was; 'Otto of course, the porter, that's what everyone calls him.' He gestured with his chin in the direction of Otto and I watched him move along the undulating ridge of sacks, bent over, but almost at a running pace, and then with a caterpillar-like movement move the sack up his back and shoulders and over his head, place it in a gap in the adjacent row up against the wall and finally push it fully into place with outstretched arms. In this position he had something of the gorilla about him, like a character from a fairytale: his arms were those of a monkey, his broad trunk rested on thighs that were much too short and fat, he had bow legs, and in their flat shoes his feet stuck sprawlingly to the precarious ground like jelly. When he turned round I realized that he had a frog-like face, that dark hair hung down over his low forehead and small eyes. It was true, I had again and again seen a figure of similar appearance, posture and physiognomy on poster columns and walls without ever really paying any serious attention to it.

In general Nazi posters all looked alike. One was invariably confronted with the same breed of brutal and doggedly erect warrior, with a flag or a rifle or a sword, in SA, SS or military uniform, or alternatively naked; they always displayed physical strength and fanatical Will; muscles, toughness and a complete absence of introspection were the characteristics of these advertisements for sport and war and obedience to the Will of the Führer. 'We are the Führer's serfs!' a secondary school teacher had declaimed with due pathos in the presence of a number of Dresden philologists shortly after Hitler took up office; ever since then the word had screamed out at me from all the posters and special-issue stamps of the Third Reich; and if women were portrayed it was as the heroic Nordic wives of heroic Nordic men. I really could be excused for paying only cursory attention to these posters, particularly because, since wearing the star, I had made every effort to get off the street as quickly as possible, as I was never safe from insults, nor from the even more embarrassing expressions of sympathy. All of these pathetically heroic posters transposed the most monotonous bits of the monotonous LTI into pictorial equivalents without enriching them visually in any way. Nowhere was there a real coming together, a mutual improvement through the juxtaposition of pictorial representation and caption in these drawings which appeared by the dozen. 'Command us Führer and we will follow!' or 'Our flags pledge victory!' impressed themselves on the mind simply as banners, as phrases in their own right, and I didn't know of any instance where a saying or word and an image belonged together sufficiently for the one to evoke the other. I had also never known a figure from a poster in the Third Reich to catch on in everyday life like the *Kohlenklau,* a combination of word and image which had seized hold of an entire workforce.

As a result I had a good look at the poster: it was true, it really was offering something new, something of a fairy-tale, a figure from a ghost story, it appealed to the imagination. In Versailles there is a fountain inspired by Ovid's Metamorphoses: the figures slipping over the rim of the fountain are partially caught up in the magic spell, their human forms have begun to turn into animal shapes. *Kohlenklau* is of the same mould; his feet are almost amphibian, the hem of his coat looks like the stump of a tail, and with the stooping posture of the skulking thief he is almost a four-legged animal. The fortunate choice of name also contributes to the fairy-tale effect of the image: on the one hand casually folksy and down to earth thanks to the use of '*Klau* {snitch}' rather than *Dieb* {thief} and on the other lifted out of the everyday and made more poetical by the bold nominalization (compare it with the word *Fürsprech* {counsel}) and the use of alliteration. Word and image etched themselves jointly on the memory like the word and emblem for the SS.

Subsequently a few attempts were made to achieve the same result, but the effect was never the same. There was the *Groschengrab* {Penny Guzzler} representing some wastefulness or other – and it is telling that I no longer know which one; good alliteration, but the word was less colourful than *Kohlenklau* and the drawing less compelling. And then there was a dripping-wet *Frostgespenst* {Frost Ghost}, who climbed in through the window auguring disaster, but here the memorable name was missing. The only one who came close to the *Kohlenklau* was the shadowy, uncannily creeping figure of the *Lauscher* {Eavesdropper}, whose admonitory presence embellished the corners of newspapers, shop windows and matchboxes for months as a warning against spies. But the related caption *Feind hört mit* {Enemy is Listening Too} – the omission of the article, an Americanism, sounded disconcerting to

German ears – was already hackneyed by the time the ghostly man first made his appearance; these words had already been seen below any number of what you might call short-story-like images depicting the wicked enemy behind a newspaper listening in on an indiscreet discussion in a café or some such place.

Kohlenklau's direct impact can be gauged from a sequence of copies and variations on the theme: subsequently there was a *'Stundenklau* {Hour Thief}', there was a minesweeper called the *'Minenklau* {Mine Thief}', in *Das Reich* there was an illustration attacking the policies of Soviet Russia captioned *'Polenklau* {Poland Thief}' . . . The *Kohlenklau* himself reappeared unchanged, but this time framed in a hand-mirror; below were the words 'Put the glass up to your face: is it you or is it not?' And if someone left the door of a heated room open there would often be the cry *'Kohlenklau's* coming !'

Further categorical proof of the unique impact of this particular poster amongst myriad others, more telling even than the nickname given to Otto the porter, came in 1944 – at a time, therefore, when the *Kohlenklau* was no longer a novel or up-to-date image – when I observed the following little scene on the street: a young woman was fighting to no avail with her disobedient little boy. The lad repeatedly snatched his hand away from hers and stood there screaming, refusing to go on. All of a sudden a man of mature years, who, like me, had seen what was going on, walked up to the little boy, put his hand on his shoulder and said in a calm but serious tone: 'Are you going to be a good boy and go home with your mother? Yes or no? If not I will take you to the *Kohlenklau!*' For a moment the boy looked at the man in horror. Then he started to howl with fear, ran to his mother, clung to her skirt and screamed, 'Home, Mummy! Home, Mummy!' There is an extremely thought-provoking story by Anatole France, I believe it is called 'Putois the Gardener'. The children of one particular family are told that Putois is a menacing character, a bogeyman, and as such he enters into their fantasies; he becomes integral to the education of the next generation, turns into a family god and a supreme deity.

Had the Third Reich lasted much longer, *Kohlenklau* – born of word and image – would have had every chance of becoming a mythical person like Putois.

Chapter 15
Knif

I had already heard the word '*Knif* {out of the question}' for the first time two years before the war. Bertold M., who had come over in order to conclude his remaining business deals in these parts before emigrating to America ('Why should I allow all my efforts here to be scotched? We'll see each other again in a couple of years!'), Bertold M. replied to my question as to whether he believed in the long-term survival of the Third Reich, '*Knif!*' And, as the somewhat specious combination of sarcasm and indifference finally gave way to bitterness – which in turn had to be concealed on account of the Berlin Bushido – he appended a vigorous '*Kakfif!*' I looked at him inquiringly and he explained patronizingly that I had become very provincial and no longer had any idea what was going on in Berlin: 'Where we are everyone uses these words all the time. "*Knif*" means "*kommt nicht in Frage* {out of the question}" and *Kakfif*, "*kommt auf keinen Fall in Frage* {absolutely out of the question}"!'

An ability to appreciate the dubious side of things and a discerning sense of humour have always been fundamental ingredients of Berlin life (which is why to this very day I fail to understand how Nazism could have thrived in Berlin); it was for this reason that in the mid-1930s the Berliners began to exploit the comic potential of the obsession with abbreviations. If you can make the comedy a little salacious then the spiced-up jokes will be doubly funny; this is how the word 'popo {literally: botty}' came to stand in for 'good-night' as an antidote to the nights spent in Berlin cellars during bombing raids: 'Penne ohne Pause oben! {kip up there without a break}'.

Later, in March 1944, it got to the point of a serious, public and official warning against the improperly excessive use of '*Stummelwörter* {stump words}', as the abbreviations were referred to on this occasion. From time to time the representative *DAZ* devoted its regular column 'In our opinion' to linguistic matters. On this occasion it reported on an official decree intended to prevent the spread of these portmanteau words, which were considered to be ruining the language. As if it were possible for them to curtail through a single decree something which they had fostered repeatedly, and indeed still were, something moreover which ceaselessly grew of its own accord without any encouragement from those who were now trying to halt its development. It was questioned whether a phonetic sequence such as '*Hersta der Wigru*' was any longer German at all; the term appeared in a dictionary of economics and stood for '*Herstellungsanweisung der Wirtschaftsgruppe* {manufacturing instructions of the commercial group}'.

In the period between the popular joke in Berlin and the preliminary observations in the *DAZ* something happened which looks distinctly like the dulling of a bad conscience and the shifting of blame. An article in *Das Reich* with the poetic title '*Hang und Zwang zur Kürze* {The Inclination and Obligation to be Brief}' lays the blame for the 'monstrosities' of abbreviation at the foot of Bolshevism; German humour resists monstrosities of this kind; there are however, it was claimed, also successful contractions, all of them (of course!) the invention of the German people, such as the widespread use of the term '*Ari*' for *Artillerie* {artillery} during the First World War.

Everything is wrong in this essay: an abbreviation is an entirely artificial coinage, and as much a product of the people as Esperanto; the people themselves usually only contribute sarcastic imitations, forms such as '*Ari*' are exceptions. And the accusation of Russian authorship in relation to the linguistic monstrosities does not stand up to close scrutiny. As a matter of fact it clearly has its origins in an article published three months previously in *Das Reich* (on 7 May). Regarding the teaching of the Russian language in those areas of Southern Italy rid of Fascism, the article alleged that 'the Bolsheviks have buried the Russian language under a flood of discordant abbreviations and neologisms . . . pupils in Southern Italy are learning slang'.

Nazism may well have copied any number of things from Bolshevism via Italian Fascism (only to turn everything it touched – like some Midas of lies – into an untruth); it did not, however, need to steal the idea of creating contractions, because they were already in vogue by the beginning of the twentieth century and increasingly after the First World War, in Germany, in every European country, worldwide.

In Berlin the KDW, the Kaufhaus des Westens, has been around for a long time, and HAPAG for even longer. There is a charming French novel entitled *Mitsou: Mitsou* is both an abbreviation for an industrial concern and the name of a kept lover; this erotic connotation is sure proof of the fact that the abbreviation had become established in France.

Italy enjoyed a number of particularly creative contractions. Here one can identify three distinct stages: the most primitive simply strings together a few letters, as with BDM;[1] the second forms a phonetic unit which can be pronounced as a word; the third, however, reproduces an existing word in the given language, whereby the original word has some connection with what is expressed by the abbreviation. The word of creation 'Fiat' (Let there be!) denotes a proud automobile of the *'Fabbriche Italiane Automobili Torino'*, and the newsreel films of Fascist Italy are called *'Luce'* (light), which contains the first letters of the federation of pedagogical films, the *Lega universale di cinematografia educativa.* When Goebbels coined the contraction *'Hib-Aktion* {Hib Campaign}' for *'Hinein in die Betriebe!* {Into the Factories!}' it became a powerful expression only in the spoken language; in print its integrity was marred by orthographic incorrectness.

We heard that in Japan a young man and a young girl who dressed and behaved in a Euro-American style had been labelled 'Mobo' and 'Mogo', *modern boy* and *modern girl.*

And along with the geographical spread of contractions there is, after all, a corresponding historical span. Is not, indeed, the password and symbol of the earliest Christian communities, Ichthys, the fish, an abbreviation of this kind, made up of the first letters of the Greek words for 'Jesus Christ, Son of God, the Saviour'?

But if the contraction is so widespread across time and space, to what extent is it a specific mark and a specific evil of the LTI?

In answering this question I need to recall the tasks ascribed to abbreviations before National Socialism.

---

[1]See note on p. 9.

Ichthys is the emblem of a secret religious group, it is suffused with the romanticism of both a secret agreement and mystical enlightenment. Hapag has a brevity which is both commercially necessary and convenient for a telegram address. I am not sure whether one can infer from the far greater age of the romantic–transcendental, spiritual instance that the need for religious expression found an appropriate means of utterance before more practical concerns – I am equally sceptical about conclusions of this kind in the realm of language and poetics; it is perhaps simply that solemn expressions like this were more likely to be accorded the honour of being preserved than those relating to everyday matters.

What is more, on closer inspection, the dividing line between the romantic and the real becomes increasingly uncertain. Anyone who uses an abbreviated technical term to refer to an industrial article, anyone who uses a telegram address, will always, more or less acutely, more or less consciously, experience the warm feeling of standing out from the crowd, of being an initiate of a distinguished community by reason of special knowledge and a special allegiance; and the experts who came up with the appropriate contraction are very well aware of this emotional effect and make the most of it. Of course it is true that the modern, universal demand for contractions grew out of the business needs of commerce and industry. And pinpointing the dividing line between industrial and scientific abbreviations is also difficult.

The birthplace of the modern wave of contractions is undoubtedly to be found in the two leading commercial and industrial nations, England and America, and it is true – hence the attack on Russian 'linguistic monstrosities' – that Soviet Russia was particularly open to the influx of abbreviations given that Lenin, with the American model in mind, had made technological progress a major priority . . . a philologist's notebook! There are so many themes for seminar papers and dissertations in these few lines, so many insights still to be gained here into the history of language and culture . . . But the modern contraction did not only develop in the specialist field of economics, but also in the realm of political economics and politics itself in the narrow sense of the word. Wherever a union, organization or party is involved there will be an abbreviation at hand, and it is here that the emotional value of the unique term becomes clearly apparent. The attempt to discover American roots for this category of contractions seems to me to be inappropriate; I don't know whether the term SPD[2] needed a foreign linguistic model. The imitation of foreign examples is, nevertheless, probably responsible for the tremendous spread of these contractions in Germany.

Here again, however, a specifically German, autochthonous dimension comes into play. The most powerful organization of Imperial Germany was the army. And the language of the military incorporated all of the different forms and styles of abbreviation, the succinct term for a piece of machinery and a group, the code word as outer protection and inner solidarity.

If I ask myself now whether and why the contraction should be counted as a principal characteristic of the LTI, the answer is simple. No linguistic style prior to Hitler German had made such an exorbitant use of this form. The modern contraction always appears with new technology and new organization. And in line with its claim to totality Nazism brings new technology and new organizations into everything. Hence the immense number of abbreviations. However, since this claim to totality also involves an attempt to control people's inner lives, because it aspires to be religion, planting the swastika everywhere, each of its contractions is also related to the old Christian 'fish': *Kradschütze*[3] {motorized infantry} or teams of MGs {machine-gunners}, members of the HJ or the DAF –[4] everyone is 'sworn into the community'.

[2]Abbreviation of *Sozialdemokratische Partei Deutschlands,* German Social Democratic Party.
[3]Abbreviation for *Kraftradschütze.*
[4]See note on p. 9.

Chapter 16
On a Single Working Day

The poison is everywhere. It is borne by the drinking water of the LTI, nobody is immune to its effects.

The envelope and paper bag factory Thiemig & Möbius was not particularly National Socialist. The boss was a member of the SS but he did whatever he could for his Jews, he spoke politely to them, he sometimes made sure they got something from the canteen. I really don't know what comforted me more thoroughly and enduringly: the arrival of a scrap of horse-meat sausage or for once being addressed as 'Herr Klemperer', or even 'Herr Professor'. The Aryan workers, amongst whom those of us with the Star of David were distributed – segregation only occurred at mealtimes and during air raid protection duty; at the workplace the ban on conversation was supposed to be a substitute for isolation, but no one adhered to it – these workers were certainly not devotees of National Socialism, at least by the winter of 1943/44 they weren't any more. Everyone feared the foreman and two or three women who were believed to be capable of denunciation, people prodded each other or exchanged warning glances when one of these notorious characters appeared; but once they were out of sight comradely co-operation was immediately restored.

Most friendly of all was the hunchback Frieda who had trained me and continued to help when I got into difficulties with my envelope machine. She had worked for the firm for more than thirty years and did not let even the foreman prevent her from shouting an encouraging word to me above the noise of the machine room: 'Don't be so pompous! I didn't talk to him, I simply gave him an instruction regarding the gumming machine!' Frieda knew that my wife was lying ill at home. In the morning I found a big apple in the middle of my machine. I looked over to Frieda's workplace and she nodded to me. A little later she was standing next to me: 'For Mama with my best wishes.' And then, with a mixture of inquisitiveness and surprise: 'Albert says that your wife is German. Is she really German?' . . .

The pleasure in the apple was gone. This Sancta-Simplicitas soul, whose feelings were entirely un-Nazi and humane, had been infected by the most fundamental ingredient of the National Socialist poison; she identified Germanness with the magical concept of the Aryan; it was barely conceivable to her that a German woman could be married to me, to a foreigner, a creature from another branch of the animal kingdom; all too often she had heard and repeated the terms *'artfremd* {alien}' and *'deutschblütig* {of German blood}' and *'niederrassig* {of inferior race}' and *'nordisch* {Nordic}' and *'Rassenschande* {racial defilement}':[1] she certainly didn't have a clear picture of what this all meant – but her feelings could not grasp the fact that my wife could be a German.

Albert, from whom she had her information, was rather better at thinking than she was. He harboured his own political opinions, and they were in no way supportive of the government, nor were they militaristic. He had lost a brother in action, he himself had so far been deferred at each army medical examination on the grounds of a serious stomach disorder. He mentioned this 'so far' every day: 'I'm still free so far – I hope this wretched war is over before they finally call me up!' On that day of the apple, which had also seen a veiled report of the success of the Allies somewhere in Italy, he discussed his favourite topic with a comrade for rather longer than usual. I was stacking piles of paper for my machine on to a trolley right next to Albert's workplace. 'I hope they don't call me up', he said, 'before this wretched war is over!' – 'Look here mate, how on earth is it going to be over? No one wants to give in.' – 'Yes of course: they will just have to realize that we are invincible; they can't break us because we are so fantastically well organized {*prima organisiert*}!' Fantastically well organized – there it was again, he had swallowed the mind-numbing drug.

---

[1] Term used to describe forbidden cohabitation between German Aryans and Jews.

An hour later the boss called me to help label the finished boxes. He wrote the labels as per invoice and I stuck them on to the towering rows of boxes which formed a wall separating us from the rest of the workers in the room. This isolation made the old man talkative. He was approaching 70 and still working; this was not how he had imagined his old age, he sighed. But these days you have to work like a slave until you're done for! 'And what will happen to my grandchildren if the lads don't come back? We haven't heard anything of Erhard from Murmansk for months, and the youngest is in a military hospital in Italy. If only peace would come . . . It's just that the Americans don't want it, they've no business being here . . . But they're getting rich through this war, this handful of Jewish pigs. It really is the "Jewish war" ! . . . There they are again !'

He had been interrupted by the wail of the sirens; we often had a full-scale alarm unexpectedly, at this time of day we often didn't hear the early warnings because they had become so common that they no longer led to an interruption of work.

Down in the huge cellar the Jewish group sat around a pillar, crowded together and clearly separated from the Aryan workforce. But the Aryan benches were not far away and the discussions from the front rows reached us. Every two or three minutes we heard the report on the situation from the loudspeaker. 'The formation has swung to the southwest . . . New squadron approaching from the north. Danger of an attack on Dresden.'

The conversation faltered. Then the silence was broken by a fat woman sitting on the front bench, a very industrious and skilful worker who operated the large, complicated machine producing 'envelopes with windows' – with a smile and a tone of calm certainly she announced, 'They won't come, Dresden will be spared.' – 'Why?' enquired her neighbour. 'Surely you don't believe that nonsense about them making Dresden into the capital of Czechoslovakia?' – 'Oh no, I have an even better reason than that to be so sure.' – 'What reason?' The answer came with an enthusiastic smile which sat awkwardly on her earthy and unintellectual face. 'Three of us saw it quite clearly. Last Sunday afternoon near the Annenkirche. The sky was clear except for a few clouds. All of a sudden one of these little clouds straightened itself out to form a face, a sharply defined, truly unique profile' (she really did say 'unique {*einmalig*}). 'All three of us recognized it at once.

My husband was the first to call out: It's Old Fritz,[2] just as he always looks in the pictures!' – 'So what?' – 'What happened then?' – 'What's all that got to do with our safety here in Dresden?' – 'How can anyone ask such a stupid question? Isn't the image which all three of us saw – my husband, my brother-in-law and I – a sure sign that Old Fritz is looking after Dresden? And what can happen to a city he is protecting? . . . You see! There's the all-clear already, we can go back up.'

Of course it was exceptional that four such revelations of the prevailing state of mind should come together all on one day. But the state of mind itself was exclusive neither to this one day nor to these four people.

None of these four was a real Nazi.

In the evening I was on air raid protection duty; the route to the Aryan control room passed just a couple of metres from my seat. While I was reading a book the Frederick the Great enthusiast called out 'Heil Hitler!' as she walked past. The next morning she came up to me and said in a kind tone, 'Forgive me for saying "Heil Hitler!" yesterday; I was in a hurry and I mistook you for someone I was supposed to greet in that way.'

None of them were Nazis, but they were all poisoned.

[2]Colloquial expression for Frederick the Great.

Chapter 17
'System' and *'Organisation'*

There is the Copernican system, there are various philosophical and various political systems. But when a National Socialist refers to *'das System* {the system}' he invariably means the system of the Weimar Constitution. In this special LTI meaning – or rather expanded to denote the entire period from 1918 to 1933 – the word became popular very quickly, considerably more popular than, for example, the historical term Renaissance. As early as summer 1935 a carpenter who was mending our garden gate said to me: 'Am I sweating! In the days of the system there used to be those nice Byron collars {*Schillerkragen*} which left your neck free. You can't get anything like that any more, everything is close fitting and wherever possible also stiff.' The man obviously didn't realize that in one single sentence he had figuratively mourned the lost freedom of the Weimar era and also figuratively poured scorn over the very same period. That the Byron collar was a symbol for freedom is self-explanatory, what is not so obvious is that the term *'System'* should harbour a metaphorical indictment.

For the Nazis the system of government in the Weimar Republic was the system *per se* because they had been in direct conflict with it, because they held it to be the worst form of government, and because they felt more antagonistic towards it than, for example, towards the monarchy. They condemned it for the paralysing effect of the splintering of the political parties. Following the first farcical sitting of the Reichstag under Hitler's tyrannical control – nothing was discussed and every government demand was accepted unanimously by a well-trained group of supernumeraries – the Party newspapers reported triumphantly that the new Reichstag had achieved more in half an hour than the old system's parliamentarianism in six months.

But linguistically – in the term itself, I mean, despite the fact that in this case it simply stands for 'Weimar parliamentarianism' – there is much more to the rejection of the system than this. A system is something which is 'assembled {*Zusammengestelltes*}', a construction, a structure built by hands and tools according to the dictates of reason. We still refer today to a railway or canal system, meaning something that is concrete and constructive. More commonly however (we do, after all, often like to refer to 'a railway network') the word is used to refer almost exclusively to abstractions. The Kantian system is a logically structured network of ideas to grasp the world in its entirety; for Kant – for the professional, trained philosopher as it were – to philosophize means to think systematically. And it is this very way of thinking which the National Socialist rejects from the innermost core of his being, which he despises out of a desire for self-preservation.

Someone who thinks does not want to be persuaded but rather convinced; someone who thinks systematically is doubly hard to convince. That is why the LTI is, if anything, less fond of the word 'philosophy' than of the word 'system'. It approaches the system with antipathy, refers to it with disdain, but does so frequently. Philosophy on the other hand is hushed up and universally replaced with '*Weltanschauung* {worldview}'.

Anschauen {viewing something} has never been an intellectual activity, the thinker does the exact opposite, he divorces his senses from the object in question, he abstracts; *Anschauen* is also never just a matter of simply looking at something with the eye as a sensory organ. The eye only sees. The word '*anschauen*' is reserved in German for a finer, more portentous and mysteriously significant – I don't know which – activity or condition: it denotes a way of seeing which involves the observer's inner being and his emotions, and it denotes a way of seeing which discerns more than simply the surface of a given object, which in a strange way also grasps its essence, its soul. As a substitute for philosophy, the word '*Weltanschauung*', already prevalent before National Socialism, lost its solemnity and acquired an everyday, business-like ring. '*Schau* {vision}', revered by the followers of Stefan George, also became a ceremonial word for the LTI – if I were writing this notebook in the form of a proper dictionary, and in the style of my beloved encyclopaedia,

I would doubtless refer to the entry on 'Barnum' – 'system' belongs in the list of abominations along with 'intelligence' and 'objectivity'.

But if 'system' is frowned upon, how does the Nazis system of government refer to itself? Because they have a system as well, after all, and are proud of the fact that absolutely every expression and situation in life is caught up in this network; that is why 'totality {*Totalität*}' is one of the foundations on which the LTI is built.

They don't have a *System,* they have an *Organisation,* they don't think systematically with the power of reason, they cull secrets from all that is organic.

I must start with the adjective which, alone amongst this family of words – and unlike the nouns '*Organ* {organ}' and '*Organisation*', and the verb '*organisierien* {to organize}' – has maintained the splendour and the aura that it had from day one. (When was day one? Without question at the dawn of Romanticism. But, of course, one always says 'without question' when questions crop up, so this will have to be dealt with separately.)

By the time Clemens hammered on my head with the *Myth of the Twentieth Century* during a house search in the Caspar-David-Friedrich-Straße, and tore up the accompanying pages of notes (fortunately without deciphering them), I had already pondered Rosenberg's Delphic central idea of the 'organic truth' in my diary. And already at that point, before the invasion of Russia, I wrote: 'How ridiculous it would be in its jumble of hollow phrases if only it didn't have such frighteningly deadly consequences!'

Rosenberg informs us that the professional philosophers always make a double mistake. First, they set out 'to find the so-called single, eternal truth'. And second they search 'along a purely logical route, drawing conclusion after conclusion from axioms of reason'. If, on the other hand, one surrenders oneself to his, Alfred Rosenberg's, strictly non-philosphical insights derived from the profundity of an omniscient mystical vision, then the 'whole bloodless, intellectual rubble heap of exclusively schematic systems is done away with' once and for all. These quotations contain the most significant reason for the LTI's antipathy towards the word '*System*' and what it denotes.

Directly following on from this, the concluding few pages of the *Myth* finally enthrone the notion of the 'organic'; orgao (οργάω) means to swell, to put out shoots, to be trained unconsciously like a plant, 'organic' is sometimes translated into German as '*wuchshaft* {sprouting}'. The single, universally valid truth which is meant to exist for an imaginary, universal humanity is replaced by the 'organic truth' which emerges from the blood of a particular race and is only valid for that race. This organic truth is not thought up and fostered by the intellect, it is not grounded in rational knowledge, but instead is to be found at the 'mysterious centre of the soul of a people and of a race {*geheimnisvollen Zentrum der Volks- und Rassenseele*}', present for the Teutons {*Germanen*} since time immemorial in the Nordic bloodstream: 'the ultimate "knowledge" of a particular race is already embodied in its earliest religious myth.' Things would not get any clearer if I assembled a mass of quotations; it is not Rosenberg's intention to make things clearer. Thought strives for clarity, magic takes place in semi-darkness.

The magic aura which surrounds the organic in these pythonic discourses, and the stupefying odour of blood in which it is shrouded, are to some extent lost linguistically if we move from the adjective to the noun and verb. The reason being that there had been 'party organs' and 'organizations' in the political sphere long before the NSDAP, and during the period in which I first heard people discussing political matters, which was in the 1890s, it would typically be said of a worker in Berlin that he was '*ein Organisierter* {an organized man}' or that he was '*organisiert* {organized}', which meant that he was a member of the Social Democratic Party. However, a party organ is not produced by the magical powers of the bloodstream, rather, it is edited with much care and attention, and an organization doesn't grow like a fruit, but is carefully built up, or, as the Nazis used to say, '*aufgezogen* {set up}'. I have definitely also come across certain writers, even before the First World War – in my diary there is a note in brackets: 'check where and when!', but even today, a year after our deliverance, it is very difficult to check such things – writers for whom an organization is a way of doing away with the organic, of taking out the soul and making a machine. Even amongst the National Socialists themselves, in Dwinger's novel on the Kapp putsch, *Auf halbem Wege* (Halfway) (1939), I found the 'miserable' bond sustained by an organization, despised for its artificiality, contrasted with the 'true', evolutionary bond of nature. But of course Dwinger only gradually descended into Nazism.

At any rate '*Organisation*' remained an honest and honoured word within the LTI, indeed it underwent a further refinement which had not existed prior to 1933, except perhaps in occasional and isolated technical contexts.

The will to totality entailed an excess of organization, right down to the *Pimpfe*,[1] no, right down to the cats: I was not allowed to make any more contributions to the Society for the Prevention of Cruelty to Cats because there was no room in *Das deutsche Katzenwesen* {The German Feline} – this really was the name of the society's newsletter, which had become a Party organ – for those mongrel creatures which resided with Jews. Later they took our pets away from us, cats, dogs, even canaries, and killed them, not just in isolated cases and out of individual malice, but officially and systematically; this is one of those acts of cruelty which will not be mentioned at any Nuremberg Trial and for which, if it was up to me, I would erect a towering gallows, even if it cost me eternal salvation.

I have not strayed as far from the subject of the LTI as it may at first appear, because it was precisely the 'German Feline' which provided the opportunity for this linguistic invention to become both popular and ridiculous. In their mania for organization and the greatest possible degree of centralization, the Nazis created collective 'umbrella organizations' over and above individual organizations; and because the *Münchener Neueste Nachrichten* still felt it could be a little daring during the first Fasching season of the Third Reich – later it became tame and finally went completely silent after two or three years – it published in its first Fasching special edition, amongst other things, a note about the 'Umbrella Organization of the German Feline'.

Although this derisory remark remained an exception and was not afforded a particularly wide circulation, an unconscious critique of the National Socialist obsession with organization, and one, in intention at least, entirely devoid of irony, grew quite organically out of the people's soul {*Volksseele*}; to put it unromantically, it appeared simultaneously and entirely naturally all over the place. The reason being once again, as I wrote at the beginning of my notebook, that language writes and thinks for us. I observed this unconscious critique in two distinct phases of its development.

As early as 1936 a young car mechanic who had managed to carry out a tricky emergency repair on my exhaust all by himself said to me,

[1]See note on p. 45.

'Didn't I organize that well!' The words '*Organisation*' and '*Organisieren* {to organize}' were ringing in his ears so insistently, and he was so saturated with the idea that every bit of work had first to be organized, i.e. had to be allocated to a disciplined group by its leader, that he couldn't even come up with an appropriate and simple expression like '*arbeiten* {to work}', '*erledigen* {to deal with}' or '*verrichten* {carry out}' or even just '*machen* {to do}' for a task which he himself undertook and completed.

I first encountered the second and decisive phase in the development of this critique during the Stalingrad days, and subsequently on numerous occasions. I asked whether it was still possible to buy good soap. The answer was 'You can't buy it, you have to organize it.' The word had fallen into ill repute, it smelled of wheelings and dealings, of black marketeering, it was tainted with exactly the same smell that the Nazi organizations themselves emitted. Which did not of course mean that the people who spoke of organizing things privately intended to admit to questionable activities. No, '*organisieren*' was a benign word which had become fashionable everywhere, it was the most commonplace expression to describe an activity which had itself become commonplace . . .

For some time now I have been writing: it was . . . it was. But who was it said only yesterday 'I must organize some tobacco for myself?' I fear it was me.

Chapter 18

I Believe in Him

When I think of professions of faith in Adolf Hitler the first person who springs to mind is always Paula von B., standing in front of me, with her grey eyes open wide in a face no longer in the first flush of youth, but delicate, and as good-natured as it was intelligent. She was an assistant in Walzel's German department, and over the years she diligently helped innumerable future elementary and secondary school teachers get hold of books and write their compulsory essays.

It should be noted at this point that Oskar Walzel may well now and then have erred somewhat from the straight and narrow path of aesthetics into the domain of the aesthete, that his predilection for the very latest trend occasionally exposed him to the danger of snobbishness, and that in his large public lectures he perhaps paid undue attention to the many women present, and the so-called afternoon-tea audience, but, despite all this, when it came to his books he was always an excellent scholar and a thoughtful man to whom literary studies owes a considerable debt. Because his whole cast of mind and attitude towards society clearly marked him out as belonging to the left wing of the bourgeoisie, his opponents liked to accuse him of 'Jewish journalese {jüdischer Feuilletonismus}'; it must consequently have come as a great surprise to them when – by this time already in Bonn and at the end of his academic career – he was able to provide the proof of Aryan status demanded by Hitler. For his wife, however, and in particular for his circle of friends, this Nuremberg note of indulgence was unattainable.[1]

---

[1] Proof of racial purity was demanded by the Nuremberg Laws on Citizenship and Race, passed in 1935.

All in all Fräulein von B. was very content to work for a boss of this kind, and his friends were her friends. For my part, it is undoubtedly thanks to her affection that I never failed to recognize Walzel's inner qualities despite his minor surface imperfections. When at a later date Walzel's successor in Dresden substituted a certain philosophical viscidity for the salon tone – it seems that the cathedraticos of literary studies are not able to manage without a touch of coquettishness, it appears inevitably to go with the job – Paula von B. adapted herself to the style of her new boss with almost the same degree of contentment; in any event her erudition and understanding were sufficient to enable her to swim with this tide as well.

She came from an officer's family which belonged to the old nobility, her father had died as a retired general, her brother returned from the world war as a major, whereupon he found a prestigious position of trust in a large Jewish firm. If anyone had asked me prior to 1933 what Paula von B.'s political opinions were, I would probably have answered as follows: obviously German and equally obviously European and liberal, despite the odd wistful reminiscence of the glorious Imperial era; but it is more likely that I would have replied that politics wasn't an issue for her, that her entire life revolved around intellectual matters, and that the practical demands of her university post prevented her from becoming an aesthete or being lost in hot air.

And then came 1933. Paula von B. had to collect a book from my department. Usually so serious she came up to me on this occasion with a cheerful face and a youthful spring in her every step. 'You look radiant! Has something good happened to you?' – 'Something very good! Do I really need to explain? . . . I feel ten years younger, no, nineteen: I haven't felt like this since 1914!' – 'And you are telling me about it? You can say all this even though you can see, read and hear how people who used to be close to you are being denounced, how books which you once respected are being condemned, how people are rejecting the very intellectual things that you used to . . .' She interrupted me a little alarmed and very lovingly: 'My dear Professor I hadn't expected you to overreact so nervously. You should take a couple of weeks' holiday and not read any newspapers. You are allowing yourself to get upset at this moment, and allowing yourself to be distracted from what really matters by minor embarrassments and blemishes which can scarcely be avoided during periods of such radical change. In no time at all you will judge things quite differently. Can I come and visit the two of you some time soon?' And with the greeting 'kind regards to your family' she exited through the door like a bouncy teenager before I could even reply.

The 'no time at all' turned into many months, during which the general perfidy of the new regime and its particularly brutal attitude towards the 'Jewish intelligentsia' became ever more apparent. Paula von B. may well have been shaken in her artlessness. We didn't see each other at the university – I don't know if she deliberately avoided me.

Then one day she did turn up at our place. She felt it to be her duty as a German to make an open confession to her friends, and hoped that she could still consider herself to be a friend of ours. '"Duty as a German" is not something you would have said in the past,' I interjected, 'what has being German or non-German got to do with highly personal or universal human questions? Or do you want to discuss politics with us?' – 'Everything is related to the issue of being German or non-German, this is all that matters; you see that's what I, what we all, have either learned from the Führer or rediscovered having forgotten it. He has brought us home again!' – 'And why are you telling us this?' – 'You must recognize, you must understand that I belong entirely to the Führer, but I don't want you to think that as a result I have renounced my affection towards you . . .' – 'And how can these two feelings be reconciled? And what does the Führer say concerning your former boss Walzel, the teacher you admired so much? And how can you reconcile this with the humanitarianism of Lessing and all the others about whom you had essays written? And how . . . but it's pointless asking any more questions.'

She had in fact simply shaken her head in response to every sentence I uttered and had tears in her eyes. 'No, it really does seem to be pointless, because everything you are asking is based on reason, and the accompanying feelings stem from bitterness about insignificant details.' – 'And what are my questions supposed to be based on if not reason? And what is significant?' – 'I've told you already: that we've really come home! It's something you have to feel, and you must abandon yourself to your feelings, and you must always focus on the Führer's greatness, rather than on the discomfort which you are experiencing at present . . . And our classical writers? I really don't think that they are at variance with him in any way, you just have to read them properly, Herder for example, and in any case they would certainly have been convinced sooner or later!' – 'And where does this certainty come from?' – 'Where all certainties come from: faith. And if all this doesn't mean anything to you, then – yes, then the Führer is right after all when he comes out against the . . . (she just managed to swallow the word Jews and continued) . . . against the sterile intelligentsia. Because I believe in him, and I had to tell you that I believe in him.' – 'Well in that case, Fräulein von B., the best thing is to postpone our friendship and the discussion about faith indefinitely . . .'

She left, and for the short time that I continued to work at the university we really did make an effort to avoid one another. After that I only saw her again on one occasion, and once heard her name mentioned in conversation.

The encounter occurred at one of the historic moments of the Third Reich. On 13 March 1938 I innocently opened the door leading to the main banking hall of the Staatsbank and started back until I was at least partially hidden by the half-open door. The reason being that inside everyone present, both behind and in front of the counters, was standing stiffly erect with outstretched arms listening to a declamatory voice on the radio. The voice announced the law governing the annexation {Anschluß} of Austria to Hitler's Germany. I remained half-hidden in order not to have to practise the salute along with everyone else. Right at the front of this gathering of people I caught sight of Fräulein von B. She was in a state of total ecstasy, her eyes sparkled, she was not simply standing to attention like the others, the rigidity of her posture and salute was more of a convulsion, a moment of rapture.

A few years later a piece of news reached the Jews' House indirectly about a number of university people. It was reported with a chuckle that Fräulein von B. was the most adamant supporter of the Führer. At the same time she was also much more harmless than many other party followers because she was not interested in denouncing people or any other sort of malice. She was just utterly enthusiastic. Currently she was apparently showing everyone a photograph which she had managed to take. On a holiday trip she had been able to admire the Obersalzberg from afar; she had not caught sight of the Führer – but she had seen his dog and had managed to take a wonderful photograph of it.

When my wife heard about this she remarked, 'I told you as early as 1933 that B. was a hysterical old maid who had found her saviour in the Führer. He relies on these old maids, or rather he relied on them until he had the power in his own hands.' – 'And my reply is the same as it was then: you may well be right about the hysterical old maids, but there must have been more to it, and it certainly wouldn't be sufficient now either, especially not now (it was after Stalingrad), despite all the instruments of power and despite all the tyranny, regardless of how ruthless it is. He must radiate faith, and this faith must communicate itself to more than just old maids. What's more, Fräulein von B. is not just any old maid. For many years (some of which were pretty difficult for her as well) we knew her to be a very sensible woman, she had a good education, she had a post to which she was well fitted, she grew up in a sensible, hard-working environment, for many years she felt at home amongst people with broad horizons – all of which should have made her relatively immune to a religious psychosis of this kind . . . I hold much store by her claim "I believe in him" . . .'

And right at the end of the war, when it was clear to everybody that total and irredeemable defeat was inevitable, when the end was nigh, I encountered this credo on two separate occasions, and in both cases without an old maid in sight.

The first was in a wood near Pfaffenhofen. It was early April 1945. We had managed to flee to Bavaria, we were in the possession of papers which would enable us to find accommodation, but for the time being each local authority passed us on to the next. We proceeded on foot with heavy luggage and were exhausted. A soldier caught up with us, picked up our heaviest piece of luggage without saying a word and followed us. He must have been in his early twenties, he had a friendly, open face, he looked strong and fit despite the fact that the left sleeve of his tunic hung empty by his side. He could see, he began, that we were having trouble carrying our things – why shouldn't he help out a 'national comrade {*Volksgenosse*}', in any case our route was the same as far as Pfaffenhofen. And then in a friendly tone he told us something about himself. He had been wounded and taken prisoner on the Atlantic Wall, he had lived in an American camp and then, as an amputee, been part of an exchange. He was a farmer from Pomerania and wanted to return home as soon as it was out of enemy hands. – 'Out of enemy hands? Do you think that's likely? The Russians are just outside Berlin, and the English and Americans . . .' – 'I know, I know, and there are many people who think the war is lost.' — 'And you don't? You've seen a lot, you must also have heard a number of things when you were abroad . . .' – 'What they say abroad is all a pack of lies.' – 'But our enemies have already entered deep into Germany, and our reserves are exhausted.' – 'You mustn't say that. Just wait and see what happens in a fortnight.' – 'How is a fortnight going to change anything?' – 'It's the Führer's birthday. Many people are saying that is when the counter-offensive will begin, and that we have only let the enemy in this far in order to be able to destroy them all the more effectively.' – 'And you believe that?' – 'I'm only a lance-corporal; I don't understand enough about warfare in order to be able to judge. But the Führer announced only recently that we are definitely going to win. And he has never lied yet. I believe in Hitler. No, God won't leave him in the lurch, I believe in Hitler.'

Although he had been very talkative up to this point, uttering this last sentence in the same uncomplicated tone as the rest, albeit perhaps rather more pensively, he now cast his eyes to the ground and remained silent. I didn't know what to reply and was glad when he left us as we came to the first houses of Pfaffenhofen.

And it happened again shortly afterwards in the little village of Unter-bernbach where we had finally found accommodation and which was occupied by the Americans shortly afterwards. Singly and in troops the remnants of the defeated regiments streamed back from the nearby front line. It was a drying-up of the army. Everyone knew that the end was approaching, and everyone wanted to avoid being imprisoned. Most of them railed at the war and longed for peace, everything else was irrelevant to them. Some of them cursed Hitler, quite a few cursed the regime and reckoned that the Führer had had something else in mind and that others were responsible for the collapse.

We talked to many people because our landlord was the most charitable soul imaginable, and for every refugee there was always a piece of bread or a spoonful of soup. One evening four soldiers from different units were sitting round the table, they were to sleep in the barn afterwards. Two of them were young students from North Germany, the other two were older, a carpenter from Upper Bavaria and an upholsterer from Storkow. The Bavarian spoke with great bitterness about Hitler and the two students agreed. At this point the upholsterer banged on the table with his fist. 'You should be ashamed of yourselves. You are behaving as if we had lost the war. Just because the Yanks have broken through here!' – 'Oh yes, and what about the Russians? . . . And the Tommys . . . And the French?' They attacked him from all sides, surely even a child could understand that it was the eleventh hour. – 'Understanding has nothing to do with it, you have to have faith. The Führer won't give in, and the Führer can't be defeated, and he has always found a way when others have said there is no way out. No, damn it, no, understanding is useless, you have to have faith. I believe in the Führer.'

_____

Thus I have heard this profession of faith in Hitler from two different social strata – from the intellectuals and, in the narrow sense of the word, from the working man – and during both periods, at the beginning and at the very end. And I unfortunately never had any reason to doubt that as well as coming from the lips, it also came from the heart. And I can also confirm now, as then, that the three confessors were undoubtedly of what one would normally consider to be average intelligence.

_____

It is self-evident that at its height the LTI was a language of faith because its objective was fanaticism. But what is strange is that as a language of faith it relied heavily on Christianity or, to be more precise, on Catholicism, despite the fact that from the very outset National Socialism fought against Christianity in general and the Catholic Church in particular, sometimes openly, sometimes secretly, sometimes in theory and sometimes in practice. The theory demolishes the Hebraic and – a technical term of the LTI – 'Syriac {syrisch}' roots of Christianity; in practice members of the SS are repeatedly expected to leave the Church, efforts are made to require the same of elementary school teachers, homosexual teachers in monastic schools are put on trial without good reason, clergymen are labelled 'political clergymen' and locked up in prisons and camps.

But the first victims of the Party, the sixteen who died in front of the Feldherrnhalle, are treated like Christian martyrs in the rituals and language accorded them. The flag which was borne at the head of their demon- stration is called the *Blutfahne* {Blood Banner}, and new SA and SS standards are consecrated by touching it. There is also of course no lack of '*Blutzeugen* {martyrs, blood witnesses}' in the accompanying speeches and articles. Even those who have experienced these ceremonies indirectly, or through the cinema, are still enveloped in a miasma simply by the pious smell of blood emanating from these expressions.

It is true, the first Christmas after the usurpation of Austria, 'Greater Germany's Christmas of 1938', is entirely de-christianized by the press: it is in every way a 'Festival of the German Soul' which is being celebrated, the 'Resurrection of the Greater German Reich' and accordingly the rebirth of the light, at which point the discussion turns to representation of the sun and the swastika, leaving the Jew Jesus entirely out of it. And when shortly afterwards a Blood Order is founded to celebrate Himmler's birthday it is specifically referred to as an 'Order of Nordic Blood'.

But taken together what comes across in these words is in fact something akin to Christian transcendence: the mysticism of Christmas, martyrdom, resurrection and the consecration of an order of knights – these ideas, be they derived from Catholicism or Parsifal, are plainly linked (and that despite their paganism) to the actions of the Führer and his Party. And the martyrs' *'ewige Wache* {eternal guard}' directs the imagination in a similar direction.

Here the word *ewig* {eternal} plays its very special part. It is one of those words in the LTI dictionary whose specifically Nazi aspect derives purely from excessive use: an inordinate number of things in the LTI are *'historisch* {historic}', *'einmalig* {unique}' and *'ewig* {eternal}'. It is possible to see *ewig* as the final rung in a long ladder of National Socialist numerical superlatives, but with this final rung heaven is reached. Eternal is an attribute reserved exclusively for the divine; by calling something eternal I elevate it to the sphere of the religious. 'We have found the path to eternity', Ley claims at the opening of a Hitler school in early 1938. In examinations for apprentices there is a common but pernicious trick-question. It reads: 'What comes after the Third Reich?' If the candidate is gullible or falls into the trap he will answer 'the Fourth', at which point he will be failed mercilessly as an inadequate disciple of the Party (even if he has an excellent knowledge of his subject). The correct answer should read: 'Nothing comes after it, the Third Reich is the eternal German Reich.'

I only noted on one occasion that Hitler referred to himself, in words unambiguously derived from the New Testament, as the German saviour – (but once again: not much reached my ears and eyes, and even now I can only undertake a very limited amount of supplementary reading). I noted under 9 November 1935: – He called those who fell at the Feldherrnhalle "My Apostles" – there are sixteen, of course he has to have four more than his predecessor – and in the funeral ceremony there are the words "You have risen again in the Third Reich".'

Even if this direct self-deification and stylistic alignment with the Christ of the New Testament was an exception, and perhaps it really did only happen on this one occasion, it remains the case that the Führer again and again underlined his uniquely close relationship with the Godhead, his special status as the chosen one, his special sonship, his religious mission. During his triumphant rise he said in Würzburg (June 1937): 'We are led by Providence, we act according to the Will of the Almighty. No one can make national and world history if he has not been blessed by this Providence.' On 'The Day of Remembrance for the Dead of the First World War' in 1940 he places his trust 'humbly in the mercy of Providence'. For years the Providence which chose him appears in almost every speech and almost every address. Following the assassination attempt of 20 July 1944 it is fate which saved him, because the nation needs him, the standard-bearer 'of faith and of trust'. On New Year's Eve 1944, when every last hope of victory has evaporated, the personal God of the days of triumph has to return, the 'Almighty' who cannot leave the just cause without victory.

But there is something else which is more important than these individual references to the Godhead. In the selection from his diary, *Vom Kaiserhof zur Reichskanzlei* (From the Kaiserhof to the Reich Chancellery), Goebbels reports on 10 February 1932 on a speech given by the Führer in the Sportpalast: 'Towards the end he built up to a wonderful, incredible rhetorical pathos and closed with the word Amen!, it sounded so natural that everybody was deeply shaken and moved by it . . . the masses in the Sportpalast were soon caught up in a frenzy . . .' This Amen demonstrates clearly that the general thrust of this rhetoric was religious and pastoral. And the phrase 'it sounded so natural' coming from the most expert listener betrays a high degree of calculated rhetoric. If you read the recipes for mass suggestion which Hitler himself discloses in *Mein Kampf you* are left in no doubt as to the deliberate nature of the seduction which lies behind the adoption of this pious, ecclesiastical register. At any rate, a religious fanatic, a madman, often develops a high degree of ingenuity to minister to his madness, and experience has shown that the most powerful and lasting suggestion is brought into play by those conmen who have already conned themselves. But Hitler himself has spared the Nuremberg judges the decision as to whether he belongs on the gallows or in a lunatic asylum, and the question here is not one of guilt but rather how he was able to have such an effect. The fact that this effect ends up being religious is partly a result of the fact that specific individual expressions echo those of Christ and partly, indeed increasingly, a result of the sermon-like, enthusiastic delivery of extended passages of these speeches.

But the main reason is that for his deification he could count on the well-organized assistance of numerous trained aides.

A few pages after the passage just quoted, Goebbels proudly reports on the 'Day of the Nation's Awakening': 'We will employ all the means of propaganda available to us with a concentration never before experienced . . .', everything 'will go like clockwork'. And the Führer speaks in Königsberg, everyone is deeply moved, and then 'with the final chord of the speech, the Netherlandish prayer of thanksgiving fills the air, drowned out in the last verse by a peal of bells from the Königsberg cathedral. Thanks to the wireless this hymn resonates through the ether across the whole of Germany.'

But the Führer can't speak every day, he mustn't, the Godhead must normally be seated on his throne above the clouds and more often speak through the mouths of his priests than he does himself. And here Hitler has the further advantage that his servants and friends can elevate him to the status of Saviour even more decisively and with fewer inhibitions than he can, praying to him even more incessantly and with more voices. From 1933 to 1945, right up until the catastrophe in Berlin, this elevation of the Führer to the status of a god, this alignment of his person and his actions with the Saviour and the Bible, took place day by day and always 'went like clockwork' and it was impossible to contradict it in any way.

My colleague Spamer, the folklorist who knows so much about the genesis and subsistence of legends, said to me one day during the first year of Hitlerism, when I was voicing my dismay at the spiritual state of the German people: 'If it were possible – (at the time he held this to be a clause of unreal condition) – to force the press, all publications and teaching to follow a single line, and if it was asserted everywhere that there had been no world war between 1914 and 1918, then within three years the whole world would believe there really hadn't been one.' When I reminded Spamer of this at our first proper reunion he corrected me: 'Yes I remember; but you have got one thing wrong; at the time I said within one year, and I believe that to be true even more so now!'

I will pick out just a very few of the countless examples of idolization. In July 1934 Göring said in a speech in front of the Berlin Town Hall: 'All of us, from the most humble member of the SA through to the Prime Minister {*Ministerpräsident*}, are what we are because of Adolf Hitler and through Adolf Hitler.' In the announcements for the election of 1938 to ratify the annexation of Austria, in the endorsement of Greater Germany, it is claimed that Hitler is 'an agent of Providence', and then, in the style of the Old Testament, 'any hand that writes No shall wither'. Baldur von Schirach determines that the town in which the Führer was born, Braunau, should become a 'place of pilgrimage for the youth of Germany'. It is Baldur von Schirach who publishes *The Song of the Faithful,* 'poems by anonymous Austrian members of the Hitler Youth from the years of persecution 1933 to 1937'; in it one reads '. . . There are so many who will never meet you, but for whom you are nevertheless the Saviour.'

Now, of course, Providence is called upon by all and sundry, not just by those who on account of their social standing and education might be allowed a little suggestibility and exuberance. Even the rector of the Dresden Institute of Science and Technology, a highly respected professor of mathematics – a man therefore from whom one would expect balanced thoughts and moderate words – even His Magnificence Kowalewski writes at the time in a newspaper article, 'He has been sent to us by Providence.'

Shortly before the assault on Russia, Goebbels strikes up a more uncompromisingly idolatrous tone once again. In his message of congratulation on 20 April 1941 he claims: 'We do not need to know what the Führer intends – we believe in him.' (In cases like this a future generation will have to be reminded again and again that absolutely no one expressed even the slightest doubt publicly about statements of this kind uttered by the Propaganda Minister.) And at New Year in 1944 Goebbels laments more loudly than the Führer himself, who has reportedly gone grey with worry at the undeserved suffering of his people, that he has been misunderstood by many. Because his love embraces all of humanity; if only they knew it 'they would take leave of their false gods forthwith and render homage to him'.

The ritualistic worship of Hitler, the radiant fog of religion surrounding his person, are intensified even more by the use of religious epithets wherever there is mention of his work, his state, his war. Will Vesper, the head of the Reich Chamber of Literature in the state of Saxony – total organization! Spamer's clause of unreal condition has lost its unreality – Will Vesper announces at a 'Book Week' in October: *'Mein Kampf* is the Holy Book of National Socialism and of the New Germany.' I don't think the originality of this sentence actually amounts to anything more than a paraphrase. Because *Mein Kampf* had always been referred to as the 'Bible' of National Socialism. For my own personal use I have a decidedly unphilological piece of evidence for this: I made no note of this particular expression – it was simply too obvious and commonplace. It goes without saying that the war, as a means of preserving not only Hitler's Reich in the narrow sense, but also the area of influence of the Hitler Religion, became known as a 'crusade', a 'holy war', a 'holy people's war', and that in this religious war there were also casualties who fell 'believing in their Führer to the last'.

The Führer as the new Christ, a special German Saviour – a major anthology of German literature from the *Edda* to Hitler's struggle, in which Luther, Goethe, *et al.* are merely intermediate stages, is entitled *The Teutonic Bible {Germanenbibel}* – his book, the true gospel of the Germans, his defensive war, a holy war: it is clear that both the book and the war owe their sanctity to the sanctity of their author, even if they themselves also enhance his aura retrospectively.

But what are the priorities with regard to the Reich as announced, created and defended by Hitler? Here Hitler is the receiver.

The word Reich has an aura of solemnity and a religious dignity absent from the many expressions with which it is in part synonymous. The *res publica,* the republic, is the concern of the people as a whole, a universally binding public order which they themselves have created communally and which they maintain, a structure entirely of this world and built on reason. That is precisely what is expressed by the Renaissance word 'the state': it denotes the solid ground, the fixed order of a unified region, it refers to something totally of this world and exclusively political. '*Reich*', on the other hand, in so far as its meaning is not restricted by use in compounds (*Königreich* {King's Reich, kingdom}, *Kaiserreich* {Emperor's Reich, empire}, *Gotenreich* {the empire of the Goths} . . .), encompasses a wider realm, embracing the spiritual and the transcendental: for Christians the next world is heaven {*Himmelreich*}, and in the most universal and simple Christian prayer the second request is *Dein Reich komme* {Thy kingdom come}. There was a gruesome joke which people told to take secret revenge on the bloodhound Himmler: it was said of his victims that he had let them into his *Himmlersches Reich* {Himmlery Kingdom}[2]. The state of which Germany was a part until 1806 is expressly referred to as '*das Heilige Römische Reich Deutscher Nation* {The Holy Roman Empire}', whereby Holy is more than just a decorative or enthusiastic epithet; it implies that the state does not merely create order in this world, but that the next world is also taken care of.

After Hitler had taken the first step towards his goal of a Greater Germany by incorporating Austria, he then, *mutatis mutandissimis,* imitating the journeys to Italy undertaken by the medieval emperors, travelled to Rome in style and with a large retinue for talks with the Duce – the headline in the German press read '*Das Heilige Germanische Reich Deutscher Nation* {The Holy Teutonic Empire}'. The rulers of the medieval empire were confirmed in their divine right by an ecclesiastical coronation, and felt themselves to be stewards of a Romano-Christian system of belief and culture. By securing a Holy Teutonic Empire, Hitler exploits the aura of the old empire for his new structure. For the time being Hitler keeps to his original doctrine of only wanting to create a German or Teutonic empire, and that the freedom of all other nations should remain inviolable.

At Christmas 1942, after he has broken promise after promise and committed robbery after robbery, and at the point when what had begun as a *Blitzkrieg* had long since become a lingering haemorrhage, an article on the philosophy of history appears in the *Frankfurter Zeitung* (with the initials srp) which adds a new fluorescent hue to the faded aureole surrounding the concept of the Reich: 'The Reich is Proving its Worth'. The article, aimed at an educated audience in its style and content, takes as its starting point the spiritual and secular order of the Holy Roman Empire. This, it is claimed, was a supranational, European order in which numerous, culturally diverse peoples were subordinate to the German Emperor. This Empire broke up with the formation of the nation states. Amongst them it was Prussia that developed the idea of the state in its purest form, 'as a moral imperative, as a spiritual position', which led to its status as the steward of Lesser Germany.

---

[2]A pun on the word *Himmel,* the German for sky and heaven.

However, when it came to the negotiations in the Paulskirche regarding a new Greater Germany, it became apparent that Greater Germany could not just be a *'völkischer Staat* {national state}', but must also take on supranational, European responsibilities. That which the men of the Paulskirche were unable to accomplish was successfully achieved by the Führer – he created the Greater German Reich. Perhaps the closed nation state seemed to him to be an option at one point (when he promised he would be satisfied with the Sudetenland). But the inherent idea of Greater Germany forced him of necessity to push ever onwards. Greater Germany can only exist 'as the centre and support of a new Reich, it bears the historical responsibility for a new universal order and for a new era in the history of the European continent, one far removed from anarchy . . . in war it must prove its allegiance to this cause'. This concluding section of the study bears the title 'Heritage and Mission'. The most criminal of all wars is hereby sanctified for the educated public by the time-honoured notion of the Reich, and the term Reich is itself filled with renewed holiness.

An intensification of this holiness into the realm of mysticism – and a frightfully simplistic form of mysticism at that, one which everyone can understand easily and unconsciously – is achieved by not simply referring to the Reich, but always to the 'Third Reich'. And here again the LTI idolizes Hitler by appropriating something that is already in existence. Moeller van den Bruck's *Das dritte Reich* (The Third Reich) bears, under the foreword to the first edition, the date December 1922. There he writes: 'The idea of the Third Reich is an intellectual world view {*Weltanschauungsgedanke*} which transcends reality. It is no coincidence that the ideas evoked by the term itself, by the name of the Third Reich, are . . . strangely nebulous, emotional and ethereal and entirely associated with the life hereafter.' Hans Schwarz, editor of the third edition in 1930, reports that 'National Socialism has taken up the call for a Third Reich, and the Oberland organization has named its periodical after it', and points out moreover in its opening lines that 'the Third Reich has a legendary power for all who seek it'.

In general, the power of legend is most potent with people who have no intellectual education or historical knowledge. Here the situation is reversed. The more someone knows about the history of literature and the history of Christianity, the more the term 'Third Reich' speaks to him of the 'life hereafter'. Those who purged the Church and religion itself in the Middle Ages, zealous reformers of the human race of later ages, men of the most diverse persuasions, have dreamed of an age which would supersede paganism and Christianity, or at least corrupt contemporary Christianity, of a perfect Third Reich, and they hoped for a Messiah who will bring it into being. Memories of Lessing and Ibsen are aroused.

But also the mass of people who know nothing of the rich heritage of this concept – these things can and indeed will be explained to them, provision is constantly being made to instruct them in questions of *Weltanschauung,* the division of labour between the ministries of Goebbels and Rosenberg has been carefully thought through – the simple masses also sense that the term 'Third Reich' is a religious intensification of the already extremely religious term Reich. Twice before there had been a German Reich, both turned out to be flawed and both foundered; but now the Third Reich has achieved perfection and will be unassailable for all time. The hand which is unwilling to serve it, or which even dares to oppose it, that hand must wither . . .

Taken as a whole the diverse phrases and expressions in the LTI which touch on the world hereafter form a net which is thrown over the imagination of the listener, dragging it into the realm of faith. Is this net deliberately woven, is it, to use the eighteenth-century expression, priestly deception? In part, certainly. It mustn't be forgotten that a yearning for faith and an openness to religion undoubtedly played a part In the case of certain initiates in the new doctrine. It isn't always possible to weigh up the guilt and innocence of the first net-makers. But the impact of the net itself, once it was there, seems to me to be incontrovertible; Nazism was accepted by millions as gospel because it appropriated the language of the gospel.

Was? – I have only traced the 'I believe in him' up to the final days of Hitler's Reich. I am now dealing day after day with people who have been rehabilitated and those who want to be. These people, regardless of how different they are from one another in other ways, have one thing in common: they all claim to be part of a special group of 'victims of fascism', they were all forced against their better judgement, and by some form of violence or other, to join the Party that they had loathed from the outset, they never believed in the Führer and never believed in the Third Reich. But recently I met my old pupil L. in the street, whom I had last seen during my final visit to the provincial library. At the time he shook my hand sympathetically; I was embarrassed because he was already wearing a swastika. Now he came up to me with delight: 'I am pleased that you have been saved and are back in post!' – 'And how are things with you?' – 'Bad, of course, I am employed as a construction worker, but I don't earn enough for my wife and child, and I am also not physically suited to this kind of work in the long term.' – 'Aren't you going to be rehabilitated? I know you well enough – I'm sure you haven't got anything criminal on your conscience. Did you hold high office in the Party? Were you politically very active?' – 'No, not at all, I was an insignificant little Pg.' – 'So why are you, of all people, not being rehabilitated?' – 'Because I haven't applied for it and can't do so.' – 'I don't understand.' Pause. To which he replied with difficulty and eyes downcast: 'I can't deny it, I believed in him.' – 'But you surely can't still believe in him now; you can see what it all led to, and all of the regime's atrocious crimes are now apparent for all to see.' An even longer pause. Then, very quietly, 'I accept all that. The others misunderstood him, betrayed him. But I still believe in HIM, I really do.'

Chapter 19
Personal Announcements as an LTI Revision Book

Birth announcement from the *Dresdner Anzeiger* of 27 July 1942: 'Volker *21.7.42.[1] In Germany's finest hour a little brother for Thorsten. With pride and joy Else Hohmann . . . Hans-Georg Hohmann, second-lieutenant of the SS reserves Dresden, General-Wever-Straße.'

Birth, the begetting of children, death: the most universal and biologically most momentous moments in any life, the natural subdivisions of all human existence. Just as trichinae gather in the joints of someone with an infection, so the characteristic features and clichés of the LTI gather in personal announcements, and I often find that everything I could otherwise study individually, in different places and from various perspectives, comes together in the personal announcements of a single day, although they only really appear in their entirety once the war with Russia is well under way and can no longer be regarded in any way as a *Blitzkrieg*. It is important to give this date, because around this time articles appeared in the press condemning excessively soft-hearted or unbridled expressions of grief at the death of those who fell honourably in the field of battle as shameful, almost unpatriotic and hostile to the state. This definitely contributed to the increasingly heroic and stoical tone of the announcements of those who died in action.

The birth announcement quoted at the beginning of this section adds an instructive new ingredient of its own to the treasure-trove of

---

[1]The asterisk here replaces the Nazi rune of life.

handed-down clichés. That the children bear names associated with the Nibelungen or Nordic mythology, that their SS father has given his essentially rather more mundane forenames a slightly Teutonic ring by the simple addition of a hyphen, that instead of the star or the word 'born' there is a rune of life –these are just a collection of the usual Nazi conventions, and in the context of my notebook also amount to nothing more than repetitions. The fact that they live in a street renamed after an air force general in Hitler's army who died before the war is a matter of luck, and not something they can take the credit for.

And 'Germany's finest hour' is almost a modest superlative amongst the superlatives which were in vogue at the time to idolize the Hitler era.

But what is instructive and new here is the pride and joy {*stolze Freude*}. What are the happy parents proud of? The ability to have children is taken for granted with SS couples – otherwise they would not have been able to get permission to marry. And a second son is also no cause for pride: much more substantial deliveries of human flesh are expected, in particular of the SS, who were habitually used for breeding purposes like thoroughbred horses and dogs. (They were also branded with a cattle stamp like animals.) So all that remains is pride and joy at the 'finest hour'. But one can only be proud of something which one is actively involved in, and there is no army rank following the SS father's name, and the usual 'at present in action' is also missing. According to the moral code of the Third Reich, it is only the wife who would be allowed to be proud, and then only on the occasion of announcing the death of a family member fighting for the Führer. 'Pride and joy' is completely meaningless in this birth announcement.

But it is this very meaninglessness which makes it so instructive. It is clearly a mechanically created analogy to the 'pride and grief {*stolzer trauer*}' in the announcements of those who died in action. The mechanical creation of analogies is evidence of the frequency and standing, or of the forceful impact, of the originals. It is absolutely self-evident to the SS couple that a personal announcement should include an expression of pride, hence the pride and joy. Whilst pride and grief were in many cases considered obligatory after the aforementioned point in time – and were now and then reinforced by the assurance that, at the request of the hero who had died in action, mourning would not be worn – the word '*sonnig* {sunny}' as a stereotypical embellishment was extremely widespread from the beginning of the war, even amongst older people. It would seem that in Hitler's Reich every Teuton was sunny all the time, just as Homer's Hera always has ox-eyes and Charlemagne in the *Chanson de Roland* always has a white beard. Only at the point when the sun of Hitlerism was already heavily veiled, and the epithet sounded as hackneyed as it did tragi-comic, was sunny used less frequently. It never disappeared entirely, and in those cases where it was avoided it was often eagerly replaced by '*lebensfroh* {full of the joys of life}'. Right at the end, a reserve group captain announced the death of his 'radiant son'.

Sonnig denotes what you might call a universal quality amongst the Teutons, pride and grief befits the patriot *per se*. But it is also possible to express in a death announcement the specifically National Socialist dimension of a particular cast of mind; indeed many different shades are possible in this context, with appropriate terms to suggest not only the greatest enthusiasm, but even (a much more difficult task) critical distance.

For most of the time the majority of those who died in action did so '*für Führer und Vaterland* {for Führer and fatherland}'. (This analogy to the old Prussian '*Für König und Vaterland* {for King and country}', with its ingratiating alliteration, was widespread from the very first day of the war; on the other hand, the attempt immediately after Hitler's accession to power to designate the 20 April '*Führers Geburtstag* {Führer's birthday}' failed. The party leadership probably felt that the analogy to '*Königs Geburtstag* {King's birthday}' seemed too monarchical, and it thus remained '*Geburtstag des Führers* {the birthday of the Führer}', which, if need be, could be made to sound a little more like old German by adopting the word order '*Des Führers Geburtstag* {the Führer's birthday}'.) Greater degrees of enthusiasm for Nazism find expression in the following phrases: 'he died in action {*fiel*} for his Führer' and 'he died for his beloved Führer', in which the Fatherland is not mentioned because it is both represented and contained within Adolf Hitler himself, just as the body of the Lord is contained within the consecrated host. And the expression of the highest degree of National Socialist fervour entails placing Hitler unambiguously in the place of the Saviour: 'He fell believing in his Führer to the last.'

If, on the other hand, someone is not at all in agreement with National Socialism, if they want to vent their antipathy or perhaps even hatred without, however, showing any demonstrable signs of opposition, because their courage doesn't quite stretch that far, then the appropriate formulation is 'our only son died for the Fatherland' without any mention of the Führer. This corresponds roughly to the greeting 'with best German wishes' at the end of a letter, which a number of half-courageous people dared to use during the first few years as a substitute for 'Heil Hitler'. It appears to me that as the number of victims increased, and the hope of victory diminished, the expressions of devotion to the Führer became correspondingly less frequent, but, despite checking this in a few newspapers, I would not like to to swear to it.

It may well be that the increasing shortage of people and material played a part, for this led increasingly to the merging of individual newspapers and their reduction in size, necessitating, in the case of personal announcements, the most concise wording possible (often through the use of abbreviations, which made them garbled almost to the point of incomprehensibility). Ultimately, as in the case of an expensive telegram, every word and every letter was carefully weighed up. In 1939, when death for the Fatherland was still a novel event and not just another part of everyday life, at a time when there was still a surplus of paper and compositors, announcements for those who had died in action filled a large square surrounded by a thick black line, and if the hero had, for example, owned a factory or shop in his private life, then the *Gefolgschaft* {workforce} would insist on putting their own announcement in the paper. For the employees of a firm, the placing of a second announcement alongside that of the widow was an essential duty, which is why the hypocritical word *'Gefolgschaft'* belongs in my revision book. If the deceased was a really big cheese, a high-ranking official, or on many different boards of directors, then there would sometimes be three, four or even more announcements of his heroic death, one below the other, and they could easily fill a good half-page of a newspaper. Here there was clearly space for emotional outpourings and expansive phrases. By the end, however, there were rarely more than two lines of the narrowest column available for a single family announcement. The black line around the individual announcements was also dropped. The dead lay squeezed together in a single black-edged rectangle as if in a mass grave.

In the final phase of the war, the birth and marriage announcements suffered from a similar, if not quite so drastic, lack of space, and invariably constituted a small group opposite the dreadfully long tally of deaths. It was not all that unusual for a strange kind of marriage to stand out from the rest, one which could just as well have been announced in the deaths column: women announcing their posthumous wedding to a fiancé who had died in action.

In a terrible indictment – terrible in terms of the mass of material presented without comment – published as early as 1944 by the Moscow Publishing House for Foreign-Language Literature, 'Hitler's Words and Hitler's Deeds' are juxtaposed; it classifies personal announcements such as the following one from the *Völkischer Beobachter* as special 'atrocities of Hitler's Germany': 'I hereby announce my posthumous marriage with Lance-Corporal Robert Haegele, radio operator, *stud.-ing., Inh. des EK II* {student of engineering, holder of the Iron Cross Second Class}, who died in action . . .' Notwithstanding the tragedy of this announcement, and of some of the 'long-distance weddings' also mentioned in this publication, they do not constitute a special characteristic of Nazism, a specific sin alongside the general sinfulness of this war of conquest, or a special case of hubris of the kind couched in the religious phrase 'died believing in Adolf Hitler to the last'. Because they may be prompted by the very thing one otherwise almost always looks for in vain during this period: humanity pure and simple, perhaps concern about the future of a child, perhaps fidelity to the name of a loved one. The underlying legal conditions were also not created by the Third Reich.

We can return to the Nazi realm proper via an observation on what you could literally call the framework. As already mentioned, the dead of the last year of the war were placed in mass graves by the newspapers as well. To be more precise, there were in each case two places of burial, literally two frames: the first and more distinguished is intended for the corpses of those who died on the battlefield in honour, a swastika adorns the top left-hand corner, next to which are the words 'They died for Germany . . .' The second frame surrounds the names of those who died merely as civilians without having served their country honourably in any way. It is noticeable, however, that an increasing number of civilians also crowd the first frame, men next to whose name a civilian job is mentioned, but no military one, men and boys too old or too young to serve even in Hitler's army, together with women and girls of all ages. These are the dead of the air raids.

If they lost their lives away from home, the place of death may be mentioned: 'During a raid on Bremen our beloved Mother . . .' If, on the other hand, they perished here, then the neighbours must not be made anxious by the admission of losses. In such cases the stereotypical LTI wording reads: 'a tragic misfortune resulted in their forfeiting their lives . . .'

Here my revision book registers the mendacious euphemism which played such an immense role in the make-up of the LTI. The fate of these victims was no more tragic than that of hares bagged in a course. After a while they were separated from those who had died on the front line by a thick dash. At which point there were three categories of corpses. The wit of the Berliners rebelled vigorously against this demotion of those who died in the air raids. The question is asked: 'What's the definition of cowardice?' And the answer: 'When a Berliner signs up to fight on the front line.'

Chapter 20
What Remains?

'And then septemberize them {*septembrisieren*} . . .' That's roughly how the line must have gone. In 1909, when I was still writing utterly unprofessionally with all ten fingers, I drew up an outline and a little anthology of German political poetry of the nineteenth century for a publisher of popular books. The line must have been in a poem of Herwegh: someone, the King of Prussia, or the reactionaries in the form of some allegorical beast, was intending to put a stop to freedom, or the revolution, or some followers of the revolution, 'and then septemberize them'. The word was unfamiliar to me, I didn't have any philological interests at the time – the famous Tobler had cured me of it completely and I hadn't come across Voßler yet so I contented myself with checking in the little Daniel Sanders, a remarkably comprehensive list of all foreign words and proper names current amongst people with a general education around 1900. It said roughly: to commit political mass murders as perpetrated during the Great French Revolution in September 1792.

The line of poetry and the word itself made an impression on me. In autumn or winter 1914 I was reminded of them, and by then I had developed a taste for linguistic questions. The *Neue Freie Presse* in Vienna wrote that the Russians had intended to 'lüttichize {*lüttichieren*}' Przemysl. This is exactly the same phenomenon as 'septemberize', I said to myself: a historical fact has made such a powerful and lasting impression that its name is universally applied to similar incidents. In an old Sachs-Villatte of 1881 I not only found that the French words *septembriseur, septembrisade* and *septembriser* were listed, but also that they were given as German borrowings (*Septembrisierer* {septem-berizer}!). A new equivalent formation was also referenced: *décembriser* and *décembriseur.* These referred to the *coup d'état* of Napoleon III on 2 December 1851, and the German translation of the verb was '*dezembrisieren*'. I came across the German '*septembrisieren*' again in a dictionary published at the beginning of the world war. The survival and spread of this word beyond the borders of its country of origin were clearly a result of the tremendous imaginative impact of the September murders; nothing that followed had been able to displace the horror of these events from memory and from tradition.

In Autumn 1914 I was already asking myself whether '*lüttichieren*' would have such a long life. In fact it didn't make any headway at all, I don't think it even made it into the Reich's linguistic corpus. The reason being undoubtedly that the assault on Liége {*Lüttich*} was followed by a series of more impressive and more bloody acts of war. A military expert will raise the objection here that the capture of Liége was a very special military action, a direct assault on a modern fortress, and that the new verb was intended to express this exceptional technical aspect; it is not, however, either the wish or the exactitude of the expert which determines the universal acceptance of a new word, but rather the mood and imagination of the public at large.

'*Septembrisieren*' may well today live on in the memories of an older generation of Germans, given that *septembriser* is an established word in the French vocabulary. '*Lüttichieren*' died away completely in the anonymous misery of war which followed Liége, in so far as it ever really came to life.

A related word, coined during the last world war, has also died out, despite the fact that, in Nazi terms at least, it looked as if it was made for eternity, and was accompanied at birth by the united clamour of Greater Germany's press and radio: the verb '*coventrieren* {coventryize}'. Coventry was an English 'armoury store', nothing more, and populated exclusively by the military, because on principle we only attacked what in every report were referred to as 'military targets', for we also only engaged in 'retaliation', had certainly not started anything, in contrast to the English who had started the air raids, and who, as 'pirates of the air', mainly directed them at churches and hospitals. German bombers had therefore 'razed' Coventry 'to the ground' and were now threatening to 'coventryize' every English town, since they all served military ends.

We learned in October 1940 that London had had to endure 'non-stop retaliatory attacks' and 'the largest bombardment ever known', that it had suffered 'the massacre of St Bartholomew's Eve'; it would be coventryized if it didn't finally surrender.

The verb *coventrieren* has been lost to view, hushed up by a propaganda machine which day after day accused the enemy before God and Man of behaving like 'pirates and gangsters' and therefore had to avoid reminding people of its own acts of gangsterism and the time when it was all-powerful; the verb *coventrieren* lies buried under the rubble of German cities.

I am reminded of *coventrieren* literally two to four times a day, depending on whether I have to leave our peaceful garden suburb to visit a public office in the city only in the morning, or also in the afternoon. As soon as I come into contact with the zone of destruction the word is there. Then it leaves me alone during lectures, meetings and consultation hours. But as soon as I set out on my return journey it jumps out at me from the gutted rooms. The tram rumbles '*coventrieren*' and footsteps beat time to '*coventrieren*'.

We are going to have a new painting and literature of ruins, but it will be different from that of the eighteenth century. In those days people luxuriated in thoughts of transience with a mixture of sweet and tearful melancholy; these derelict medieval castles and monasteries, or even the temples and palaces of the ancient world, had been destroyed so many centuries previously that the sadness at their fate had become a general human anguish, one which was thoroughly philosophical and thus extremely gentle and really rather pleasant. But here . . . your missing relatives may be lying beneath this enormous expanse of rubble, in this hollow space bounded by four walls everything that you gathered over decades has been reduced to ashes. Irreplaceable things: your books, your piano . . . No, they don't lend themselves to gentle melancholy these ruins of ours. And, when the bitterness at this sight evokes the word '*coventrieren*' a desolate train of thought is summoned up. It is called crime and punishment.

But in my case this is the obsessiveness of the philologist. The masses no longer know anything about Coventry and '*coventrieren*'. For them two less foreign-sounding expressions have carved themselves on the memory in the face of this destruction from the air. I really can refer to the masses here, because when we were on the run following the catastrophe in Dresden we passed through many different provinces, and on the main roads we met soldiers and refugees from all the different regions and strata of society in Germany. And everywhere, on woodland paths scattered with chaff {*Stanniol*} in the Vogtland, on wrecked Bavarian railway lines, in the heavily damaged Munich university, in a hundred different bunkers, in a hundred different villages, from the mouths of country folk and city dwellers, from workers and academics, anywhere where one was reminded of the airmen, in moments of boredom waiting for the all-clear, and at times of immediate danger, I heard again and again: 'And Hermann said, if a single enemy airman reaches us my name is Meier!' And this long sentence was often reduced to the sarcastic cry of 'Hermann Meier!'

Anyone who remembered Göring's assurance had retained a degree of gallows humour. Those who had become truly embittered quoted Hitler's threat that he would wipe out {*ausradieren*} the English cities.

'*Ausradieren*' and 'my name is Meier': the Führer and his Reich Marshal never summed themselves up more succinctly or more accurately, the one in his true nature as megalomaniac criminal, the other in his role as the people's comedian. One shouldn't make prophecies, but I reckon that '*ausradieren*' and 'Meier' will survive.

Chapter 21
German Roots

Amongst the tiny handful of books that I was allowed to take with me to the Jews' House, all of them specialist works connected with my subject, was Wilhelm Scherer's history of German literature, which I came across during my first semester as a '*stud. germ.*' in Munich, and which I have since studied again and again and often consulted. Now, when I turned to Scherer I was often, indeed regularly, even more impressed with his independence of mind, his objectivity, the range of his knowledge than I had been in earlier times, when I had taken some of these virtues for granted in an academic. Again and again certain sentences and certain judgements provided me with completely different insights than in the preceding years; the terrible change that had come over Germany meant that one saw earlier expressions of the German character in a different light.

How was the terrible disparity possible between contemporary Germany and every single period of Germany's past? I had always found the *traits éternels,* the abiding features of a national character of which the French speak, to be borne out in practice, or at least that's what I believed, and I had always stressed them in my own work. Was it all wrong? Or were the Hitlerites right when they laid claim, for example, to Herder, the humanitarian? Was there any intellectual connection between the Germans of the Age of Goethe and the people who supported Adolf Hitler?

During the years I was engaged in culture studies {*Kulturkunde*}, Eugen Lerch threw a mocking word my way, one which was later to be quoted frequently, he claimed I had invented the '*Dauerfranzosen* {long-life Frenchman}' (just as one speaks of *Dauerwurst* {long-life sausage; salami}). And when I subsequently saw how shamefully the Nazis went about their business armed with a completely false kind of culture studies, using it to elevate the Germans to a master race, both by right and as God intended, and to degrade other peoples to the status of lesser creatures, I was both ashamed and dismayed at having played a role, indeed a leading one, in this movement.

But throughout all the soul-searching I was repeatedly able to establish that I had a clear conscience: how I pounced on Wechßler's *Esprit und Geist* (Esprit and Spirit), that ridiculously chauvinist and weighty tome penned by a Berlin professor responsible for the miseducation of a legion of secondary schoolteachers. But the issue wasn't my clear conscience, which is of no interest to anybody, but rather the existence or non-existence of abiding character features.

At the time, Tacitus was a highly popular and much-quoted personality: in his *Germania* he had painted such a nice picture of the German ancestors, and there was a direct succession from Arminius and his followers, via Luther and Frederick the Great, to Hitler with his SA and SS and HJ. One of these historical analyses provoked me into checking what Scherer had to say about *Germania.* I came upon a paragraph which astonished and, to some extent, rescued me.

Scherer maintains that in Germany intellectual rises and declines take place with uncompromising thoroughness, and that they lead to great heights and great depths: 'a lack of moderation seems to be the bane of our intellectual development. We soar upwards and then fall correspondingly far. We are like the Teuton who has lost all his possessions in a game of dice, puts his own freedom on the last throw, loses this as well and willingly allows himself to be sold as a slave. This, adds Tacitus, who is telling the story, shows the extent of Teutonic tenacity, even for a bad cause; they themselves call it loyalty.'

At the time this made it clear to me that the best and the worst of the German character can be traced back to one common and abiding trait. That there is a connection between the bestiality of Hitlerism and the Faustian excesses of classical German literature and German idealist philosophy. And five years later, when the catastrophe had occurred, when the full extent of all the bestialities and the real depth of Germany's fall were clear for all to see, I was sent back to that passage of Tacitus by a tiny detail and a passing remark on it in Plievier's *Stalingrad.*

Plievier talks about a German road sign in Russia: 'Kalatsch on the Don, 3200 km to Leipzig.' He notes: 'A strange triumph, and, even if a thousand kilometres had been added to the real distance, it was all the more an authentic expression of this pointless and immoderate venture.'

I would like to bet that the author didn't have either Tacitus's *Germania* or Scherer's scholarly literary history in mind when he wrote this. Rather, in immersing himself in contemporary German degeneration, and in searching for its ultimate cause, he has of his own accord hit upon the same characteristic feature of immoderation and the defying of all limits.

'*Entgrenzung* {disregarding boundaries}' denotes the definitive frame of mind and behaviour of the Romantic, regardless of whether his Romantic nature manifests itself in religious yearning, in artistic form, in philosophizing, in everyday life, in morality or in criminality. For many hundreds of years every German activity bore the stamp of Romanticism, before the concept and word had even been invented. This is particularly apparent to the Romance scholar, because in the Middle Ages France was constantly the master and provider of material for Germany, and whenever Germany got hold of a French theme it invariably transgressed the confines of the original in this direction or that.

In the context of Scherer's reflections, Plievier's remark, lit upon innocently and without scholarly purpose, links the army of the Third Reich to the Teutons of Arminius. This is a very vague assertion, and I have continually been plagued by the question of the concrete connection between Nazi perfidy – for which the LTI's own coinage '*Untermenschentum* {subhumanity}' is entirely appropriate – and Germany's intellectual past. Could I really be satisfied with the notion that all of these terrible things were mere imitations and importations, a virulent Italian disease, just as centuries before the first wave of the imported French disease had wreaked havoc with such virulence?

But everything was not only so much worse in our case, it was also fundamentally different from and more poisonous than in Italy. The Fascists claimed to be the legal successors of the ancient Roman state, they believed themselves destined to restore the ancient Roman Empire; however, Fascism did not teach the lesson, with all its dire consequences, that the inhabitants of the regions to be won back were biologically inferior to the successors of Romulus, and that it was both natural and necessary that they persist in this inferior state for all time and without any hope of redemption – at least not until it was reinfected by its godchild, the Third Reich.

But then came the objection which for years I had raised again and again: am I not exaggerating the role of anti-Semitism within the Nazi system because I myself was so terribly affected by it.

No, I didn't exaggerate it, it is now clear for all to see that it was at the very core of Nazism and in every way the decisive factor. Anti-Semitism is the crux of the rancour displayed by that depraved petty-bourgeois Austrian, Adolf Hitler, politically anti-Semitism is his parochial central idea, given that he began to think about politics in the era of Schönerer and Lueger. Anti-Semitism is from start to finish the Party's most effective means of propaganda, the most effective and popular concrete manifestation of its racial doctrine, and for the German masses is indeed indistinguishable from this racial theory. For what do the German masses know about the danger of *'Verniggerung* {niggering}' and how detailed is their personal knowledge of the supposed inferiority of the peoples in the east and south? But everybody knows a Jew. For the German masses anti-Semitism and racial doctrine are synonyms. And all the excesses and demands of the national arrogance, every conquest, every act of tyranny, every atrocity, and even mass murder, are explained and justified by this scientific, or rather pseudo-scientific, racial theory.

After learning about the camp in Auschwitz and its gas chambers, after reading Rosenberg's *Myth* and Chamberlain's *Foundations*,[1] I no longer doubted the central and decisive importance of anti-Semitism and racial theory for National Socialism. (One question, however, can only be answered in individual cases, namely whether racial dogma is the real starting point for anti-Semitism or merely its pretext and veil in those instances where anti-Semitism and racial doctrine are not naively held to be the same.) Were it to be proved that this was a specifically German poison, one oozing out of German intellectualism, then evidence of expressions, customs and political measures appropriated from abroad would be of no use: if that was the case, then National Socialism

---

[1]Houston Stewart Chamberlain's historical study *Die Grundlagen des neunzehnten Jahrhunderts* (Munich, 1899) was translated into English by John Lees as *The Foundations of the Nineteenth Century* (London, 1910).

was no imported scourge but rather a degeneration of the German character itself, a diseased manifestation of those *traits éternels.*

Anti-Semitism, as a form of hostility with social, religious and economic causes, has cropped up across the ages and amongst all nations, sometimes here, sometimes there, sometimes in a mild form, sometimes more virulently; to ascribe it specifically and solely to the Germans would be unjust.

There are three things that make anti-Semitism in the Third Reich something entirely new and unique. First, the pestilence flares up, more searingly than ever before, at a time when it appears to have long since become a thing of the past. What I mean is that there were certainly anti-Semitic excesses here and there prior to 1933, just as there were occasional outbreaks of cholera and the plague in European ports; but just as one apparently could be confident that within the civilized world there was no longer a danger of epidemics destroying whole cities, as in the Middle Ages, so it also seemed completely impossible that Jews could once again be deprived of their rights and persecuted as they had been in the Middle Ages. And the second unique feature, together with this anachronistic dimension, is the fact that this anachronism did not come along in the guise of the past but as something utterly modern, not as a people's revolt, a mad frenzy or spontaneous mass murder (although at the outset spontaneity was used as a pretext), but highly organized and with all the technical details completely worked out; because anyone who today commemorates the murder of the Jews thinks of the gas chambers in Auschwitz. However, the third and most crucial innovation consists of embedding the hatred of the Jews in the idea of race. In earlier times the animosity towards the Jews was directed at a group which stood outside the Christian faith and Christian society; the adoption of the country's religion and customs served as a compensation and (for the succeeding generation at least) as a blurring of differences. Displacing the difference between Jews and non-Jews into the blood makes any compensation impossible, perpetuates the division and legitimizes it as willed by God.

These three innovations are all closely related to one another, and all three point to the fundamental trait reported by Tacitus, the 'tenacity, even for a bad cause'. Anti-Semitism as a matter of ancestry is ineradicably tenacious; thanks to its claim to being scientific it is not an anachronism, but rather entirely appropriate to modern ways of thinking, and as a result it considers it almost self-evident that it should use the most scientific methods at its disposal. That it should do so with extreme cruelty again goes hand in hand with the fundamental trait of excessive tenacity.

In Willy Seidel's *Der neue Daniel* (The New Daniel), written in 1920, one encounters, alongside the idealistic German, the figure of Lieutenant Zuckschwerdt, the representative of that stratum of German society which made us so detested abroad and which at home *Simplizissimus* attacked in vain. The man isn't incompetent, all things considered he can't really be labelled a villain, and he certainly isn't a sadist. But he has been ordered to drown some kittens, and on his removing the sack from the water one of the little animals is still whimpering. He then smashes it to 'strawberry jam' with a stone and shouts at it, 'You stupid creature – I'll show you the meaning of thoroughness!'

One might expect that the author, who clearly depicted this representative of a degenerate section of the population for the sake of fairness, would remain faithful to his judgement right to the end, just as in Rolland there are two Frances and two Germanies. But no, at the end there is forgiveness and sympathy for the painstaking cat murderer and he is transfigured into something altogether more positive, whilst the Americans are condemned increasingly harshly in this novelistic exercise in setting nation against nation. And the reason for such leniency and harshness is that in the case of the Germans there is always racial purity, whilst the Americans are of mixed race – the inhabitants of the city of Cincinnati for example are described as 'this population half corrupted by inbreeding or unduly infiltrated by Indian and Jewish blood', and on another occasion a Japanese traveller's description of America is quoted approvingly: *that Irish-Dutch-Nigger-Jew-mess.*[2] Here already, immediately after the First World War, and prior to Hitler's very first appearance, in an author who is clearly a pure idealist, perspicacious and someone who on numerous occasions successfully maintained impartiality, one has to ask oneself whether the racial doctrine is anything more than a pretext and means of disguising a fundamentally anti-Semitic attitude; it is impossible not to ask this question when a reflection on the war runs as follows: whilst the battle for Verdun and the Somme rages back and forth indecisively without

[2]Klemperer gives this phrase in English.

making any progress, 'the master of impartiality hops around from one opposing party to the other with his goatee and his blank Semitic eyes and counts; this was global journalism'.

What distinguishes National Socialism from other forms of fascism is a concept of race reduced solely to anti-Semitism and also fired exclusively by it. It is from here that it distils all its poison. Absolutely all of it, even in the case of foreign political enemies whom it cannot dismiss as Semites. It therefore turns Bolshevism into Jewish Bolshevism, the French are beniggered and bejewed, the English can even be traced back to that biblical line of Jews considered lost, and so on.

The fundamental German attribute of excess, of inordinate single-mindedness, of reaching out for the infinite, provided this concept of race with the most fertile of grounds. But is it actually a German invention? If one traces its theoretical manifestations back, there is an unbroken line leading by way of important figures such as Rosenberg and the Englishman-turned-German Houston Stewart Chamberlain to the Frenchman Gobineau. His *Essai sur l'inégalité des races humaines,* which appeared between 1853 and 1855 in four volumes, preaches first and foremost the superiority of the Aryan race, the pre-eminent and indeed exclusive claim to humanity of unadulterated Germanic civilization, and the threat posed to it by the all-pervasive, incomparably inferior Semitic blood, a thing barely deserving of the name human. Here are all the ingredients required by the Third Reich for its philosophical justification and its policies; all subsequent pre-Nazi consolidation and application of this teaching invariably goes back to Gobineau, he alone is, or appears to be (I leave this question open for the present), the person responsible for conceiving this bloody doctrine.

Even in the last hours of Hitler's Reich a scientific attempt was made to find German precedents for the Frenchman. A substantial and painstakingly researched study appeared in the Publications of the Reich Institute for the History of the New Germany: *The Idea of Race in German Romanticism and its Origins in the 18th Century.* Hermann Blome, its sincere and foolish author, in fact proved the very opposite of what he believed he had proved. His aim was to turn the eighteenth century, Kant and German Romanticism into scientific precursors and accomplices of the Frenchman. In so doing he started with the false assumption that anyone who studied the natural history of mankind or the subdivision of different races and their characteristics must be a precursor of Gobineau. But the division of mankind into races was not what was original about Gobineau, but rather that he discarded the generic term 'mankind' in favour of the notion of independent races, and that within the white stock he distinguished in the most incredible manner between a Teutonic master race and a pestilent race of Semites. Are there any forerunners to Gobineau in this?

Certainly, according to Blome, both Buffon as a 'pure scientist' and Kant as a 'philosopher working scientifically' grasped and used the term 'race', and in the years that followed, prior to Gobineau, a number of new observations were made in the field of racial research and certain remarks can also be found which place the whites above those of a different colour.

But right at the beginning a regretful observation is made which then reappears throughout the book with minor variations: throughout the eighteenth and up until the middle of the nineteenth century racial studies were unable to make any significant progress (significant in the National Socialist sense of course!) because they were hampered by prevailing humanitarian ideals. What great things Herder could have achieved with his fine ear for the myriad voices of the people and powerful understanding of what it meant to be German (and out of which Nazi literary history almost managed to fashion a real Pg), had he not been compelled by an 'idealistically coloured attitude to identify and stress repeatedly a unity of mankind over and above its diversity'! That depressing 116th letter 'to promote humanity' with its 'principles for a natural history of mankind'! 'Above all one is to be impartial like the guardian spirit of mankind itself; one is to have no favourite amongst the tribes, and no favourite amongst the peoples of the world.' And 'The natural scientist does not presume there to be any hierarchy amongst the creatures he observes; he loves and values them all equally. It is the same with the natural scientist who studies mankind' . . . And what is the use of 'detecting a predominance of scientific interests' in the work of Alexander von Humboldt when 'in the context of racial matters an idealistic view of humanity typical of his age stopped him from attempting to draw racial conclusions'.

Thus the aim of this Nazi author to trace the racial teachings of the Third Reich back to German thinkers has essentially failed. And it can also be proved from another angle that anti-Semitism based on the idea of race was not present in Germany before the arrival of Gobineau. In his study on 'The Origins of Antisemitism in German Thought', published in *Aufbau* (1946, no. 2), Arnold Bauer points out that those student fraternities which set great store by all matters German and Romantic 'did not as a matter of principle exclude Jews from their ranks'. Ernst Moritz Arndt only wanted Christian members, but saw the baptized Jew as a 'Christian and national of equal standing'. 'Jahn, the father of gymnastics, who was notorious for being exceedingly Teutonic, did not even consider baptism to be a prerequisite for membership of a fraternity.' And the fraternities themselves rejected baptism as a condition of membership at the founding of the Alliance of German Student Fraternities. According to Bauer, and here he concurs with the Nazi students studying for their doctorates and postdoctoral qualifications, this demonstrates the lasting effect of the 'intellectual legacy of the humanists, the tolerance of someone like Lessing and the universalism of someone like Kant'.

And yet – and this is why this chapter belongs to my LTI, despite the fact that I have only now got to know Blome and, of course, the study by Bauer – I am forced to stick to the opinion that I formed during those evil years: these racial teachings, twisted and distorted into a unique privilege of the Teutons and justification for their monopoly on the human race, and which ultimately became a hunting licence for the most atrocious crimes against humanity, have their roots in German Romanticism. Or put another way: the Frenchman who invented them is an adherent, a follower, a pupil – I don't know to what extent a conscious one – of German Romanticism.

I repeatedly dealt with Gobineau in my early writings and I was thus thoroughly familiar with his nature. I have to take the scientists' word for it that as a scientist he was misguided. But I can easily believe it; because there is one thing that I myself know for sure; namely that Gobineau was never by nature a scientist, that he was never one for the sake of science itself. Science was always in the service of his own egotistical *idée fixe,* it was solely there to provide incontrovertible evidence in support of this obsession.

Count Arthur Gobineau has a more important part to play in the history of French literature than in the history of science, but characteristically this role was first recognized by the Germans rather than his compatriots. In all the periods of French history through which he lived – he was born in 1816 and died in 1882 – he felt himself to have been robbed of what he saw as his hereditary *droit du seigneur* as a nobleman and of his chance to develop to the full his potential as an individual, robbed by the rule of money, the bourgeoisie, and the masses calling for equality, by the reign of all that he termed democracy, a thing he detested and considered to be responsible for the demise of mankind. He was convinced that he was a pure-blooded and direct descendant of the French feudal aristocracy and the Frankish *ancienne noblesse.*

There is of course in France an ancient conflict of political theories which has had serious consequences. The feudal aristocracy asserted: we are the legitimate heirs of the Frankish conquerors, consequently we have *droit du seigneur* over our subjects, the Gallo-Roman population, furthermore we are not subjects of our Frankish king, because under Frankish law the king is only *primus inter pares* and in no way ruler over aristocrats with equal rights. The crown jurists on the other hand considered the absolutist king to be the successor to the Roman emperors and his subjects to be the Gallo-Roman successors of the former Romans. In line with this theory France returned after the revolution, having rid itself of its Caesarian oppressors, to a form of government based on the model of the Roman Republic – there was no place here for aristocratic masters of the Frankish variety.

Gobineau, by nature a writer, started out as a pupil of the French Romantic school, which was characterized by a penchant for the Middle Ages and opposition to the everyday world of the sober bourgeois. For him, being an aristocratic loner, a Frank and a Teuton were one and the same. From an early age he pursued German and oriental studies. Both linguistically and in its literature, German Romanticism had established a connection with the Indian prehistory of Germanic civilization and an Aryan common ground between the different European peoples. (Scherer's book, which accompanied me to the Jews' House, lists in his annals under 1808 Friedrich Schlegel's *The Language and Wisdom of the Indians* and under 1816 Franz Bopp's *A Comparison of the System of Conjugation in Sanskrit with that of Greek, Latin, Persian and Germanic Languages.*) The construction of the Aryan has its roots in philology rather than science.

Moreover, in the realm of science Gobineau is also decisively influenced, or rather decisively misled, by German Romanticism. For just as it breaks and blurs boundaries in reaching out for the infinite, it also allows hypothetical and symbolic speculation to encroach on science. Accordingly, as someone who exaggerates his Teutonism all the more keenly for the very reason that he has chosen it, the French author is tempted, or rather encouraged, to embellish his scientific facts with a little speculation, or interpret them philosophically, indeed he is almost given an excuse for drawing out of them that which he wants to see confirmed. Namely, the overemphasis on Teutonism. In the case of Gobineau it is a product of internal political pressure, whilst in the case of the Romantics the cause is Napoleonic oppression.

It has been said that it was the humanitarian ideal which saved the Romantics (or, according to the Nazis, prevented them) from drawing the obvious conclusions from their sense of being the Chosen Teutonic People. But inflamed into nationalism and chauvinism, the awareness of national identity burns through this protective shield. The sense of a common bond linking humanity is entirely lost; anything of real human value is to be found in one's own people, but for Germany's enemies – 'The Final Judgement: let them die! /Yours is not to reason why!'

For the writers of the wars of liberation it is the Frenchman who is the enemy of the Germans and who must be killed; but, although there is much that can be said against him, and one can categorize his Latin ancestry as inferior to pure Teutonism, it is not possible to declare him a creature of another race. Thus at the point where German Romanticism restricts its previously limitless horizons to an extreme narrowness of vision, this process manifests itself merely as a rejection of everything foreign and the glorification of all that is exclusively German, not yet as racial arrogance. It has been pointed out that Jahn and Arndt numbered German Jews amongst the Germans, and did not prevent them from becoming members of the patriotic, hyper-German fraternities.

True – but thirty years later, prior to the publication of the *Essai sur l'iné-galité des races,* in his 'Speeches and Glosses' of 1848, the erstwhile humanitarian Arndt complains in a passage triumphantly quoted by the National Socialist Blome, 'Jews and their companions, whether baptized or not, work tirelessly together with the most extreme and radical elements on the Left to subvert and destroy anything which embraces the human and sacred qualities we Germans hold dear, to subvert and destroy every patriotic feeling and fear of God . . . Listen for a moment and take a look at where this poisonous Jewish humanitarianism would lead us if we did not have anything of our own, anything truly German, to counter it with . . .' It is no longer a question of liberation from the enemy without, it is now a political and social battle at home, and already the enemies of the pure German are 'the Jews, whether baptized or not'.

It remains a matter of interpretation whether one considers this form of anti-Semitism, one which extends beyond the issue of baptism, to be racially motivated at this point; but it is undoubtedly the case that the humanitarian ideal embracing all of mankind has been left behind and that the ideal of Germanness is in direct opposition to 'poisonous Jewish humanitarianism'. (Just as in the LTI – most frequently in Rosenberg and, likewise, in the case of Hitler and Goebbels – the word *Humanität* {humanitarianism} is never used without ironic inverted commas and is frequently reinforced with a scathing epithet.)

To satisfy my philological conscience I attempted during the Nazi period to produce a series of connections linking Gobineau to German Romanticism and have today firmed it up a little. I am myself, as before, absolutely convinced that there is a close affinity between Nazism and German Romanticism; I believe that the one was an inevitable result of the other, even if there had never been the Frenchman-turned-Teuton Gobineau, whose love of the Teutons was in any case more directed towards the Scandinavians and the English than the Germans. Because all of the distinctive features of National Socialism are present in Romanticism in embryonic form: the dethronement of reason, the animalization of man, the glorification of the idea of power, of the predator, of the blond beast . . .

But is this not a terrible indictment of the intellectual movement to which German art and literature (in the broadest sense of the word) owe so many of their humane values?

The terrible indictment is justified despite all the values formulated by Romanticism. 'We soar upwards and then fall correspondingly far.' The definitive characteristic of the German intellect is boundlessness {*Grenzenlosigkeit*}.

Chapter 22

A Sunny *Weltanschauung* (Chance Discoveries Whilst Reading)

In the Jews' Houses books are precious possessions – most of them have been taken away from us, getting hold of new ones and the use of public libraries is forbidden. If an Aryan wife uses a lending library in her own name and the Gestapo finds us in possession of one of the books we are fortunate to get away with a good thrashing – on a couple of occasions I was myself fortunate enough to get away with it in this way. What we have, and are allowed to have, are Jewish books. The definition is not rigid, and since all of the valuable private libraries have now been 'taken into safe keeping {*sichergestellt*}' – LTI, because the representatives of the Party never steal or rob – the Gestapo no longer sends experts.

On the other hand we are not particularly attached to the few books that remain; because many a copy has been 'inherited', which means in our own special language that it was left abandoned when its owner suddenly disappeared in the direction of Theresienstadt or Auschwitz. With the result that it brings home very forcefully to the new owner the fate which can befall him too any day and, especially, any night. Thus every book is lent by everyone to everyone else without further ado – we of all people certainly do not need a sermon on the transience of earthly possessions.

I myself read whatever falls into my hands; I am primarily concerned with the LTI, but it is remarkable how often books which either appear to be, or indeed really are, totally unrelated to the theme have something to contribute, and it is even more remarkable how many fresh insights one can gain in a different situation from books which one thought one knew back to front. So it was that in the summer of 1944 I came across Schnitzler's *Weg ins Freie* (The Road to the Open), and glanced through the novel without expecting to gain much from it, the reason being that I had written a lengthy study of the writer many years before, around 1911 I believe, and had read, discussed and worried about the problem of Zionism during the last few years until I was blue in the face. As a result I had all the issues in the book at my fingertips. But then a tiny section, ostensibly only a passing remark, did in fact stay with me as a new acquisition.

One of the main characters gets angry about the 'idle chitchat about *Weltanschauung* {*Weltanschauungsgerede*}' which has now – i.e. around the beginning of our century – become so fashionable. The man defines *Weltanschauung* as 'evidently meaning the will and the ability to see the world as it really is, i.e. view it without being swayed by any preconceived opinion, without the urge to deduce some new law from every experience or attempt to integrate it into some pre-existing one . . . But for these people *Weltanschauung* is nothing more than a superior form of staunchness {*Gesinnungstüchtigkeit*} – staunchness in the midst of the infinite, so to speak.'

In the next chapter, and it is there that one recognizes how the earlier *aperçu* fits into the actual theme of this Jewish novel, Heinrich ruminates further: 'Believe me, Georg, there are times when I am jealous of people who have a so-called *Weltanschauung* . . . but in our case, we can be guilty and innocent, cowards and heroes, fools and wise men all at once, depending on which bit of our psychological make-up prevails.'

The desire to interpret the term '*anschauen* {to view}' without a hint of mysticism, as seeing clearly what is actually there, the indignation and envy at those for whom *Weltanschauung* is a fixed dogma, a protective rope that you can hold on to in any situation where you can no longer rely on your own mood, judgement or conscience – according to Schnitzler all of this is characteristic for the Jewish spirit, as it doubtless also is for the mentality of large sections of the Viennese, Parisian and European intelligentsia at the turn of the century. The emergence of the 'idle chitchat about *Weltanschauung*' (in the sense of something 'illogical') can be explained as part of the incipient opposition to decadence, impressionism, scepticism and the undermining of the idea of a continuous and therefore responsible self.

What really struck me when reading these passages was not so much the question of whether this was a specifically Jewish or more general problem of decadence at work here. What I really asked myself was why, at the time when I read the novel for the first time, when the world it portrayed was the real one I was living in, I had paid so little attention to the emergence and increasing popularity of the new word. The question was not long in coming. At the time the word '*Weltanschauung*' was restricted to an oppositional group comprising certain New Romantics, it was a clannish word and not part of everyday language.

And I also asked myself how this clannish word from the turn of the century came to be a linguistic mainstay of the LTI, whereby the most insignificant Pg and the most uneducated member of the petty bourgeoisie would talk about his *Weltanschauung,* or behaviour based on it, at every possible opportunity; and then I asked myself about the nature of the National Socialist 'staunchness in the midst of the infinite'. It had to be something utterly comprehensible to all and suitable for every occasion, something which served a useful organizational purpose, because in the constitution of the *Deutsche Arbeitsfront* {German Labour Front}, the DAF, which I once set eyes on in the factory, in this statute of an 'Organization for all hands' there was expressly no reference to 'insurance premiums' but rather '*Beiträgen zu einer weltanschaulichen Gemeinschaft* {contributions to an association with a *Weltanschauung*}'.

What attracted the LTI to this word was not the idea of it being a translation into German of the foreign word 'philosophy' – the LTI did not, by any means, want to translate everything into German – no, but what it did see expressed here was the all-important antithesis of philosophical activity. Because philosophizing involves the exercise of reason, of logical thought, something which Nazism views as the most deadly enemy of all. The requisite antithesis of clear thinking is not, however, to see properly in the sense that Schnitzler defines the verb *schauen* {to see}; that would also get in the way of the constant National Socialist rhetoric of deception and stupefaction. Instead it finds in the word *Weltanschauung* the insight {*das Schauen*}, the vision {*die Schau*} of the mystic, i.e. the vision {*Sehen*} of the inner eye, the intuition and revelation of religious ecstasy. The vision of the Saviour from whom the laws of our world arise: this is the innermost meaning and the deepest yearning articulated by the word *Weltanschauung* as first used by the New Romantics and then adopted by the LTI. I keep returning to the same verse and the same formula: 'On a single patch of ground/Weed and flower both are found' . . . and: the German root of Nazism is called Romanticism . . .

However: before German Romanticism narrowed itself down from being *deutsch* {German} to *teutsch* {Teutonic} it entered into an intimate relationship with things foreign; and whilst Nazism on the one hand exaggerated the nationalistic ideas of Teutonic Romanticism, it was also, like the original German version, extremely receptive to anything useful it could glean from elsewhere.

A few weeks after reading Schnitzler I finally managed to get hold of Goebbels's *From the Kaiserhof to the Reich Chancellery.* (By 1944 the shortage of books had even become a serious problem for Aryans; poorly supplied and overrun, the lending libraries only took on new customers by dint of entreaty and on special recommendation – my wife was 'registered' at three different places and always carried my request slips in her handbag.) In these 'diary entries', which triumphantly report on successful propaganda and are themselves fresh propaganda, Goebbels notes the following on 27 February 1933: 'The grand propaganda campaign for the Day of the Nation's Awakening is now arranged down to the last detail. It will go off like a marvellous show {*Schau*} across the whole of Germany.' Here the word *Schau* has nothing whatsoever to do with inwardness and mysticism, in this case it is brought into line with the English word *show,* which denotes a display, a splendid spectacle, here it is entirely determined by the idea of the circus, the American Barnum show.

The corresponding verb, '*schauen* {to see}', has, depending on your standpoint, either got nothing or everything to do with Schnitzler's 'seeing properly {*richtig sehen*}'. Because this is a directed gaze, a gratification and engaging of the sensual eye, the garishness of which ultimately leads to blindness. Romanticism and well-advertised commerce, Novalis and Barnum, Germany and America: both of these are present in the LTI's *Schau* and *Weltanschauung,* and are as inseparably connected as mysticism and pomp and circumstance in the Catholic mass.

And I ask myself what this Saviour, exalted by the DAF and its *Weltanschauung,* actually looks like, and I realize that here too, in his most striking features, there is a meeting of the German and the American.

A year prior to wrestling with Schnitzler's passage on *Weltanschauung* I had, in a similar vein, already noted down a few sentences from Lily Braun's *Memoiren einer Sozialistin* (Memoirs of a Socialist) and related them to my theme. (This heirloom was pervaded in a particularly awful way with the imagined stench of a gas chamber. 'Died in Auschwitz of an inadequate cardiac muscle' I read on the death certificate of the man who had involuntarily bequeathed it . . .) I noted the following in my diary: '. . . In Münster Alix entered into a religious dispute with a Catholic priest: "The idea of Christianity? . . . The Catholic Church has nothing whatsoever to do with it! And that is precisely what I love and admire about it . . . we are heathens, sun worshippers . . . Charlemagne understood that almost at once, along with his missionaries. They often enough had their own fair share of Saxon blood in their veins. Which is why, instead of shrines to Wotan, Donar, Baldur and Freya, they had the temples of their numerous saints; this is why they raised the Mother of God, symbol of the creation of life, onto the heavenly throne rather than her crucified son. This is why the servants of the man who had nowhere to lay his head decorated their vestments, altars and churches with gold and precious stones and took art into their service. From Christ's point of view their Anabaptists were right when they destroyed the images, but the vigorous character of their national comrades {*Volksgenossen*} put them in the wrong."'

A Christ unsuited to Europe, the affirmation of Teutonic dominance within Catholicism, the emphasis on a positive attitude to life, on the cult of the sun, together with the Saxon blood and the vigorous character of the national comrades – all of that could just as well be in Rosenberg's *Myth*. And the fact that, despite all of this, Braun is not a Nazi, and neither anti-intellectual nor anti-Jewish, merely gives the Nazis a broader base when it comes to their parading of swastikas as a Teutonic symbol, their worshipping of the sun wheel and their constant insistence on sunny Teutonism. '*Sonnig* {sunny}' was rampant at the time in the announcements of those who died in action. I was therefore entirely convinced that this epithet was rooted firmly at the heart of the old Teutonic cult and derived solely from the vision of the blond Saviour.

Until, that is, I discovered a good-natured female worker at the factory keenly reading a forces' postal service booklet during a breakfast break and, on my request, was lent the pamphlet. It was one of the series '*Soldaten-Kameraden* (Soldiers-Comrades)' published in huge numbers by the Hitler press Franz Eher, and consisted of a series of short stories under the overall title *Der Gurkenbaum* (The Cucumber Tree). They all disappointed me insofar as I had expected a publication of the Eher press in particular to contain the Nazi poison in its most concentrated form. He had, after all, injected the army with more than enough of it in other booklets. But Wilhelm Pleyer, whom I later got to know better as a Sudeten German novelist without my initial impression being significantly changed either for the better or for the worse, was both as a writer and as a man a very minor Pg indeed.

The fruits of the 'Cucumber Tree' consisted of extremely uninspired and entirely harmless so-called humoresques. I was just about to put them to one side having gained nothing from them when I came across a mawkish story about happy parents, about a happy mother. It told the story of a very lively, very blonde, golden-haired, sunny-haired little girl: the lines were brimful of blonde hair, sun and a sunny mentality. The little girl had a special relationship with the sun's rays and was called Wiwiputzi. How did she come by this strange name? The author asks himself this as well. It may well be that the three i's made the word seem particularly bright, or that the first three letters reminded him of *vif,* lively, or that there was something else which struck him as poetical and life-affirming about this invented word – be that as it may, he answered his own question as follows, '*Ersonnen?* {Thought up?}[1] No, it just appeared of its own accord – *ersonnt* {conjured up by the sun}.'

When I gave the worker her book back I asked her which of the stories she had liked the most. She replied they were all nice, but the best was the one about Wiwiputzi.

'If only I knew where he got the idea for the play on the word sunny {*das Spiel mit dem Sonnigen*}.' The question had slipped out almost against my better judgement and I immediately regretted it – what, after all, was this entirely unliterary woman supposed to answer? All I would do would be to embarrass her. But strangely enough the answer came

---

[1]*Ersonnen* is the past participle of the (irregular) verb *ersinnen,* to devise or think up. In this context it reverberates with the word *Sonne,* sun. *Ersonnt,* at the end of the sentence, is the past participle of the fanciful (regular) verb *ersonnen,* literally to bring something into being by the sun.

right away, without a moment's thought: 'Well, I suppose he must have been thinking of *Sonny Boy*!'

For once that was really the *vox populi*. Of course I couldn't organize a questionnaire, but at that moment I was intuitively sure, and still am today, that the film *Sonny Boy* {The Singing Fool} – who after all knows that *sonny* means a little boy and has absolutely nothing to do with 'sunny'? – that this American film was at least as responsible for the plague of sunniness as the cult of the Teutons.

Chapter 23

If Two People do the Same Thing . . .

I know exactly the moment, and the very word, that expanded, or was it narrowed, I'm not sure which, my philological interest from the literary to the specifically linguistic. The literary context of a text suddenly stops being important, is lost, and one becomes fixated on a single word or a single form. Because on close examination it is the single word which reveals the way a particular epoch thinks, the universal way of thinking in which the ideas of an individual are rooted, which influences and perhaps even steers him. It is true that the single word and single turn of phrase can have entirely contrary meanings depending on the context in which they appear, and that brings me back to the literary aspect, the entirety of the given text. Reciprocal elucidation is necessary, cross-checking between a single word and the document as a whole . . .

It occurred at the point when Karl Voßler expressed his rage at the expression *Menschenmaterial* {human material, manpower}. Material, he said, refers at most to the skin and bones and the entrails of an animal; to speak of human material is to stick to mere matter and to ignore the spiritual, the essentially human aspects of a human being.

At the time I did not entirely agree with my teacher. It was two years before the Great War, I had never encountered the true awfulness of war, I didn't believe it could possibly break out again in the heart of Europe, I thought of military service pretty much as a fairly innocent form of physical and sporting training; and if an officer or military doctor referred to good or bad human material it didn't strike me as any different from a civilian doctor dealing with a 'case' or an 'appendix' before lunch. In any event one didn't come into direct contact with the soul of the new recruit Tom, or, for that matter, with the souls of Dick and Harry who had fallen ill, for an instant one simply concentrated for professional reasons on the purely physical side of human nature. After the war I was more inclined to see in 'human material' an uncomfortable correspondence with 'cannon fodder', the same cynicism, here in a more conscious form, there in a more unconscious one. But even today I am still not fully convinced of the brutality of this discredited expression. Why shouldn't someone with the highest ideals refer to the literal material value of an individual or a group in the case of a specific profession or sport? For analogous reasons, I can't see anything particularly heartless in the fact that in the official language of the prison service prisoners are referred to by numbers rather than their real names: their status as human beings is not thereby automatically negated, rather they are considered as objects to be administered, and only viewed as numbers as far as lists are concerned.

Why therefore is it different, why does a palpable and undeniable brutality come to light when a female warder in Belsen concentration camp explains to the war crimes trial that on such and such a day she dealt with sixteen *'Stück' Gefangenen* {'head' of prisoners}? In both of the former cases we are dealing with the professional avoidance of reference to the person, with abstraction, *Stück* {piece, head}, on the other hand, involves objectification. It is the same objectification expressed by the official term 'the utilization of carcasses {*Kadaververwertung*}', especially when widened to refer to human corpses: fertilizer is made out of the dead of the concentration camps and referred to in the same way as the processing of animal carcasses.

Dictated by an embittered hatred, behind which lies a burgeoning despair in the face of helplessness, this objectification is articulated still more deliberately in a stereotypical phrase which cropped up in military despatches, above all in 1944. They repeatedly point out that gangs can expect to be shown no mercy; in the case of the expanding French Resistance in particular there was for a time routine mention of the fact that umpteen people had been *'niedergemacht* {massacred}'. The verb *'niedermachen'* betrays the fury directed at the adversary, but at least in this case he is still thought of as a hated enemy, as a person. But then one reads every day: umpteen people have been *'liquidiert* {liquidated}'. *Liquidieren* derives from the language of commerce, as a loan word it is a degree or two colder and more objective than its respective German equivalents; a doctor *liquidiert* {charges} a particular sum for his efforts, a businessman puts his business into liquidation {*liquidiert*}. In the former case we are dealing with the conversion of medical effort into cash value, in the latter the final settlement, the giving up of a business. When people are liquidated they are settled or terminated as if they were material assets. In the language of the concentration camps it is said of a group that it 'was led to its final solution {*der Endlösung zugeführt*}' when it was shot or sent to the gas chambers.

Should this objectification of the individual personality be seen as a special characteristic of the LTI? I don't think so. This is because it is only applied to people to whom National Socialism has already denied membership of the human race proper, people who, as members of a lesser or inimical race, or as subhumans, have been excluded from that true brand of humanity exclusive to the Teutons or those of Nordic blood. Within this recognized circle of people, on the other hand, it lays particular emphasis on individual personality. To demonstrate this fact I wish to single out two irrefutable pieces of evidence.

The military no longer speak of the people under the command of a particular officer or in a company, but rather of the men {*Männern*}; every lieutenant reports –I ordered my men {*Männern*} . . . On one occasion a moving and emotional obituary appeared in the *Reich* written by an old university professor for three of his favourite students who had died as officers in action. In it were also reproduced letters written by these officers from the field. The old professor again and again expressed his enthusiasm for the German loyalty among men and for the heroism of the officers and their '*Mannen* {men, liegemen}', he revelled in this expression made poetic by its Old German ring; in the letters from the field written by his pupils on the other hand, the phrase used was, without exception, '*unsere Männer* {our men}'. In this case the contemporary linguistic form was used without a second thought – the young people no longer felt that they were saying anything novel or poetic with the new designation.

In general the LTI was ambivalent about Old German forms. On the one hand it was obviously quite fond of the link with tradition, the Romantic predilection for the German Middle Ages, the attachment to the pristine world of the Teutons prior to its corruption by the Romans; on the other hand it wanted to be both contemporary without any historical ballast and progressively modern. What is more, in the early days Hitler had fought against those nationalistic Germans who were fond of giving their own language a manifestly Old German ring, viewing them as embarrassing rivals and enemies. Thus the German designations for the months of the year, which were promoted for a while, never caught on and were never used officially. On the other hand several runes and all kinds of Teutonic first names acquired a better standing and became commonplace . . .

The desire to emphasize the individual personality is expressed even more clearly than in the word '*Männer*' in a new formulation adopted universally in bureaucratic language, one which degenerated into unintentional comedy. There were no clothing or ration coupons for Jews, they were not allowed to buy anything new and were only given second-hand things by special clothing and household stores. Initially it was relatively easy to get something from the clothing store; later a petition was necessary, which was passed from the appointed 'legal adviser' of the district, and the Jewish division of the Gestapo, to the police headquarters. On one occasion I received a form card with the notification: 'I have made a second-hand pair of working trousers available to you. To be collected . . . etc. The Chief of Police.' The underlying principle being that no decision of any kind should be made by an impersonal office, but by the appropriate person in charge. The result was that all official communications were translated into the first person and ordained by a personal god. I, the financial director in person, and not the tax office X, ordered Friedrich Schulze to pay three Marks and fifty Pfennig for failure to pay on time; I, the Chief of Police, sent out a fine amounting to three Marks; and last but not least I, the Chief of Police, personally even granted the Jew Klemperer a second-hand pair of trousers. Everything *in majorem gloriam* of the Führer principle and the individual personality.

No, National Socialism did not want to depersonalize or objectify those it regarded as human beings, namely the Teutons. It is merely that a leader also needs people to lead, those on whose unconditional obedience he can rely. It is telling how often during the twelve years the word '*blindlings* {blindly}' appeared in oaths of allegiance, and in telegrams and resolutions paying homage or expressing support. *Blindlings* is one of the linguistic pillars of the LTI, it denotes the ideal manifestation of the Nazi spirit with regard to its leader and respective subordinate leaders, and it is used almost as often as '*fanatisch*'. But in order to carry out an order blindly I mustn't even begin to think about it.

Thinking about something always means delays and scruples, it could even lead to criticism, and finally to the refusal to carry out an order. The basic principle underlying all military training lies in the inculcation of a series of automated movements and actions, in order that the individual soldier and individual squad carry out the orders of their superior just as a machine springs into action at the press of a button, independent of external circumstances, independent of internal considerations, and independent of the dictates of instinct. National Socialism certainly does not want to encroach upon the individual personality, on the contrary, it seeks to reinforce it, but that does not preclude it (as far as it is concerned!) from mechanizing this personality at the same time: everyone should be an automaton in the hand of his superior and leader, and at the same time he should also be the one who presses the button to activate the automatons under his own control. This construction disguises universal enslavement and depersonalization, and explains the excessive number of LTI expressions lifted from the realm of technology, the mass of mechanizing words.

It is of course essential in this context to disregard the growth of technical terms experienced by all languages of the civilized world since the beginning of the nineteenth century, one indeed which is still being experienced today, and which is a logical consequence of the rapid spread of technology and its increasing importance in day-to-day life. Rather, it is in this case a matter of technical expressions being applied to non-technical areas, in which they then function as a means of bringing about mechanization. In the German language this was only very rarely the case before 1933.

In effect, the Weimar Republic only transported two expressions from the specialized domain of technology into the common language: *verankern* {to anchor} and *ankurbeln* {to crank} were the fashionable catchwords of the period. To such an extent indeed that they very soon became the butt of sarcasm and were used to caricature unpopular contemporaries; thus Stefan Zweig was able to write the following in his *Kleine Chronik* (Little Chronicle) at the end of the 1920s: 'His Excellency and the Dean vigorously cranked up {*ankurbeln*} their contacts.'

It is open to question as to whether, and, if so, to what extent, *verankern* can be regarded as a technical image. A navigational term with a hint of poetry, it cropped up here and there long before the Weimar Republic, and only distinguished itself a fashionable word through the excessive use made of it during the period. This widespread usage was undoubtedly prompted by a much discussed official utterance: it was stressed that the National Assembly wanted to make certain that the law governing works committees was 'anchored in the constitution'. From that point on everything imaginable and unimaginable was anchored into something or other. The inner, unconscious motive behind the fondness for this image was undoubtedly a deep desire for stability: everyone had had their fill of the crashing waves of revolution; the ship of state – an ancient image (*fluctuat nec mergitur*) – was to lie at anchor in a safe haven.

Only the verb *ankurbeln* was gleaned from technology in the narrow, modern sense of the word; it undoubtedly derives from a scene which one encountered on the street again and again in those days: the automobile engine still lacked a starter, and everywhere drivers endeavoured with a great deal of effort to start their machines with a hand-crank.

What both images, the semi-technical and the entirely technical, have in common, however, is the fact that they were only ever applied to objects, situations and activities, never to people. During the Weimar Republic all kinds of businesses were reflated {*ankurbeln*}, but never the managing director himself, all kinds of institutions were anchored, as were various authorities, but never a finance director or a minister himself. The really decisive step towards a linguistic mechanization of life is only taken at the point where the technical metaphor is applied directly to a person or, in the words of an expression popular since the beginning of this century, aimed at him {*eingestellt*}.

I ask myself parenthetically whether *eingestellt sein* {to be disposed towards something} and *Einstellung* {attitude, view} – today every housewife has a particular view on the subject of sweeteners and sugar, every boy has a different attitude towards boxing and track and field events – should also come under the rubric of linguistic mechanization. Yes and no. These expressions originally had to do with focusing a telescope on an object at a particular distance, or tuning a motor to rotate at a specific speed. But the first transference of this meaning to a different field was only partly metaphorical: science and philosophy – philosophy in particular – seized hold of the expression; precise thinking, the thought apparatus, is focused {*eingestellt*} sharply on an object, the technical undertone is definitely preserved, intentionally so indeed. The public at large are likely to have first picked up on the word from philosophy. To be considered cultured one had to have an '*Einstellung* {view}' on vital matters. To what extent people were generally still aware by the beginning of this century of the technical, or at least of the purely rational, meaning of these expressions can scarcely be ascertained with any accuracy. In one particular satirical sound film the coquettish heroine sings that her life is *'von Kopf bis Fuß auf Liebe eingestellt* {focused on love from head to toe}',[1] which speaks for a knowledge of this original meaning; but at the same time a patriot who believes himself to be a writer, and who is later celebrated as one by the Nazis, sings of his feelings being entirely *'auf Deutschland eingestellt* {tuned in to Germany}'. The film was based on Heinrich Mann's tragi-comic novel about a senior schoolmaster; the man of verse celebrated by the Nazis as an early supporter and fighter in the Freikorps bore the not particularly Teutonic first name Boguslav or Boleslaw – what is the use of a philologist whose books have been stolen and whose notes have been partially destroyed?

The explicit mechanization of the individual himself is left up to the LTI. Its most characteristic, and probably also earliest, creation in this field is *'gleichschalten* {to force into line}'. You can see and hear the button at work which forces people – not institutions and impersonal authorities – to adopt the same, uniform attitude and movements: teachers in various institutions, various groups of employees in the judiciary and tax authorities, members of the *Stahlhelm* and the SA, and so on, are brought into line almost *ad infinitum*.

This word is so horrendously representative of the basic attitude of Nazism that it is one of the few expressions accorded the honour of satirization by Archbishop Cardinal Faulhaber, as early as winter 1933 in his advent sermons. In the case of the Asiatic peoples, he explained, religion and the State had been *gleichgeschaltet* {forced into line}. At around the same time as the high dignitaries of the Church, cabaret artists also plucked up the courage to shed comic light on this verb. I remember a compère on a so-called mystery tour who, during a coffee stop in a forest, told the group of tourists that they had now been *gleichgeschaltet* with nature, a remark which earned him a round of applause.

In the LTI there is no other appropriation of technical words which could reveal the tendency to mechanize and automate more fully than *'gleichschalten'*. It was used throughout the twelve years, albeit more

---

[1] In the English version of this song, from the film *The Blue Angel,* the line is rendered 'Falling in love again'.

frequently at the beginning than at the end because, quite simply, all of the forcing into line {*Gleichschaltungen*} and automations had soon been carried out and become a matter of course.

Other expressions appropriated from the field of electrical engineering have less grave consequences. If, now and then, people refer to *Kraftströmen* {power currents} which coalesce in a natural leader or which he himself emanates – it is likely that, with minor variations, much the same was said of both Mussolini and Hitler – then these are metaphorical expressions which imply magnetism as much as electrical engineering, and are thus associated with Romantic sensations. This is particularly noticeable in the case of Ina Seidel, who turned to the same electrical metaphor in both her purest creations and her most sinful – but Ina Seidel is a sad chapter in her own right.

But should it really be considered Romantic when Goebbels misrepresents a trip to the bombed cities in the west by claiming that he who had originally intended to instil courage in the victims had in the end himself been 'recharged {*neu aufgeladen*}' by their unshakeable heroism? No, this is plainly nothing more than the old habit of degrading people to the status of machines.

I say plainly because in the other technical metaphors used by Goebbels and the Propaganda Minister's circle direct references to the realm of the mechanical abound without the slightest recollection of any power currents {*Kraftströme*}. Again and again working people are compared with machines. Thus, for example, there is a reference in the *Reich* to the governor of Hamburg working like 'a motor which always runs at full tilt {*ein immer auf Hochtouren laufender Motor*}'. However, unlike this comparison, which still draws a clear distinction between the image and the object with which it is compared, a Goebbels sentence such as the following provides more compelling and serious evidence of this intrinsically mechanizing attitude: 'In the foreseeable future we will be running at full tilt again {*zu vollen Touren*} in a range of areas.' We are thus no longer being compared with machines, we have become machines ourselves. We: that is Goebbels, that is the Nazi government, that is the totality of Hitler's Germany which, in dire distress and critically depleted of energy, is to be spurred on; and this powerful preacher doesn't just compare himself and his faithful followers with machines, no, he identifies them with them. A more dehumanized way of thinking than the one exposed here would not be conceivable.

Given that this mechanizing linguistic usage grabs hold directly of the individual, it is hardly surprising that it endlessly embraces things outside its domain which are more easily within its grasp. There is nothing that can't be started up {*anlaufen*} or overhauled {*überholen*}, just as a motor is overhauled after it has run for a long time or a ship is overhauled after a lengthy voyage, there is nothing which can be channelled in or out of somewhere {*hinein-, herausschleusen*}, and of course – oh language of the fledgling Fourth Reich! – everything and anything can be set up {*aufziehen*}. And if it is time to extol the indomitable will to live demonstrated by the inhabitants of a bombed city, the *Reich* proclaims as philological evidence the popular expression of the local Rheinland or Westphalian population: 'Everything is back on track {*Es spurt schon wieder*}.' (I had this specialist term from the field of automobile construction explained to me: the wheels on a vehicle stay on the right track.) And why is everything on the right track again? Because everyone is 'working to their full capacity {*voll ausgelastet*}' thanks to the excellent organization all-round. '*Voll ausgelastet*', a favourite expression of Goebbels during the last years, is also undoubtedly a term lifted from the language of technology and applied to the people themselves; it sounds simply less aggressive than the motor running at full tilt because human shoulders can also be used to capacity {*auslasten*} like some load-bearing structure or other. Language brings everything to light. The constant encroachment and spinning out of technological terms, the revelling in them: In the Weimar Republic there was only the cranking up {*Ankurbeln*} of the economy, the LTI didn't just add the idea of running it at full tilt, but also 'the well-adjusted steering {*die gut eingespielte Lenkung*}' – all of this (which I have in no way exhausted here lexicographically) bears witness not only to the *de facto* disregard of individuality, something purportedly valued and nurtured, but also to the will to subjugate the independent thinker, the free human being. And this evidence cannot be invalidated by any number of protestations that it is precisely the individual personality which is to be developed in total contradistinction to the 'de-individualization' striven for by Marxism, and which in turn finds its true apotheosis in Jewish and Asiatic Bolshevism.

But does language really bring it to light? A word keeps coming into my mind which I now hear again and again as the Russians attempt to rebuild our decimated school system: people are endlessly quoting Lenin's remark that the teacher is the engineer of the soul. But this is also undoubtedly a technological image, indeed the most technological of all in fact. An engineer deals with machines. If he is seen as the ideal man to tend the soul, then I can only conclude that the soul is regarded as a machine . . .

Do I have to? The Nazis always pontificated about the fact that Marxism is materialism, and that Bolshevism surpasses even socialist doctrine in its materialism by attempting to imitate the industrial methods of the Americans, and by appropriating their technical way of thinking and feeling. How much of all this is actually true?

Everything and nothing.

It is certainly the case that Bolshevism served its apprenticeship under American technology, that it proceeded with great enthusiasm to mechanize its own country, a process bound to make the biggest possible impression on the language. But why did it mechanize its country? In order to attain for its people more humane living conditions, to reduce the burden of work and provide a physical basis from which they could prosper intellectually. The wealth of new technical terms in their language thus testifies to something diametrically opposed to what it reveals about Hitler's Germany: it points to the weapons employed in the battle for the liberation of the mind, whilst in the case of Germany I am forced to conclude that the imposition of technological terms implies an enslavement of the mind.

If two people do the same thing . . . the most trivial of sayings. But in my philologist's notebook I intend to underline this home truth from my own discipline: if two people use the same expression there is absolutely no reason why they should have the same intentions. In fact I want to underline it today again and again. Because it is absolutely essential that we learn about the true spirit of different nations, nations we have been isolated from for so long and about which we have been told so many lies. And we have been told more lies about Russia than any other . . . And nothing gives us better access to the soul of a nation than its language . . . And yet: *Gleichschalten* and *Ingenieur der Seele* {engineer of the soul} – both are technical expressions, but whilst the German metaphor points to slavery, the Russian one points to freedom.

Chapter 24
Café Europe

12 August 1935. 'It is certainly right on the edge – you can see across to Asia –but it is still in Europe', Dember said to me two years ago when he told me about his appointment to the University of Istanbul. I can still see his contented smile, the first after weeks of bitterness following his dismissal, or rather, to be more precise, his being hounded out. Today I can still remember how this smile and the happy ring to his voice highlighted the word 'Europe'; because today I received from the Bls the first news since they emigrated. In the meantime they must have made it to Lima since their letter was sent from Bermuda. I find it very depressing: I am envious of these people's freedom, the broadening of their horizons, I am jealous of him because of the chances he has to influence people – and instead of just being happy they complain about seasickness and being homesick for Europe. I have knocked off a few lines of verse to send them:

Thank the Lord with all your might
For furnishing your means of flight
Across the sea from grief and fright –
To where your woes are truly small;
To spew a little in the sea
From a ship that cruises free
Is hardly worth a word at all.
Lift your weary eyes to view
The Southern Cross beyond the blue;
Far from all the woes of the Jew

Your ship has bridged the ocean.
Do you yearn for Europe's shore?
It greets you in the tropics more
For Europe is a notion!

13 August 1935. Walter writes from Jerusalem: 'Please in future simply use the following address: *Café Europe.* I'm not sure how long I'll stay at my present address, but I can definitely always be reached at the *Café Europe.* I am much happier here – by which I mean Jerusalem as a whole and this café in particular – than I was in Tel Aviv; there the Jews want to keep themselves very much to themselves and to be Jews and nothing more. Things are altogether more European here.'

I'm not sure if I am giving undue weight to today's letter from Palestine as a result of yesterday's correspondence; but it seems to me that my uneducated nephew has got closer to grasping the essence of 'Europe' than my scholarly colleagues, whose yearnings can never be separated from the geographical space.

14 August 1935. I can never be proud of some idea or other for longer than a single day; at that point it fades away as I realize – the curse of the philologist – where I got it from. The notion of Europe is borrowed from Paul Valéry. For my own satisfaction I can add: cf. Klemperer's *Modern French Prose.* In those days, twelve years ago now, I gathered together, in a special chapter, French opinions on Europe and commented on them – how they despairingly lament the way in which the continent has torn itself limb from limb in war, how they determine its true nature in terms of the development and spread of a particular culture, of a particular attitude of mind and will. In his Zurich speech of 1922, Paul Valéry referred quite explicitly to a concept of Europe distinct from the geographical entity. For him Europe consists of all those places permeated by the trinity of Jerusalem, Athens and Rome, as he himself puts it: Hellas, ancient Rome and the Rome of Christianity, but Christian Rome obviously embraces Jerusalem; even America is for him 'a formidable creation of Europe'. But in the same breath in which he presents Europe as the supreme world power he adds: I have not expressed this accurately, it is not Europe which rules, but rather the European spirit.

How can one long for a Europe which is no longer Europe? And Germany is certainly not Europe any more. And for how long are the bordering countries going to be safe? I myself would feel safer in Lima than in Istanbul. And as far as I'm concerned, Jerusalem is too close to Tel Aviv, which has rather a lot in common with Miesbach . . .

(Note for today's reader: during the Weimar Republic a daily newspaper was published in the Bavarian town of Miesbach which didn't so much prepare the ground for the *Stürmer* as steal its thunder.)

*

Following these notes the word *Europa* doesn't crop up once in my diary for almost eight years, despite the fact that I kept a watchful eye on everything that struck me as a distinctive feature of the LTI. Of course I'm not trying to say that there wasn't here and there something written about Europe or the state of Europe. That would be all the more incorrect given the fact that Nazism worked with a counterfeit notion of Europe inherited from its progenitor Chamberlain, one which played a central role in Rosenberg's *Myth* and which was consequently repeated parrot-fashion by all party theoreticians.

It can be said of this idea that it was treated in much the same way as the politicians of racial purity dealt with the German population: it was '*aufgenordet* {nordified}'. According to Nazi doctrine, everything European stemmed from the Nordic peoples or Northern Teutons; every plague, every menace came from Syria or Palestine; in cases where it was impossible to deny the Greek and Christian origins of European culture, the Hellenes and even Christ were of blond-haired-blue-eyed-Nordic-Teuton origin. Those aspects of Christianity which did not fit neatly into Nazi ethics and political doctrine were weeded out for being Jewish, or Syrian, or Roman.

But even in this distorted form, both the concept and word *Europa* were the preserve of a small educated elite, and in the main as notorious as the despised terms 'intelligence {*Intelligenz*}' and 'humanitarianism {*Humanität*}'. Because there was always the danger that memories of the old notion of Europe could be awakened, which would inevitably lead to peaceful, supranational and humanitarian ways of thinking. It was also possible, on the other hand, to do without the notion of Europe entirely, by making Germania into both the fountain of all ideas about Europe and the sole source of true-blooded Europeans. In this way Germany was severed from all cultural ties and responsibilities, it stood alone and godlike, with divine rights over all other peoples. Of course one often heard that Germany had to defend Europe against Jewish-Asiatic Bolshevism. And when Hitler set off with much pomp and circumstance on 2 May 1938 for a state visit to Italy, the press repeatedly claimed that the Führer and Duce were together to create 'The New Europe', notwithstanding the fact that the internationalizing term 'Europe' was immediately offset by the headline 'The Holy Teutonic Empire {*Das heilige Germanische Reich deutscher Nation*}'. During the pre-war years of the Third Reich the word 'Europe' was certainly not used often enough, with a sufficiently emphatic new meaning, or enough emotional fervour, to justify its being registered as a characteristic term of the LTI.

It was only with the onset of the Russian campaign, and then definitively with the ensuing retreat, that it gained a new and ever more desperate currency. Whilst Europe had up until this point only on rare occasions been 'protected from Bolshevism', and then only in the context of what might be termed weekend cultural analysis, this phrase, or similar ones, became so routine that they cropped up every day in the newspapers, and were often repeated in different contexts. Goebbels invents the image of the onslaught of the Steppes, and by appropriating the noun from the technical vocabulary of geography, warns everyone of the danger that Europe will be turned into steppes {*Versteppung*}, and from this point on *die Steppe* {the steppe} and *Europa* become part of the unique lexicon of the LTI, usually in combination.

But by this point, the concept of Europe has undergone a strange back-formation. In Valéry's observations, Europe was detached from its original geographical space, indeed from any kind of physical space; it referred to the region intellectually shaped by the aforementioned trinity of Jerusalem, Athens and Rome (or, from a more Latin point of view, once by Athens and twice by Rome). Now, in the last third of the Hitler era, it has nothing to do with an abstraction of this kind. Of course there is talk of the ideas of the Occident that are to be defended against the forces of Asia. But people are not only careful to avoid propagating once again, as had been the case during the rise of Nazism, the idea of a Nordic–Teutonic European people, they also rarely waste a sentence on addressing Valéry's more accurate notion of Europe. I only call it more accurate because his exclusively Latin attitude and western point of view are too narrow to be entirely precise: ever since Tolstoy and

Dostoyevsky made their impact on Europe (and Vogüé's *Roman Russe* appeared as early as 1886), ever since Marxism evolved into Marxism-Leninism, and banded together with American technology, the focus of European thought has shifted to Moscow . . .

No, the Europe about which the LTI talks daily, its new keyword *Europa,* can only be understood spatially and materially; it denotes a restricted area which it regards with altogether more concrete criteria than was previously the case. For Europe is now no longer simply fenced off from Russia – whilst also laying claim to large areas of its land as part of Hitler's continent by right – but is also at loggerheads with Great Britain.

It was all very different at the beginning of the war. 'England is no longer an island' it was claimed. Incidentally, the phrase was coined well before Hitler, I found it in Disraeli's *Tancred* and in the writings of the political travel writer Rohrbach, who promoted the Baghdad railway and Central Europe; nevertheless, the dictum will always be associated with Hitler. In those days, during the victory celebrations following the invasion of Poland and France, all of Hitler's Germany expected an imminent landing in England.

The hopes were dashed, and England, blockaded and defenceless, was replaced by the blockaded and defenceless Axis; and from this point the slogan was the 'unblockadable {*blockadefeste*}', 'economically self-sufficient Europe {*autarke Europa*}', the 'honourable continent' betrayed by England, threatened on all fronts by the Americans and Russians, and destined to be enslaved and dulled. The definitive expression for the LTI, both lexically and conceptually, is 'Fortress Europe {*Festung Europa*}'.

In spring 1943 a book by Max Clauß entitled *Tatsache Europa* (The Fact of Europe) appeared with official approval ('This work is listed in the National Socialist bibliography'). The title alone points to the fact that a rambling, speculative notion of Europe is not the issue here, but rather something utterly concrete, the beleaguered European space. The issue is 'the new Europe that is on the march today'. The role of the real enemy is played in this work by England, more so even than Russia. The theoretical starting point is provided by Coudenhove-Kalergi's book *Pan-Europa,* which appeared in 1923, and in which England is portrayed as the supreme European power, and Soviet Russia as the threat to European democracy. Coudenhove is thus an ally rather than enemy of the Nazi author, at least as far as antagonism towards the Soviets is concerned. It is not, however, simply the political positions of the two theoreticians which are at issue here. Clauß quotes Coudenhove's commentary on his unifying emblem: 'the sign, under which the Pan-Europeans of all states will be united, is the Sun Cross: the red cross on a golden sun, the symbol of humanitarianism and reason'. What matters in the present context is neither Coudenhove's lack of appreciation of the fact that it is precisely Russia, which he himself excludes, that bears the European torch, nor his defence of English hegemony. All that matters here is the fact that for Coudenhove it is the idea of Europe, and not the geographical space, which is placed centre stage – on the cover of the Nazi book, on the other hand, one is faced with the space, the map of the continent – and that this idea is referred to as humanitarianism and reason. The book *The Fact of Europe* ridicules the 'will-o'-the-wisp of Pan-Europe', and deals exclusively with 'reality' or, to be more precise, what in Hitler's Germany was officially endorsed as a lasting reality at the beginning of 1943: 'Reality, the organization of this enormous continent with a basis in the East freed by force, reality, the release of prodigious powers to secure Europe, come what may, against the threat of a blockade.' Germany remains at the heart of this continent as a 'power which imposes order {*Ordnungsmacht*}'. This word also belongs to the late phase of the LTI. It is a euphemistic pretext for the use and abuse of power. It wields ever greater power, the weaker the position of its ally and Axis partner, Italy, becomes; it does not embrace an idealistic, non-geographical goal.

Regardless of how often the name Europe crops up in the press and speeches of the final years – and this happens increasingly, and with growing fervour, as the situation for Germany gets worse and worse – it only ever has one single meaning: Germany, the 'power which imposes order', defends 'Fortress Europe'.

In Salzburg an exhibition is mounted with the title 'German Artists and the SS'. The headline above a report on it reads 'From the Vanguard of the Movement to the Defenders of Europe'. Shortly before this, in Spring 1944, Goebbels writes: 'The peoples of Europe ought to thank us on bended knees' for fighting to protect them, perhaps they don't even deserve it! (I only noted down the beginning of this sentence verbatim.)

On one occasion however, amidst all the materialists concerned only that Hitler's Germany's should have control over European lands, a writer and idealist does take to the floor. In the summer of 1943 the *Reich* publishes an Ode to Europe in an archaic metre. The author is Wilfried Bade, and his recently published volume of poems is entitled *Tod und Leben* (Death and Life). I don't know anything else about the author or his work, as far as I know they may both have sunk without a trace; I was affected at the time, and still am when I am think of it, by the clear articulation and energy of one of the odes. In it Germany is, as it were, a god in the guise of a bull who has seduced the beautiful Europa, and of this looted and exalted figure it is said: '. . . You are in one/Mother, lover and daughter too/a great secret, / scarcely to be divined . . .' But the young idealist and friend of the ancient world does not abandon himself to this secret any further, for he knows a remedy for all spiritual difficulties: 'Yet in the splendour/of swords everything is simple, and nothing/remains a mystery.'

What an enormous discrepancy there is between this and the idea of Europe during the First World War! 'Europe, I cannot bear to see you perish in this madness, Europe, I will scream into the ears of your butchers your true identity!' writes Jules Romains – and the poet of the Second World War finds nobility and a deadening of pain in the splendour of swords!

———

Life admits of combinations no novelist would allow himself, for in a novel they would appear too fanciful. I had collected my notes on Europe from the Hitler period and was considering whether we could now return to a purer notion of Europe, or whether we would drop the concept entirely, because in Moscow, the place still ignored by the Frenchman Valéry, the most unadulterated European thinking is now being directed literally 'at everyone', and, as far as Moscow is concerned, there is just the world and no longer the special province of Europe – when all of a sudden I received the first letter from Jerusalem from my nephew Walter, the first for six years. It was no longer sent from the *Café Europe.* I don't know whether the café exists any longer, but I read the absence of its address as symbolically as I previously had its existence. Because the content of the letter also noticeably lacked the European dimension that had been there before. 'You may have read something about it in the newspapers (it said), but you can't begin to imagine what our Nationalists are up to here. Is that why I left Hitler's Germany?' . . . So the *Café Europe* in Jerusalem really did have nowhere to stay any more. But this belongs to the Jewish chapter of my LTI.

Chapter 25
The Star

Today I ask myself again the same question I have asked myself and all kinds of people hundreds of times; which was the worst day for the Jews during those twelve years of hell?

I always, without exception, received the same answer from myself and others: 19 September 1941. From that day on it was compulsory to wear the Jewish star, the six-pointed Star of David, the yellow piece of cloth which today still stands for plague and quarantine, and which in the Middle Ages was the colour used to identify the Jews, the colour of envy and gall which has entered the bloodstream; the yellow piece of cloth with 'Jew' printed on it in black, the word framed by the lines of the two telescoped triangles, a word consisting of thick block capitals, which are separated and given broad, exaggerated horizontal lines to effect the appearance of the Hebrew script.

The description is too long? But no, on the contrary! I simply lack the ability to pen precise, vivid descriptions. Many was the time, when it came to sewing a new star onto a new piece of clothing (or rather an old one from the Jewish clothing store), a jacket or a work coat, many was the time that I would examine the cloth in minute detail, the individual specks of the yellow fabric, the irregularities of the black imprint – and all of these individual segments would not have been sufficient, had I wanted to pin an agonizing experience with the star on each and every one of them.

A man who looks upright and good-humoured comes towards me leading a young boy carefully by the hand. He stops one step away from me: 'Look at him, my little Horst! – He is to blame for everything!'. . .

A well-groomed man with a white beard crosses the road, greets me solemnly and holds out his hand: 'You don't know me, but I must tell you that I utterly condemn these measures.' . . . I want to get onto the tram: I am only allowed to use the front platform and then, only if I am travelling to the factory, and only if the factory is more than 6 kilometres from my flat, and only if the front platform is securely separated from the inside of the tram; I want to get on, it's late, and if I don't arrive punctually at work the boss can report me to the Gestapo. Someone drags me back from behind: 'Go on foot, it's much healthier for you!' An SS officer, smirking, not brutal, just having a bit of fun as if he were teasing a dog . . . My wife says: 'It's a nice day and for once I haven't got any shopping to do today, I don't have to join any queues – I'll come some of the way with you!' – 'Out of the question! Am I to stand in the street and watch you being insulted because of me? What's more: who knows whether someone you don't even know will get suspicious, and then when you are getting rid of my manuscripts you'll accidentally bump into them!' . . . A removal man who is friendly towards me following two moves – good people with more than a whiff of the KPD –[1] is suddenly standing in front of me in the Freiberger Straße, takes my hand in both of his paws and whispers in a tone which must be audible on the other side of the road: 'Well, Herr Professor, don't let it get you down! These wretched brothers of ours will soon have reached rock bottom!' This is meant to comfort me, and it certainly warms the heart; but if the wrong person hears it over there, my consoler will end up in prison and it will cost me my life, via Auschwitz . . . A passing car brakes on an empty road and a stranger pokes his head out: 'You still alive, you wretched pig? You should be run over, across your belly! . . .'

No, the individual segments would not be sufficient to note down all the bitterness caused by the Jewish star.

On the Georgplatz there used to be a statuette of Gutzkow on the grass, all that is left of it now is the plinth in the furrowed earth; I had a particularly soft spot for this bust. Who nowadays has heard of the *Ritter vom Geist* (Knights of the Mind)? I had the pleasure of reading all nine volumes for my PhD dissertation, and many years previously my mother had told me that as a girl she had lapped it up as the most modern novel around, despite the fact that it was really proscribed

---

[1] Abbreviation of *Kommunistische Partei Deutschlands,* the German Communist Party.

reading. But it is not the *Knights of the Mind* which I am reminded of when I pass the bust of Gutzkow. Rather, the *Uriel Acosta*, which I saw in the Kroll as a 16-year-old. By that time it had been dropped almost entirely from the repertoire, and it was the duty of every critic to say that it was a bad play and point only to its weaknesses. I, on the other hand, was shattered by it, and one sentence in particular has stayed with me throughout my life. On a number of occasions when I encountered anti-Semitic reactions I felt I could relate to it particularly strongly, but it really only got to the heart of my very own existence for the first time on that 19 September. It reads: 'I would truly like to submerge myself in the multitude and go with the great flow of life!' It is true, I was already cut off from the multitude in 1933, and indeed so was the whole of Germany from that point; but all the same: as soon as I had left the flat behind me, and the street in which everyone knew me, I could submerge myself in the great flow, not without fear, of course, because at any moment anyone with malicious intent could recognize and insult me, but it was nevertheless a submersion; now, however, I was recognizable to everyone all the time, and being recognizable isolated and outlawed me; the reason given for the measure was that the Jews had to be segregated, given that their cruelty had been proved beyond doubt in Russia.

Now, for the first time, the ghettoization was complete: prior to this point, the word 'Ghetto' only cropped up on postmarks bearing such addresses as 'Litzmannstadt Ghetto' – it was reserved exclusively for conquered lands abroad. In Germany there were isolated Jews' Houses into which the Jews were crowded together, and which from time to time were provided with a sign on the outside bearing the name '*Judenhaus* {Jews' House}'. But these houses were situated in Aryan districts, and were themselves not occupied exclusively by Jews; it was for this reason that one sometimes saw the declaration on other houses 'This House is Free of Jews {*judenrein*}'. This sentence clung to a number of walls in thick black letters until the walls themselves were destroyed in the bombing raids, whilst the signs proclaiming 'Fully Aryan Shop {*rein arisches Geschäft*}', the hostile 'Jewish Shop!' daubings on display windows, together with the verb '*arisieren* {to aryanize}' and the pleading words on the shop door 'Entirely Aryanized Business!' very soon disappeared, because there were no more Jewish shops, and nothing left that could be aryanized.

Now that the Jewish star had been introduced, it made no difference whether the Jews' Houses were scattered or gathered together into their own district, because every star-bearing Jew carried his own Ghetto with him like a snail with its shell. And it was irrelevant whether or not Aryans lived in his house together with the Jews, because the star had to be stuck above his name on the door. If his wife was Aryan she had to put her name away from the star and add the word 'Aryan'.

And soon other notices began to appear here and there on the doors leading off the corridors, Medusa-like notices: 'The Jew Weil lived here.' At which point the postwoman knew she didn't have to worry about his address; the letter was returned to sender with the euphemistic remark 'addressee gone away'. The result being that 'gone away {abgewandert}', with its dreadful special meaning, definitely belongs in the lexicon of the LTI, in the Jewish section.

This section is full of official expressions and terms which were familiar to those at whom they were directed, and who used them constantly in conversation. It started off with 'non-Aryan' and 'to aryanize', then there were the 'Nuremberg Laws for the Preservation of the Purity of German Blood', followed by the 'full Jews' and 'half-Jews' and 'mixed marriages of the first degree' and other degrees, and 'Jewish descendants {Judenstämmlinge}'. And, most importantly, there were the 'privileged {Privilegierte}'.

This is the only invention by the Nazis where I am not certain whether the authors were fully aware of the diabolic nature of their contrivance. The privileged only existed amongst groups of Jewish factory workers: the preferential treatment they received consisted of not having to wear the star or live in the Jews' House. Someone was privileged if they lived in a mixed marriage and had children from this marriage who were 'brought up as Germans', which means they were not registered as members of the Jewish community. Perhaps this section, which in action repeatedly led to inequalities and grotesque hairsplitting, was really only created in order to protect sections of the population deemed useful to the Nazis; but in practice nothing was more divisive and demoralizing for the Jewish population than this regulation. And how much envy and hatred it provoked! There are few sentences that I have heard uttered more frequently and with more bitterness than this one: 'He is privileged.' It means: 'He pays lower taxes than we do, he doesn't have to live in the Jews' House, he doesn't wear the star, he can almost drop out of sight . . .' And how much arrogance, how much pathetic gloating – pathetic because ultimately they were in the same hell as we were, albeit in a better district of hell, and in the end the gas ovens devoured the privileged as well – how much emphatic distance was couched in the three words 'I am privileged'. Now, when I hear of accusations levelled by one Jew at another, of acts of revenge with serious consequences, my first thought always turns to the universal conflict between those who bore the star and the privileged. Of course in the cramped living conditions of the Jews' House – shared kitchen, shared bathroom, shared hall for different groups – and the close-knit groups of Jewish workers in the factories, there were innumerable other sources of friction; but it was the distinction between privileged and non-privileged which ignited the most poisonous resentments, because what was at stake was the most loathed thing of all, the star.

Again and again, and with only minor variations, I find sentences in my diary such as the following: 'All the worst characteristics of people come to light here, it's enough to make you an anti-Semite!' From the second Jews' House onwards, however – I got to know three – outbursts of this kind are always accompanied by the rider: 'It's a good thing that I have now read Dwinger's *Die Armee hinter Stacheldraht* (The Army behind Barbed Wire). The people herded together in the Siberian compound of the First World War are not Jews at all, they are racially pure Aryans, German military men, German officers, yet what happens in this compound is exactly the same as what happens in our Jews' House. It has nothing to with race or religion, it is the herding and the enslavement . . .' 'Privileged' is the second worst word in the Jewish section of my lexicon. The worst remains the star itself. Sometimes it is viewed with gallows humour: I am wearing the *Pour le Sémite* is a widespread joke; sometimes people claim not only to others, but also to themselves, that they are proud of it; right at the very end people pinned their hopes on it: it will be our alibi! But for most of the time its shrill yellow illuminates the most agonizing of thoughts.

And the 'covered star' phosphoresces more poisonously than any other. According to Gestapo regulations the star has to be worn uncovered, above the heart, on the jacket, on the coat, on the work coat, it must be worn at any place where there is the possibility of an encounter with Aryans. If you open up your coat on a humid day in March so that the coat flap is folded back over your chest, if you carry a briefcase under your left arm, if as a woman you wear a muff, then your star is covered, perhaps unintentionally, and only for a few seconds, or perhaps even intentionally so that just for once you can walk the streets without stigma. A Gestapo officer will always assume that you intended to cover the star, and the punishment is the concentration camp. And if a Gestapo officer wants to demonstrate his zeal, and you cross his path, then the arm carrying the briefcase or wearing the muff may as well be hanging right down to your knees, and it doesn't matter how correctly the coat is buttoned up: the Jew Lesser or the Jewess Winterstein has 'covered up the star', and, within three months at the most, the community will receive a formal death certificate from Ravensbrück or Auschwitz. It will state the cause of death precisely, even with variations and an individual touch; it may say circumspectly 'died of an inadequate cardiac muscle' or 'shot attempting to escape'. But the real cause of death is the covered star.

Chapter 26
The Jewish War

My neighbour on the front platform looks at me piercingly and says quietly but commandingly into my ear: 'You are getting out at the main station and coming with me.' It is the first time this has happened to me, but, from the stories of other people who wear the star, I know what it's all about. It all passes off without serious consequences, they are in a jolly mood and see me as harmless. But since I can't know this in advance, and since even lenient and jovial treatment by the Gestapo is not something to be relished, the incident is extremely exhausting. 'I want to get rid of this one's fleas', my dog-catcher says to the porter, 'let him stand here with his face to the wall until I call him.' So I stand on the stairs for about a quarter of an hour with my face to the wall, and passers-by hurl abuse and advice at me such as 'Hang yourself you Jewish dog, what are you waiting for?'. . . 'Not been flogged enough yet?' . . . At long last the order comes: 'Up here, but make it sharpish . . . quick march!' I open the door and remain standing in front of the nearby desk. He addresses me in a friendly way: 'You've never been up here before have you? Really not? That's your good fortune – you've a lot to learn . . . Two steps from the table, stand to attention and announce yourself properly: "Jew Paul Israel Dirty Pig or whatever, here!" So, back out again, left, right! left, right! and heaven help you if you don't announce yourself *zackig* {smart} enough! . . . Well, it wasn't very *zackig*, but good enough for a first attempt. So, out with the fleas. Hand over your identity card and papers, empty your pockets, you've always got something stolen or from the black market on you . . . What, you're a professor? You wretch, how dare you think you can teach us anything!

You deserve to be sent to Theresienstadt for such impertinence alone . . . No! You're nowhere near 65 yet, you'll end up in Poland. Not even 65 – and yet so green about the gills, so doddery and always gasping for air! My God, you must have lived it up in your time, you look 75!' The inspector is in a good mood.

'You're in luck that we haven't found anything prohibited on you. But God help you if things look different in your pocket next time; you'll be on your way if there's even the tiniest cigarette, even if you've got three Aryan wives . . . Fall out, on the double!'

I already have my hand on the door handle when he calls me back: 'At home you're all praying for the Jewish victory, aren't you. Don't gawp at me like that, and don't answer either, because I know you do. It's your war – what? You're shaking your head? Who are we at war with then? Open your mouth when you're asked a question, you're supposed to be a professor aren't you?' – 'With England, France and Russia, with . . .' – 'Oh shut up, that's a load of rubbish. We're at war with the Jews, it's the Jewish war. And if you dare shake your head once more I'll hit you so hard you'll have to go straight to the dentist. It's the Jewish war, the Führer said so, and the Führer is always right . . . get out!'

The Jewish war! The Führer didn't come up with this idea, he had certainly never heard of Flavius Josephus, he simply noticed one day in the newspaper or in a shop window that the Jew Feuchtwanger had written a novel called *Der jüdische Krieg* (The Jewish War).[1] It is probably like this with all the characteristic words and expressions of the LTI: England is no longer an island, *Vermassung* {de-individualization}, *Versteppung* {to turn into steppes}, *Einmaligkeit* {uniqueness}, *Untermenschentum* {subhumanity}, etc. – they have all been appropriated from somewhere, yet they are also all new, and will remain forever part of the LTI, because they all entered the common language from secluded corners of intimate, technical or group-specific usage and were contaminated through and through with Nazi ideology.

The Jewish war! I shook my head when I heard it, and listed each individual country at war with Germany. And yet, from the point of view of National Socialism, the term is entirely appropriate, indeed in a much broader sense than was intended at the time; because the Jewish war had begun with the 'takeover of power' on 30 January

---

[1]Published in England in 1932 under the title *Josephus*.

1933, and on 1 September 1939 had only undergone an escalation of hostilities {*Kriegserweiterung*}, to use what later temporarily became a fashionable LTI term. I have long resisted the assumption that we – and it was precisely because I had to say 'we' that I considered it a narrow and conceited self-deception – that we should really be at the centre of Nazism in this way. But it really was the case, and the way in which this situation came about is clear for all to see.

One only has to consult carefully the relevant pages in the chapter 'Apprenticeship and Suffering: the Vienna Years' in *Mein Kampf*, in which Hitler describes his 'conversion to anti-Semitism'. Although much of it is clearly vague, embellished and fabricated, there is one thing which is undoubtedly true: this completely uneducated and insecure man first comes across politics at the hands of the Austrian anti-Semites Lueger and Schönerer, whom he looks up to from the perspective of the gutter. In the most primitive way, he categorizes all Jews – he will call them 'the Jewish people' until the day he dies – as Galician pedlars; in the most primitive way he vilifies the appearance of the greasy old man wearing a kaftan; in the most primitive way he heaps the sum of all imaginable depravities onto this person he has elevated to the status of an allegorical figure, the 'Jewish people' indeed, and on whom he vents his anger in the midst of extreme bitterness at his lack of success during the period in Vienna. In every malignant 'tumour of cultural life' he inevitably finds 'a little Jew {*Jüdlein*} . . . like a maggot in a rotting corpse'. And all Jewish activities in every field are, as far as he is concerned, a pestilence, 'worse than the Black Death of old' . . .

'*Jüdlein*' and 'Black Death', an expression of scornful derision and an expression of terror, of panic-stricken fear: these are the two distinct styles that will always crop up with Hitler whenever he refers to the Jews, which means in every one of his speeches and addresses. He never grew out of his initial childish and infantile attitude to the Jews. Herein lies a considerable part of his strength, because it unites him with the dullest section of the population, which, in the age of the machine, is plainly not made up of the industrial proletariat, nor does it consist exclusively of the peasantry, but rather derives from the concentrated masses of the petty bourgeoisie. For them anyone who dresses differently or speaks differently is not simply a different person, but a different animal from a different sty with whom there can be no accommodation, and who must be hated and hounded out. Race, as a scientific and pseudo-scientific concept, only appeared in the middle of the eighteenth century. But as a feeling of instinctive antagonism towards anything foreign, a tribal animosity towards it, the sense of race belongs to the earliest stage of human development; it is overcome at the point where the individual horde of people learns not to regard the neighbouring horde as an entirely different pack of animals.

But whilst Hitler's anti-Semitism is a correspondingly basic feeling, rooted in the man's intellectual primitiveness, the Führer also possesses, seemingly from the outset, a large measure of that calculating guile which doesn't seem to accord with an unsound mind, but so often seems to go hand in hand with it. He knows perfectly well that he can only expect loyalty from those who inhabit a similarly primitive world; and the simplest and most effective means of keeping them there is to nurture, legitimize and as it were glorify the instinctive hatred of the Jews. In the process he plays on what is the weakest spot in the cultural thinking of the nation. When did the Jews at last emerge from their segregation, from their special sty, and when were they last integrated into the nation as a whole? The emancipation goes back to the beginning of the nineteenth century, but is only implemented fully in Germany during the 1860s, and in Galician Austria a tightly knit group of Jews doesn't want to relinquish its unique way of life, and thereby repeatedly provides those who speak of an un-European people, an Asiatic race of Jews, with the concrete illustrative material and evidence they are looking for. And just at the point when Hitler is formulating his first political opinions, the Jews themselves set him on the path best suited to him; it is the time of the rise of Zionism; it does not make much of a mark at the time in Germany, but in Vienna, during Hitler's years of apprenticeship and suffering, it is already noticeable. Here it amounts to – and I quote *Mein Kampf* again – a 'major movement of no mean proportions'. If you base anti-Semitism on the notion of race, you don't only give it a scientific or pseudo-scientific foundation, but also a basis in traditional folk history {*eine ursprünglich volkstümliche Basis*} which makes it indestructible: because a man can change his coat, his customs, his education and his belief, but not his blood.

But what is to be gained from nurturing an indestructible hatred of the Jews retrogressively embedded in the dullness of instinct? An enormous amount. Such an enormous amount in fact, that I don't consider anti-Semitism to be a specific application of their universal racial dogma, but rather am convinced the universal racial doctrine was only taken on and formulated in order to justify anti-Semitism in the long term and scientifically. The Jew is the most important person in Hitler's state: he is the best-known Turk's head of folk history {*der volkstümlichste Türkenkopf*} and the popular scapegoat, the most plausible adversary, the most obvious common denominator, the most likely brackets around the most diverse of factors. Had the Führer really achieved his aim of exterminating all the Jews, he would have had to invent new ones, because without the Jewish devil – 'anyone who doesn't know the Jew, doesn't know the devil' it said in the *Stürmer* display cases – without the swarthy Jew there would never have been the radiant figure of the Nordic Teuton. Incidentally, the Führer would not have had any great difficulty inventing new Jews, given that the English were repeatedly referred to by Nazi authors as descendants of the lost biblical lineage of the Jews.

Hitler's fanatical guile is demonstrated by his perfidious and shamelessly blatant instructions to the propagandists of the Party. The golden rule is always: don't let your listeners engage in critical thought, deal with everything simplistically! When referring to various enemies, some people could jump to the conclusion that you, the individual, are perhaps in the wrong – the answer is to reduce everything to a common denominator, bracket everything together, show them the common ground! The Jew can provide all of this graphically, and in a way that the people can relate to. In so doing it is important to observe the use of the personifying and allegorical singular. Once again not an invention of the Third Reich. Traditional folk songs, historical ballads, and also the down-to-earth language of the soldier in the First World War are all partial to expressions such as 'the Russian', 'the Briton', 'the Frenchman'. But in referring to the Jew, the LTI extends the use of the allegorizing singular article well beyond the former domain of the landsknecht.

Der Jude – the word is even more prominent in everyday Nazi usage than *'fanatisch'*, but even more common than the word *'Jude'* is the adjective *'jüdisch* {Jewish}', because it is the adjective above all which has the bracketing effect of binding together all adversaries into a single enemy: the Jewish-Marxist *Weltanschauung*, the Jewish-Bolshevist philistinism, the Jewish-Capitalist system of exploitation, the keen Jewish-English, Jewish-American interest in seeing Germany destroyed: thus from 1933 every single hostility, regardless of its origin, can be traced back to one and the same enemy, Hitler's hidden maggot, the Jew, who in moments of high drama is referred to as 'Judah' or, with even greater pathos, *'Alljuda* {Universal Judah}'. And whatever actions are taken, they are, from the very outset, defensive measures in an unavoidable war, the Jewish war – from 1 September 1939 *'aufgezwungen* {imposed}' is the customary adjective to accompany the word 'war', but ultimately 1 September didn't bring about anything new, only a continuation of the murderous Jewish attacks on Hitler's Germany, and we, the peace-loving Nazis, are only doing what we have done up to now – defending ourselves: since this morning 'we are returning enemy fire' as our first war bulletin puts it.

However, this Jewish desire to kill is not a product of deep-seated reflection or particular interests, not even of a hunger for power, but of the Jewish race's innate and 'profound hatred {*Haß*}' of all that is Nordic and Teutonic. This profound *Haß* felt by the Jews is a cliché which circulated throughout the twelve years. There is no protection against innate hatred other than the elimination of the hater: thus it is a logical step to proceed from the stabilization of racially motivated anti-Semitism to the necessity of exterminating the Jews. Hitler only once spoke of 'wiping out {*Ausradieren*}' the English cities, it was a unique utterance which, as in all his uses of the superlative, can be explained in terms of his unrestrained megalomania. *'Ausrotten* {to exterminate}', on the other hand, is a common verb, it belongs to the general vocabulary of the LTI and finds its home in the Jewish section, it denotes a goal to be aimed at zealously.

Racially motivated anti-Semitism, for Hitler initially a feeling resulting from his own primitiveness, is the central concern of Nazism, well thought-out and carefully developed into a coherent system, right down to the last detail. In Goebbels's *Kampf um Berlin* (Battle for Berlin) there is the following passage: 'You could describe the Jew as a repressed inferiority complex made flesh. This is why the best possible way to sting him is to refer to him by his real name. Call him a wretch, rogue, liar, criminal, murderer or killer. Beneath the surface he will barely be affected. But look him straight into the eye long and hard and then say: you're a Jew aren't you! And you will be amazed to discover that he immediately looks insecure, embarrassed and guilty . . .' A lie (this it has in common with a joke) is all the more effective, the more truth it contains. Goebbels's observation is accurate, but for the mendacious word 'guilty'. Someone spoken to in this way would not become aware of any guilt, but his previous security would turn into total helplessness, because the ascertainment of his Jewishness would cut the ground from under his feet and deny him any chance of mutual understanding, or of fighting a battle as an equal.

Anything and everything in the section of the LTI relating to the Jews is geared to segregating them as completely and irreconcilably as possible from everything German. One moment they are characterized as the Jewish people, as the Jewish race, the next as global Jews or international Jewry; in both cases what counts is their non-Germanness. They are no longer allowed to practise as doctors and lawyers; and since they themselves need a few doctors and lawyers, who have, of course, to come from their own ranks given that the Germans are not supposed to have any more contact with them, these medics and jurists who are only allowed to deal with Jews are given special names, they are called *Krankenbehandler* {medical workers} and *Rechtskonsulenten* {legal consultants}. In both cases the intention is not only to segregate, but also to belittle. In the case of the consultant this is more apparent because a distinction had been drawn in the past between *Winkelkonsulenten* {shady legal advisers} and academic or state-licensed lawyers; *Krankenbehandler* only sounds disparaging because it withholds the official and customary job title.

In some cases it isn't easy to determine why a particular expression sounds disdainful. Why is the Nazi term '*Judengottesdienst* {the Jews' religious service}' belittling? It implied nothing more than the neutral '*jüdischer Gottesdienst* {Jewish religious service}'. I suspect that the reason is that it is somehow reminiscent of exotic travel journals, of some African native cult or other. And here I am probably on the right track: the Jews' religious service is dedicated to the God of the Jews, and the God of the Jews is a tribal god and tribal idol and not, at least not yet, the one, universal deity to whom the Jewish religious service is dedicated. Sexual relations between Jews and Aryans are referred to as *Rassenschande* {racial defilement, literally: racial shame}, the Nuremberg synagogue, which he has destroyed during a 'ceremony', is referred to by Streicher, the leader of the Franconians, as the *Schande von Nürnberg* {Nuremberg's shame}, and he calls synagogues in general robbers' caves – no analysis is necessary to explain why this sounds insulting rather than just frosty. Explicit abuse directed at the

Jews is also exceedingly common; it is rare to come across the word 'Jew' from either Hitler or Goebbels without its being accompanied by such adjectives as *gerissen* {cunning}, *listig* {wily}, *betrügerisch* {deceitful}, *feige* {cowardly}, and there is also no lack of traditional terms of abuse which relate to physical attributes including *plattfüßig* {flat-footed}, *krummnasig* {hook-nosed}, *wasserscheu* {water-shy}. For the more educated palate, the terms *parasitär* {parasitic} and *nomadisch* {nomadic} are to hand. If you want to accuse an Aryan of the worst thing imaginable you call him a slave of the Jews, if an Aryan woman doesn't want to be separated from her Jewish husband she is a Jew's whore, if you want to hit out at the dreaded intelligentsia you can refer to hooknosed intellectualism.

Is it possible to discern any change, development or differentiation in the use of this invective during the twelve years? Yes and no. The poverty of the LTI is prodigious, it uses exactly the same obscenities in January 1945 that it had already used in January 1933. And yet, despite the consistency of the ingredients, a change is discernible, indeed terribly so, if you consider a speech or a newspaper article in its entirety.

I return for a moment to the *Jüdlein* {little Jew} and the Black Death in Hitler's *Mein Kampf,* the contemptuous tone and the fearful tone. One of the most commonly repeated and paraphrased remarks of the Führer is his threat to wipe the smile off the faces of the Jews, which later turned into the equally common declaration that it really had been wiped off their faces. This is true, and is confirmed by the bitter Jewish joke that Hitler was only as good as his word when it came to the Jews. But the smile was also gradually wiped off the face of the Führer and the entire LTI, or rather it becomes increasingly twisted and forced, before turning into a mask behind which mortal agony and, finally, desperation attempt in vain to hide. During the final years of the war one never comes across the comic diminutive *Jüdlein* but instead one senses the dread of the Black Death behind all the expressions of contempt and affected arrogance, and through all the boasting and bragging.

The most powerful expression of this situation may well be an essay published by Goebbels on 21 January 1945 in the *Reich* entitled 'The Authors of all the Misfortune in this World'. It claims that the Russians, who have already reached the outskirts of Breslau, and the Allies on the western border, are nothing but 'mercenaries in the global conspiracy of a parasitic race'. The Jews are driving millions of people to their death out of repulsion at our culture 'which they sense is far superior to their own nomadic conception of the world', out of repulsion at our economy and our social institutions because they don't any longer allow them 'freedom of movement for their parasitic roaming' . . . 'wherever you hunt you'll hunt out the Jews!' But the smile has already been 'thoroughly' wiped off their faces on a number of occasions! And so even now 'Jewish dominion will be overthrown'. All the same: Jewish dominion and the Jews – no *Jüdlein* any more.

One might ask whether this endless assertion of Jewish malice and inferiority, and the claim that the Jews were the sole enemy, did not in the end dull the mind and provoke contradiction. The question would immediately broaden out into the more all-embracing one regarding the value and endurance of Goebbels's propaganda as a whole, leading finally to the question of the correctness of National Socialism's fundamental thinking in the field of mass psychology. With great insistence and a high degree of precision right down to the last detail, Hitler's *Mein Kampf* preaches not only that the masses are stupid, but also that they need to be kept that way and intimidated into not thinking. One of the main means of doing this is to hammer home incessantly the same simplistic lessons, ones which cannot be contradicted from any angle. And think how many threads there are connecting the soul of the (invariably isolated) intellectual to the masses that surround him!

I am reminded of the little pharmacist with the Lithuanian-East Prussian name from the last three months of the war. She had passed her difficult first degree, had received a good all-round education, was a passionate opponent of the war and certainly not a supporter of the Nazis – she knew perfectly well that it was nearly all over for them, and she longed for the end. When she was on night duty we used to have long conversations together, she sensed our views and gradually dared to voice her own. We were on our flight from the Gestapo, living under a false name, our friend in Falkenstein had provided us with shelter and rest, we slept in the back room of his pharmacy underneath a picture of Hitler . . .

'I never liked his arrogant attitude towards other nations,' said little Stulgies, 'my grandmother is Lithuanian – why should she, why should I be any less worth than some pure German woman?' – 'Yes, their entire doctrine is based on purity of blood, on the Teutonic privilege, on anti-Semitism . . .' – She interrupted me: 'In the case of the Jews he may well be right, that's a somewhat different case.' – 'Do you personally know . . .' – 'No, I've always avoided them, they give me the creeps. You hear and read such a lot about them.'

I tried to think of an answer which would combine caution and enlightenment. The young girl was at most 13 when all the Hitler business broke out – how could she know better, where could one pick up the thread? . . .

At that point a full-scale alert was sounded as usual. It was better not to go down into the cellar as it contained carboys of explosive liquid. We huddled up against the solid pillars on the stairs. We weren't really in any great danger, the target for the pilots was usually the much more important town of Plauen. Today, however, there was a nasty and horribly long minute. Heavy squadrons flew over us at short intervals, so tightly packed and so low that everything around us quaked and trembled at the deafening noise. Bombs could explode at any moment. Images of the night in Dresden passed before my eyes, and the same sentence kept going through my mind: the thrashing of the wings of death, it's not a hollow phrase, the wings of death really do thrash. Squeezed up against the pillar and curled up into a ball, the young girl breathed loudly and heavily, it was a barely suppressed groaning.

Finally they were gone, we could straighten up and return from the dark and cold stairs into the light and warmth of the pharmacy, like coming back to life. 'Let's go to bed now,' I said, 'experience has shown that there won't be another alert before tomorrow morning.' Suddenly, and with a burst of energy as if she were ending a lengthy dispute, the otherwise gentle little woman replied, 'And it is the Jewish war after all.'

Chapter 27
The Jewish Spectacles

My wife used to bring military despatches back from the city. I myself never stood around in front of notices or loudspeakers, and in the factory we relied on the previous day's report, because to ask an Aryan about the latest telegrams would have amounted to a political discussion, and that could have led straight to the concentration camp.

'Is Stalingrad finally over?' – 'Yes sir! A two-bedroom flat with a bathroom was conquered in a heroic struggle and defended despite seven repeated counter-attacks.' – 'Why are you poking fun?' – 'Because they'll never make it, they'll bleed to death in the process.' – 'You see everything through Jewish spectacles.' – 'Now you're using that special Jewish language yourself.'

I was ashamed of myself. As a philologist I was always at pains to observe the linguistic peculiarities of every situation, and every circle of people, and to speak entirely neutrally without any colouring – and now some of my surroundings had rubbed off on me. (The result is that you damage your sense of hearing and your ability to register differences.) But I did have an excuse. It is quite impossible for a group to be forced together into a particular situation without developing its own linguistic peculiarities – especially when the force applied is genuine and malevolent – and the individual can't escape the process. We came from a wide range of different regions, classes and professions, none of us was impressionably young, some were already grand-parents. Just as thirty years previously I had toyed with the idea of a

Hotel Labruyères – I had a post as language assistant at the University of Naples, and we were long-term guests at a hotel on the coast through which tourists passed all the time – so I now, and with greater justification, thought of a series of Jewish 'characters {*Charaktere*}'. There were two doctors and a senior official from a district court and three lawyers and a painter and a grammar schoolteacher and a dozen businessmen and a dozen manufacturers and a number of technicians and engineers and – a great rarity amongst the Jews! – an entirely unskilled worker, almost illiterate; there were supporters of assimilation and Zionists, there were people whose forebears had lived in Germany for centuries, and who with the best will in the world could never have shed their German identity, and then there were others who had only very recently arrived from Poland and whose mother tongue, which they hadn't even begun to relinquish, formed the basis of their jargon, rather than the German language. But now we were simply the group of Dresden people who had to wear the star, the group of factory workers and street-cleaners and the occupants of the Jews' Houses and the prisoners of the Gestapo; and, as in prison or in the army, there was an immediate sense of mutuality which obliterated earlier common ground and individualities, and propagated new linguistic habits with the force of a physical inevitability.

On the evening of the day which had brought the first surreptitious news of the fall of Mussolini, Waldmann knocked on Stühler's door. (We shared the kitchen, hall and bathroom with the Stühlers and Cohns – there were barely any secrets.) Waldmann had 'previously {*vorher*}' been a wealthy fur trader, now he worked as the doorman of the Jews' House and also had to help with the disposal of corpses from the Jews' Houses and the prison. 'Might I be allowed to come in?' he called. 'Since when have you been so polite?' came the answer from within. And Waldmann replied immediately, 'The end is at hand, and I must get used to the proper tone for addressing my customers again, so I am starting with you as of now.' He was completely serious and definitely not trying to be funny; the hope in his heart yearned to return to the language of his former social standing. 'You've put your Jewish spectacles on again,' said Stühler at the door (he was a ponderous man who had experienced many disappointments), 'you just wait and see, he got over Röhm and Stalingrad – he won't stumble over Mussolini either.'

Du and *Sie* were strangely muddled up in our circles.[1] Some, especially those who had taken part in the First World War, used *Du* as they had previously done in the army; the others stuck firmly to *Sie,* as if they could thereby maintain their old position. The affective dual nature of *Du* became particularly clear to me during these years; if an Aryan worker spontaneously addressed me with the *Du* form – he needn't have said any especially reassuring words – I always found it very comforting, as a recognition of the fact that we were fellow human beings; if it was used by the Gestapo, who addressed us with the *Du* form on principle, it always felt to me like a slap in the face. Moreover, the worker's *Du* wasn't only a pleasure to me because it embodied a protest against the impediment of the star; for when it was used in the factory itself – where it was never really possible to enforce the complete isolation of the Jewish workforce, despite all the Gestapo regulations to that end – I always interpreted it as a sign of the diminished, or at least moderated, distrust vis-à-vis the bourgeois and academic.

The variations in speech dependent on class are by no means merely of aesthetic significance. Rather, I am convinced that the unfortunate mistrust between intellectuals and proletarians is largely a result of their different linguistic habits. There were so many occasions during these years when I said to myself: how on earth shall I put it? Workers like to use fruity expressions relating to digestion in every sentence. If I did the same he would notice it didn't come naturally and regard me as a hypocrite trying to ingratiate myself; however, if I talk naturally, or as I was taught in the nursery and at school, he will think me arrogant or a jumped-up so-and-so. The changes in our way of speaking as a group were by no means just a matter of partially conforming to the most uncouth aspects of the language of the workers. We took on expressions associated with the social standing and customs of the workers. If somebody was missing from their workplace you didn't ask if he was ill, but rather if he was 'on the sick-list', because you only had a right to be ill if you got a medical certificate from the health-insurance doctor. In days of yore the question as to one's earnings

---

[1] In the preceding exchange Stühler had addressed Waldmann with the informal *'du'* mode of address, whilst Waldmann had used the more formal *'Sie'*. In tone the difference is comparable to the distinction in English between being on first name terms and using a person's surname.

would be responded to as follows: I earn such and such an amount, or my annual salary comes to this or that. Now everyone said: I take home 30 Marks each week; and if someone was better off, it was said that he got a fatter wage packet. If we said that someone had a heavy load, then heavy was invariably meant in physical terms; the man was pulling heavy boxes or pushing heavy carts . . .

Alongside these expressions lifted from the everyday language of the workers there were others in circulation which were either a product of gallows humour or the obligatory game of hide-and-seek engendered by our situation. In the case of these expressions, it is not always easy to say whether they merely had a local meaning or were, to use a philological term, standard Germanic. In the early days in particular, when imprisonment and the camps were not necessarily synonymous with death, you were not imprisoned but 'gone away {*verreist*}'; you were not in a concentration camp {*Konzentrationslager*}, and not in the KZ, to use the customary abbreviation, but rather in the '*Konzertlager* {concert camp}'. The verb *melden* {to present oneself} acquired a horrible new meaning. 'He has to present himself' means he has been summoned to the Gestapo, and presenting oneself in this way was always associated with mistreatment, and increasingly with a one-way journey. Together with the accusation of covering up the star, a popular pretext for ordering people to present themselves was the charge of spreading horror stories {*Greuelnachrichten*}. A simple verb had developed for this activity, *greueln* {to spread horror}. If someone had listened to foreign news (and that happened every day) it reached us from Kötzschenbroda. In our language Kötzschenbroda really meant London, Moscow, Beromünster and independent broadcasters. If a piece of news seemed dubious, it came from the *Mundfunk* {mouth radio} of the JMA, which stood for *Jüdische Märchenagentur* {Jewish Fairy-tale Agency}. When you referred to the fat Gestapo officer responsible for Jewish matters {*Angelegenheiten*} – no, interests {*Belange*}, also one of the tainted words – in the Dresden region, he was invariably called the Pope of the Jews {*der Judenpapst*}.

Gradually, this adaptation to the language of the workers, and the use of expressions which sprung from the new context, is joined by a third characteristic. The number of Jews gets increasingly smaller, the young disappear in the direction of Poland and Lithuania, the old to Theresienstadt. Only a very small number of houses are needed to accommodate the remainder in Dresden. This also finds expression in

the language of the Jews; it is no longer necessary to give the full address
of the individual Jews, one simply gives the street numbers of the few
surviving houses, situated in different parts of the city; he lives in 92,
in 56. Then the dwindling remainder of the Jews is decimated – in fact
far more than decimated – once again: the majority are forced to leave
the Jews' Houses, they are herded into the barracks of the Hellerberg
Jewish camp, and from there the journey continues a few weeks later
to the extermination camps themselves. The only ones left behind are
those living in mixed marriages, the most Germanized Jews who, for the
most part, don't belong any more to the Jewish community, dissidents
or 'non-Aryan Christians', a name which was subsequently forbidden
and disappeared. It is obvious that they have little or no knowledge of
Jewish customs and rituals, and even less of the Hebrew language. And
here we have the third characteristic of their language, one that is hard
to define but all pervasive: with a certain sentimentality, tempered by a
good sense of humour, they turn to childhood memories and try together
to revive what has been forgotten. This has nothing to do with piety or
Zionism, it is simply a flight from the present, a form of relaxation.

We all stand around together during the breakfast break; someone
talks about how in 1889 he joined the Liebmannsohn grain factory in
Ratibor as an apprentice and about the strange German that his boss
spoke. The strange expressions – the faces of some of those listening
light up, memories are awakened; others have this or that explained to
them. 'When I was an apprentice in Krotoschin', said Wallerstein, but
before he could tell his story Grünbaum, the foreman, interrupts him:
'Krotoschin – do you know the story of the scrounger of Krotoschin?'
Grünbaum is the best when it comes to telling Jewish jokes and
anecdotes, he is tireless and invaluable, he shortens the day, he helps
us cope with the worst depressions. The story of the newcomer who
couldn't serve in the synagogue because he hadn't learned to write
German, and who then became a celebrated businessman in Berlin, will
be Grünbaum's swansong, because next morning he is missing, and a
few hours later we know that he has been 'collected {*geholt*}'.

From a philological point of view, *holen* {to collect} is closely related
to *melden,* but it has been in use for longer and more extensively. The
LTI meaning of the reflexive verb '*sich melden* {to report}' is only really
revealed secretly in the confrontations between the Gestapo and the
Jews; Jews, Christians and Aryans, on the other hand, are all collected

{*geholt*}, indeed *en masse,* by the military authorities in the summer of 1939. Because in its special LTI sense, *holen* means to dispose of something unobtrusively, be it in prison or in barracks, and, given that on 1 September we will be the innocent party who is attacked, the entire mobilization beforehand is a clandestine, night-time collection {*Holen*}. However, the connection between *holen* and *sich melden* within the LTI lies in the way in which two aweful processes with serious consequences are hidden behind bland, everyday names, and, on the other hand, in the fact that these events have become so numbingly routine that they are referred to as everyday, commonplace processes rather than shown up in all their grim severity.

So Grünbaum was collected, and three months later Auschwitz sent his urn, and it was buried in the Jewish cemetery. During the final stage of the war, when wholesale gassings became routine, the polite return of these urns obviously stopped, but for a long time it was to some extent our Sunday duty – and even almost our Sunday pleasure – to take part in these burials. Often two or three urns had arrived; whilst commemorating the deceased, there was the opportunity to meet companions in misfortune from the other Jews' Houses and other factory groups. By this time there hadn't been a minister for a long time, but the Jew with his star who had been appointed custodian of the cemetery read an obituary, strung together the conventional clichés taken from the sermons, and of course behaved as if the man had died an entirely natural death; then a Hebrew prayer for the dead was recited, in which everyone present took part in so far as they were able. The majority were not. And if someone in the know was asked what it meant he would reply: 'The meaning is roughly as follows . . .' – 'Can't you translate it word for word?' I interrupted. – 'No, I can only remember the sound of it, I learned it so long ago, I didn't really have any proper connections with all that . . .'

When Grünbaum's time came he had an unusually large cortège. As we followed the urn from the chapel to the place of burial, the man next to me whispered, 'What was the name of the post which the celebrated businessman in Krotoschin didn't get – it was shammes wasn't it? For poor Grünbaum's sake I shall never forget that story!' And he memorized it in time with our walking pace: 'Shammes in Krotoschin, shammes in Krotoschin.'

The racial doctrine of the Nazis also coined the term *Aufnorden* {to nordify}. Whether the nordification was successful I am not in a position

to judge. But they definitely brought about an *Aufjudung* {judaification} –
even in those who struggled against it. It was entirely impossible to take
off the Jewish spectacles, one saw every occurrence and every report
through them, and read every book through them. The only problem
was that the spectacles kept changing. At the outset, and then for a long
time, the lenses showed everything cloaked in a rose-tinted mantle of
hope. 'It's not half as bad as it looks !' Many a time I heard this comforting
expression when I took the reports in the military despatches of victories,
and the number of enemy soldiers captured, inconsolably seriously. But
then, when things really were going badly for the Nazis, when they could
no longer cover up their defeat, when the Allies approached the German
borders and then crossed them, when city after city was pounded by
enemy bombs – only Dresden seemed to be taboo – it was at that point
that the Jews swapped their lenses. The fall of Mussolini was the last
event they saw with the old glasses. But when the war continued, their
confidence was shattered and turned into its very opposite. They no
longer believed in the imminent end of the war, against all evidence to
the contrary they believed the Führer must have magic powers, more
magical than those of his increasingly doubtful followers.

We sat in the Jewish cellar of our Jews' House, which also contained
a special Aryan cellar; it was shortly before Dresden's day of catastrophe.
We sat through the full-scale alert bored and shivering rather than
frightened. From experience we knew that nothing ever happened to us,
the raid was undoubtedly directed again at the tormented city of Berlin.
We were less depressed than we had been for a long time; during the
afternoon my wife had been listening to London with loyal Aryan friends,
moreover, and indeed most importantly, she had got to know Thomas
Mann's last speech, a beautifully humane speech certain of victory. We
are normally not very receptive to sermons, they tend to put us in a bad
mood – but this one was truly uplifting.

I wanted some of my good mood to rub off on my fellow sufferers, I
moved from one group to the next: 'Have you heard today's bulletin? Do
you know Thomas Mann's latest speech?' Everywhere I was rebuffed.
Some of them were afraid to talk about forbidden matters: 'Keep it to
yourself, I don't want to end up in a concentration camp.' The others
were embittered: 'And even if the Russians are on the edge of Berlin,'
Steinitz said, 'the war will still go on for years, anything else is hysterical
optimism!'

For years we had divided people up into optimists and pessimists as if we were two separate races. In response to the question 'What type of person is he?' you always got the answer 'He is an optimist' or 'He is a pessimist', which from the mouth of a Jew was of course synonymous with 'Hitler will fall very soon' and 'Hitler will hold his ground'. Now there was nothing but pessimists. Frau Steinitz went one better than her husband: 'And even if they do take Berlin it won't make any difference. All that will happen is that the war will continue in Upper Bavaria. For three years at least. And it doesn't make any difference to us whether it's three or six years. We won't survive it anyway. It's time you finally broke your old Jewish spectacles!'

Three months later Hitler was a dead man and the war was over. But it is true, the Steinitzes, and many others who sat with us that evening in the Jewish cellar, didn't survive it. They lie buried under the ruins of the city.

Chapter 28

The Language of the Victor

Every day it was a slap in the face once again, worse than the *Du* and the Gestapo's swear-words, I never prevailed against it with protest or explanation, I never became inured to it, I never found a single one of my Labruyère types who managed to avoid this humiliation.

You really were well trained intellectually and a commendable and passionately interested Germanist, poor Elsa Glauber, a real assistant to your Professor and a helper and supporter of your students in the department; and when you got married and had children you remained a philologist, a purifier of language and a teacher – almost excessively so, rogues used to call you 'Mr Privy Councillor' behind your back!

And you helped me out for so long with your beautiful library of classics, kept in such an amusing way! Jews – in so far as they were allowed to use books at all – were only allowed to own Jewish books, and Mrs Privy Councillor was very fond of her collection of the German classics, all in the best editions. She had left the university a dozen years previously, and was the wife of a highly cultured businessman, to whom the Gestapo had allocated the agonizing office of chairman of the Jewish community, and who was thus the responsible, helpless middleman, situated between the henchmen and their victims, and tormented from both sides. And then Elsa's children began, under her leadership, to read the precious books. How had she managed to save her treasure from the perpetually snooping Gestapo? Very simply and morally! By conscientious honesty. If the editor of the volume was called Richard

M. Meyer, Elsa Glauber would lift the shroud surrounding the M. and replace the abbreviation with the first name Moses; or she highlighted the fact that the Germanist Pniower was a Jew, or she informed those who were on the look-out, that the real name of the famous Gundolf was the Jewish name Gundelfinger. There are so many non-Aryans amongst the Germanists that under the protection of these editors the works of Goethe, Schiller and many others became 'Jewish books'.

Elsa's library had also retained its order and spread, because the expansive villa of the chairman had been declared a Jews' House, with the result that although the family had to restrict themselves to a few rooms, they were still able to live in their own four walls. I was able to make good use of the Jewish classics, and with Elsa it was possible to talk shop both reassuringly and seriously.

Of course we talked a lot about our desperate situation. I couldn't say whether Elsa was a better Jew or a better German patriot. Both ways of thinking and feeling were heightened under the pressure of circumstance. A poignant tone easily entered into the most sober of everyday conversations. Elsa often talked about how she made certain that her children were growing up properly in the Jewish faith and that at the same time, despite the present humiliation, they lived and breathed their belief in Germany, or what she invariably referred to as 'eternal Germany'. 'They must learn to think the way I do, they must read Goethe like the Bible, they must become fanatical Germans!'

There it was, the slap in the face. 'What must they become, Frau Elsa?' – 'Fanatical Germans like me. Only fanatical Germanness can cleanse our Fatherland of this current un-Germanness {Undeutschheit}.' – 'But don't you know what you are saying? Can't you see that "fanatical" and "German" – I mean your "German" – are an explosive combination, that, that . . .', with a fair degree of bitterness and in a sketchy and unordered way, albeit all the more vehemently, I threw at her everything I have noted down here in the section entitled 'Fanatical'. And finally I said to her: 'Don't you realize that you are speaking the language of our mortal enemies and thus admitting defeat and thus putting yourself at their mercy and thus betraying that very Germanness of yours? And if you don't realize it, you, with your education, you who stand up for eternal, immaculate Germanness – then who on earth is going to sense it and avoid it? It's entirely natural that in our troubled isolation we should have developed a special language, that we ourselves should use official terms from the Nazi dictionary originally coined to refer to us, that here and there we should come across an extension of jargon with Hebrew terms. But this subjugation to the language of the victor, of this victor!' . . .

Elsa was quite taken aback by my outburst, she completely lost the hauteur of the Privy Councillor, she agreed and promised that she would improve herself. And the next time she proclaimed her 'fanatical love' – in this case for *Iphigenie* – she corrected herself at once in a soothing way; 'Oh dear, I'm not supposed to say that; I've just got so used to it since the radical changes {*Umbruch*}.'

'Since the *Umbruch*?' – 'Do you frown on that as well? But you are definitely wrong about that one. It's a beautiful, poetic word, it has the fragrance of freshly ploughed fields,[1] it can't have been invented by those Hitler people, it must come from somewhere in the George circle.' – 'Certainly, but the Nazis have taken it over because it goes so well with "blood and soil", with the "glorification of the sod {*Verherrlichung der Scholle*}" and "being rooted to the soil {*Bodenständigkeit*}", they have infected it so much by touching it with their filthy hands that for the next fifty years no decent person . . .'

She interrupted me and went on the counter-attack: I was a purist, a school teacher and intransigent, a – 'don't be too angry' – a fanatic.

Poor Elsa Glauber – we never found anything out about what happened to her and her entire family; 'they were taken away from Theresienstadt', that is the last we heard of her. And because I want to pay tribute to her here without disguising her identity – for despite her tendency to be an aesthete, and despite her Privy Councillor pretensions, she was a person who deserved respect and to whose courageous intellect I owe a good deal – this obituary is also an indictment.

But this indictment of one individual, a philologist, to some extent exonerates all of the others who committed the same sin without thinking as much about language. Because they all committed it, and each and every one of them is listed in the black book of my memory with their own peculiar vocabulary.

There was young K., a businessman with no literary interests, but completely wrapped up in his Germanness, christened in the cradle and

---

[1]As well as referring metaphorically to radical changes, *Umbruch* also means the literal upheaval of the soil in ploughing up a field.

a Protestant as a matter of course, he had no connection with the Jewish religion and not the least comprehension of Zionism, and certainly no feelings of goodwill towards it – yet he adopted the expression 'the Jewish nation {*das Volk der Juden*}' and used it repeatedly, just as Hitlerism did, in the sense that there is a German nation and a French nation, and as if 'global Jewry {*Weltjudenschaft*}' – he also repeated this dubious Nazi abbreviation – knowingly and deliberately constituted this unified nation.

And then there was K.'s complete opposite in every physical and psychological respect, S., born in Russia, with the features of a Mongol, a relentless enemy of Germany and of all Germans, because in every German he saw a dedicated National Socialist, and also a Zionist nationalist of the most extreme kind – and when he spoke up for the rights of this Jewish nationalism he spoke of his '*völkisch* {national} interests'.

Dentist, no, dental worker {*Zahnbehandler*} F., on the other hand, an incredibly loquacious man in the face of his defenceless patients – how is one supposed to respond with a gaping mouth? – just as much an enemy of all Germans and everything German as S., but without any connection to Zionism or even Jewishness itself, and governed by a foolishly excessive Anglomania resulting from a visit to England which had coincided with a particularly happy time in his private life. Every instrument, every piece of clothing, every book, every opinion had to come from England or else they were, without exception, no good at all, and if they came from Germany, even from the Germany of bygone days, they were totally depraved. Because the Germans were simply 'of inferior character {*charakterlich minderwertig*}'. It never entered his mind (just as it now seems not to have entered the minds of the devotees of the new age) that with his favourite word '*charakterlich*' he was popularizing a new coinage of the Nazis. According to Nazi pedagogy, everything boiled down to the cast of mind {*Gesinnung*}, the unadulterated Nazism of its pupils, with cast of mind valued as the categorically important thing in each and every situation, over and above talent, skill and any kind of knowledge. As far as I can see the spread of this new adjective has to be a result of the language spoken in the classroom, the need to gain examination and school-leaving certificates: the grade 'of good character' thus meant 'irreproachably National Socialist', which opened the door to any chosen career.

Our dental worker's strongest and most verbose antipathy was reserved for our medical worker. The latter's greatest hour had been the First World War, during which he had been a captain in the medical corps. He lived and breathed the language of the officers of 1914, and innocently augmented it with every expression circulated by Goebbels. He had overcome innumerable 'bottlenecks {*Engpässe*}' and 'mastered crises {*Krisen gemeistert*}' on numerous occasions!

A colleague of our Jewish doctor used the LTI out of quite different motives, and in a completely different way. Prior to 1933 Dr P. had felt himself to be a German and a doctor, nothing more and nothing less, and wasted no time thinking about the problems of religion and race, he had held Nazism to be a delusion or an illness which would pass without any dire catastrophe. Now he had been thrown out of his job entirely, worked as a forced labourer in a factory, and was the foreman of a group to which I belonged for a long time.

Here his bitterness expressed itself in a strange way. He appropriated all of the Nazis' anti-Jewish expressions, and especially those of Hitler, and uttered them so incessantly that he himself could probably no longer judge to what extent he was ridiculing either the Führer or himself, or whether this self-deprecating way of speaking had simply become second nature.

He was in the habit of never speaking to any member of his Jewish group without prefixing his name with the term 'Jew'. 'Jew Löwenstein, you are to use the small cutting machine today.' – 'Jew Mahn, here is your medical certificate for the tooth Jew {*Zähnejuden*}' (by which he meant our dentist). The members of the group initially responded with humour, and then accepted it as a matter of course. Some of them were allowed to use the tram, some had to go on foot. Consequently a distinction was drawn between *Fahrjuden* {travel Jews} and *Laufjuden* {foot Jews}. The washing facilities in the factory were very uncomfortable. Some used them, whilst others preferred to wait until they got home to clean themselves. As a result a distinction was drawn between *Waschjuden* {washing Jews} and *Saujuden* {filthy Jews}. Those subsequently transferred to the group may have found this rather tasteless, but they didn't take it seriously enough to make an argument out of it.

When we discussed some problem or other relating to our situation during meal breaks, our foreman would quote the relevant sentences of Hitler with such conviction, that one was forced to regard them as his own sentences and his own convictions. Mahn would report, for example, that the evening patrol in number 42 passed off without incident. The police, he added, were in a state of open conflict with the Gestapo, the older officers being, without exception, Social Democrats. (In summer we had to be at home by 9.00, in winter by 8.00; enforcement of this rule was the job of the police.) Dr P. explained immediately: 'It is the aim of Marxism to hand the world over systematically to the Jews.' On another occasion the topic was a joint-stock venture. In a tone of utter conviction the doctor added: 'By using shares the Jew surreptitiously forces his way into the cycle of national production and turns it into an arena for sharp business practices.' Later, when I had the opportunity to study *Mein Kampf* in detail, certain long sentences seemed very familiar to me; they matched precisely the expressions of our foreman, which I had recorded on pieces of paper ready for my diary. He knew long sentences of the Führer's by heart.

We put up with with the quirks, or rather obsessions, of our foreman sometimes with a sense of humour, sometimes with resignation. To me it seemed symbolic of the whole subjugation of the Jews. Then Bukowzer joined us and the peace was at an end. Bukower was an old man who suffered a lot and had a violent temper; he deplored the Germanness, liberalism and European spirit of his past, and became extremely agitated if he heard the Jews themselves utter a single word of ill will or even lukewarmness towards Judaism. The remarks of our foreman caused the veins on his temples and entirely bald head to stand out like thick cords, and over and over again he shouted: 'I won't let you defame me {*diffamieren*}, I won't put up with you defaming our religion!' His fury provoked the doctor into further quotations, and on occasion I was afraid that Bukowzer would have a heart attack. But all he did was scream and pant Hitler's favourite word, that posh foreign expression 'I won't be defamed! {*diffamieren*}'. The enmity between these two slaves of the LTI was only laid to rest on 13 February: they lie buried under the ruins of the Jews' House in the Sporergasse . . .

Had this enslavement only surfaced in everyday speech it would at least have been understandable; one is less careful about what one says there, is more dependent on what is constantly in front of one's very eyes and ringing in one's ears. But how do things stand with the printed language of the Jews, which is checked many times over and fully answerable? Authors measure their words when writing them down and then ponder them twice more when proofreading.

Right at the outset, when a few Jewish periodicals were still being published, I once read the following title of a funeral oration: 'In memory of our leader {*Führer*} Levinstein'. The *Führer* in this case was the chairman of a community. An embarrassing lapse of taste I told myself – however, one can recognize that there are mitigating circumstances in the case of an orator, even a funeral orator, who tries to say something topical.

Now, during the 1940s, there hadn't been any Jewish periodicals or public Jewish sermons for a long time. Instead there was specifically Jewish modern literature in the Jews' Houses. The gradual drifting apart of the Germans and the German Jews had begun in Germany immediately after the First World War, Zionism had gained a foothold in the Reich. All kinds of emphatically Jewish publishers and book clubs were founded, publishing exclusively Jewish history and philosophy books, along with literary works by Jewish authors on Jewish and German-Jewish themes. These publications were frequently sold on subscription and in series – I think that a literary historian of the future wanting to embrace cultural, historical and sociological factors will have to reflect on this method of publication and circulation – and we still had a sizeable quantity of these publications, which of course were non-Aryan. Our friend Steinitz in particular had a wide selection of these things; for him it had been a kind of educational and spiritual duty to subscribe to every one of these series offered to him. In his collection I found the writings of Buber, Ghetto novels, the history of the Jews by Prinz and that of Dubnow, etc.

The first book I came across here was a volume from the Jewish Book Club: Arthur Eloesser, *Vom Getto nach Europa: das Judentum im geistigen Leben des 19 Jahrhunderts,* Berlin 1936 (From the Ghetto to Europe: The Jews in 19th Century Intellectual Life). Without ever knowing him personally I had literally grown up with Arthur Eloesser. During the 1890s, when my interest in literature was beginning to stir, he was the theatre critic of the *Vossische Zeitung,* which at the time seemed to me to be one of the most high-ranking and desirable posts imaginable. If I had to assess Eloesser's achievement today, I would say that in those days it was entirely consistent with the 'Auntie Voß {*Tante Voß*}' of that period (which had not yet been taken over by Ullstein); his achievement was not thrilling but solid, not revolutionary but decently liberal. What's more, it can be said quite unequivocally that his reviews were entirely free of nationalistic partiality and always had an eye on

Europe – just as, if I remember correctly, Eloesser wrote a competent
doctoral thesis on the drama of the French Enlightenment – and they
were always, as a matter of course, entirely German in outlook; no one
could have imagined that they were not written by a German. And now,
what a change! The hopelessness of a man who has failed and become
an outcast, from the first line to the last. This is to be taken literally,
because the motto of the book, borrowed from an American relative
of the author, reads *'We are not wanted anywhere'*, in German: *Juden
überall unerwünscht!* {Jews are not wanted anywhere}. (During the early
Hitler years there were circumspect notices on restaurant windows
proclaiming *'Juden unerwünscht!* {Jews not wanted}' and *'für Juden
verboten* {no entry to Jews}'. Later this prohibition was universal so there
was no need for a notice.) And at the very end he talks about the funeral
of Berthold Auerbach, the devout Jew and warm-hearted German
patriot who died in early 1882. In Fr Theodor Vischer's commemorative
speech it was said that he would rise again from the dead, but Eloesser
adds in conclusion: 'But the age of the writer and his friends, the age of
liberalism as a world-view {*Weltanschauung*}, and of the German Jew
who set his hopes on it, was already buried under the same soil.'

It's not the helpless resignation with which this liberal, completely
assimilated man of letters accepts his elimination, it's not even the
way in which in desperation he half turns to Zionism which amazed
and shocked me the most about Eloesser's book. The despair and
the search for a new support were all too understandable. But the
slap in the face, the continually repeated slap! In this civilized book,
the language of the victor has been adopted with an obsequiousness
which again and again uses the characteristic forms of the LTI. The
simplistic herding together of people into the singular: the German Jew
who set his hopes on something; the simplistic reduction of humanity:
the German people – these crop up again and again . . . When the
transition is made in Berlin from the Enlightenment of Nicolai to critical
philosophy, it is described as *'einen starken Umbruch* {an extremely
radical change}'. . . In matters of culture the Jews believed themselves
to be *'gleichgeschaltet'* with the Germans . . . Michael Beer's *Paria*
(Pariah) is a *'getarntes* {covert}' play and Heine's 'Almansor' a *'getarnter
Jude* {covert Jew}' . . . Wolfgang Menzel strives for a comprehensive
'Autarkie {autarky}' of intellectual life in Germany . . . Börne survives
'kämpferische {attacking, aggressive}' years of manhood, he is not

led astray by any melody or mystical *'Anruf des Blutes* {call of the blood}' of the kind heeded by Heine and Disraeli. . . . A belief in the burden of social conditioning had *'ausgerichtet* {ordained}' the course of modern realist drama . . . And of course *'das Gesetz des Handelns* {the injunction to act}' is also there, an expression which probably derived from Clausewitz, and which was done to death by the Nazis. And *'aufziehen'* and *'volkhaft* {of the people}' and *'Halbjude* {half-Jew}' and *'Mischling* {half-caste}' and *'Vortrupp* {advance guard}' *e tutti quanti . . .*

Right next to Eloesser's book – because it was in the same series and came out in the same year – stood a 'Novel in Short Stories' by Rudolf Frank: *Ahnen und Enkel* (Forebears and Grandchildren). Here the LTI has slithered into the very core of the work *{nach innen gerutscht}*, as it says in my diary, and if I were now to express it in a more polished way I still couldn't put it any better. Clearly, the Nazi vocabulary was evident in such words as *'Sippe* {clan}', *'Gefolgschaft* {workforce}', *'aufziehen'* etc., which seemed all the more strange given that the author deliberately imitated Goethe's narrative style. But he had fallen prey to the language of the victor in a much more fundamental way than simply in terms of form. He talks (poetically, by the way, and for the most part inadequately) about German émigrés of 1935 who settle in Burma and feed and satisfy their homesickness with memories of their ancestors' experiences in the homeland . . . Contemporary events in Germany are only referred to in a single, short sentence; in it the author answers the question as to why his people travelled from their beloved Rheinland to exotic climes: 'They had their reasons, for they were Jews.' Everything else which dealt with Germany was in the style of a historical novella, invariably telling the story of Jews with a keen sense of tradition who are also enthusiastically German, if not hyper-German *{deutschtümelnd}*. One would have expected that at some point in the discussions and attitudes of these emigrants, with their inherited love of Germany, there would have been a trace of rightful hatred towards those who had driven them out. Far from it, rather the reverse! It was recognized as a tragic destiny to harbour in one and the same heart a love of classical German and of classical Hebrew. The fact that one had been expelled from the German paradise could hardly be blamed on the Nazis, given that in the main one felt and judged the same way as they did.

Mixed marriages between Germans and Jews? 'No, no! What God hath put asunder shall no man join together!' —[2] We sing 'the nostalgic song of the writer from Düsseldorf',[3] the wistful 'I know not the reason why {*Ich weiß nicht, was soll es bedeuten*}' heaven help him! 'We were nomads and remain nomads. Nomads against our will.' We aren't able to build any houses of our own, we always adapt ourselves to the prevailing style (it is what from the Nazi point of view would be called parasitic), now, for example, we will build a synagogue in the style of a pagoda, and our nomadic settlement will be called the 'Land of Tabernacles {*Laubhüttenland*}'. – '*Deine Hand dem Handwerk!* {Put your hands to work}' read one of the LTI banners during the early Nazi years, and Hitler and his accomplices repeatedly accused the Jews of being traders and eggheads. Frank's book celebrates a Jewish family which has practised the same craft for four generations, portrays them as a moral example, explicitly preaches the lesson of returning 'to nature and craft' and brands the filmmaker who intends to start filming again in Burma – 'you just wait and see what kind of production I'll mount {*aufziehen*} for them' – a renegade and reprobate. – A Jew, accused in the historical novellas of contaminating a well, drinks from all the waters in his area in order to cleanse himself, fourteen cups in all, 'and the water of the rivers and springs flowed into him. It flowed through his veins, his body and into the very core of his being and feeling.' And when he is exonerated, and receives a house to live in on the Rhine, he swears he will never leave it 'and bows down to the ground of whose juices he has drunk'. Would it be possible to acknowledge the *Blubo*[4] doctrine more poetically than this? – And when, at length, we read that a young mother and her very young daughter are about to present their new homeland with a child, and we are then told, with an embarrassingly comic gravity which the author seems not to appreciate, that here are 'Two mothers . . . striding along like sisters . . . bearing a new generation into their fertile land' – do we not sense a total assent to the Third Reich's teachings on breeding and the role of women?

---

[2]Klemperer renders this in a colloquial form: '*Naa, naa! Was Gott ausanand tan hat, soll der Mensch net zamme fügen!*'
[3]Heinrich Heine. The song is from the *Buch der Lieder,* Book of Songs.
[4]An abbreviation of *Blut und Boden,* blood and soil.

I read the book to the end only with great reluctance. A literary historian does not have the right to throw a book away because he finds it repugnant. The only character in it I warmed to was the sinful Fred Buchsbaum, who in Burma remains as faithful to his career as a filmmaker as he had in his homeland; he didn't allow himself to be deflected from his true nature, as a man of Europe, as a man of the present; he made comic films but he didn't put on a comic act to himself or others. No, even if everyone had adopted the language of the victor in the Jews' Houses, it was merely an unthinking enslavement, and certainly didn't amount to an assent to their teachings or a belief in their lies.

I was reminded of this one Sunday morning. Four of us were standing in the kitchen, Stühler and I were helping our wives with the washing up. Frau Stühler, the upright Bavarian, whose appearance revealed her robust Bavarian origins, was comforting her impatient husband: 'As soon as you can travel for your clothing company again – it'll happen one day! – we'll get another maid.' For a while Stühler dried his plates vociferously and without saying a word. Then he said, with passionate insistence: 'I'll never travel again . . . they are quite right, it's unproductive, it's just sharp practice {*geschachert*} . . . I'll do gardening or something . . . I want to be close to nature {*naturnah*}!'

The language of the victor . . . you don't speak it with impunity, you breathe it in and live according to it.

Chapter 29
Zion

We regularly used to barter with Seliksohn: he was a diabetic and brought us potatoes in exchange for tiny quantities of meat and vegetables. Before long he was showing a real liking for us both, which always touched me quite a bit, although I never really understood it, given that he hated everything German and considered any German patriot amongst those who wore the star – there were only a few left – to be a fool or a hypocrite. He himself was born in Odessa and had only come to Germany during the First World War at the age of 14; his goal was Jerusalem, despite the fact that – or, as he put it, precisely because of the fact that – he had attended a German school and university. Again and again he tried to convince me of the senselessness of my position. After every imprisonment, every suicide, every news of a death in the camps, i.e. whenever we met, which was increasingly frequently because our discussions became ever more lively, he would say: 'And you still want to be a German and you even love Germany? Before long you'll be declaring your love to Hitler and Goebbels!'

'They're not Germany, and love – that doesn't get to the heart of the matter. Incidentally I've found something nice on this subject today. Have you ever come across the name Julius Bab?'

'Yes, he was one of the literary Jews in Berlin wasn't he? A dramaturge and critic.'

'Well in Steinitz's library there is a privately published edition of his – God knows how it ended up there. Fifty or so poems, published as a manuscript for his friends only, because he didn't feel he was a truly creative poet, and always sensed the borrowed melody behind his own verse. A highly respectable modesty and not out of place; you continually recognize George at one moment and Rilke the next, he doesn't really speak with his own voice. But one verse touched me so much that I almost entirely forgot that it was artistically derivative. I noted it down in my diary. I'll read it to you, and I'll soon know it by heart given how often I think of it; two poems to Germany, one from 1914, the other from 1919, begin with the same confession:

> *Und liebst du Deutschland? – Frage ohne Sinn!*
> *Kann ich mein Haar, mein Blut, mich selber lieben?*
> *1st Liebe nicht noch Wagnis und Gewinn?!*
> *Viel wahllos tiefer bin ich mir verschrieben*
> *und diesem Land, das ich, ich selber bin.*

> {And do you love Germany? A question without meaning!
> Can I love my hair, my blood, my very being?
> Is love no longer risk and profit?!
> Far more blind and profound is my devotion to myself
> and to this land which is, in fact, myself.}

Were it not for the fact that the line about risk and profit sounds so like George, I could have become quite envious. This is exactly how it is, and not only for the author and me, but for many thousands of others as well.'

'Autosuggestion, self-delusion in the most genuine cases, often enough a downright lie, and between these two extremes any number of intermediate stages.'

'And who wrote the most beautiful German poem of the First World War?'

'You surely don't mean Lissauer's affected hymn of hate.'

'Don't be ridiculous ! However: *"Unten am Donaustrand hocken zwei Raben* {Two ravens are perched down on the banks of the Donau}" . . . (I hope I have quoted it accurately); isn't this song, written by the Jew Zuckermann, an absolutely genuine German folk song?'

'Just as genuine, i.e. just as artistically recreated and just as spurious as the Lorelei, and you know about Heine's reconversion to Judaism, but you have probably never heard of Zuckermann's Zionism and Zionist poems. It really is true what they put on the noticeboard at your university and elsewhere: "When a Jew writes German he lies!"'

'It's enough to make you despair, none of you are immune to the language of the victor, not even you, despite the fact you see all Germans as enemies!'

'He speaks more of our language than we of his! He learned from us. It's just that he distorts everything into lies and duplicity.'

'How come? He learned from us? What do you mean?'

'Do you remember the first public appearances in 1933? When the Nazis staged the enormous demonstration against the Jews here? "One-way street to Jerusalem!" and "The white stag chases away the Jews", and what was written on all the banners and the pictures and posters that people carried around? A Jew joined in the demonstration bearing a placard on a long pole, and on the placard it said: "Kick us out!" '

'I've heard the story before and assumed it was a sour joke.'

'No, it really happened, and this "Kick us out" is older than all this Hitler business, and it's not that we speak the language of the victor, but rather that Hitler learned from Herzl.'

'Do you really believe that Hitler read anything by Herzl?'

'I certainly don't think he ever read anything seriously. He was forever picking up snippets of common knowledge, forever just madly repeating parrot-fashion, and overstating whatever he could use for his maniacal system, but this is precisely the genius or demonic nature of his madness, or perhaps the criminality within him – call it or explain it as you please – namely that he invariably presents whatever he has picked up in such a way that it will have a rousing effect on primitive people and, moreover, transform those who do in fact enjoy, or at least enjoyed, certain intellectual faculties, into primitive herding animals once again. And at the point in *Mein Kampf* where he first talks about his animosity towards the Jews, about his experiences and insights in Vienna, he immediately goes on about Zionism, which was something that couldn't be ignored in Vienna. Once again he distorts everything in the most shabby, ridiculous and trashy manner; the black-haired Jewish boy lies in wait for the Aryan blonde with a satanic grin on his face in order to defile in her the whole German race, all with the intention of leading his own inferior race, the Jewish people, to their goal of world domination – although I am quoting from memory these are, I assure you, his exact words in all salient points!'

'I know. I could in fact recite the passage even more accurately, because our foreman is big on quotations from Hitler, and this is one of his favourite passages. It then goes on to say that after the First World War the Jews brought the Negro to the Rhine in order to spoil the white master race by forced bastardization. But what has that got to do with the Zionists?'

'He definitely got the idea from Herzl of seeing the Jews as a people, as a political entity, and of categorizing them as "global Jewry {*Weltjudentum*}" '.

'Isn't that a frightful accusation you are levelling at Herzl?'

'It's not Herzl's fault that a bloodhound robbed him, and that the Jews in Germany didn't listen to him in good time. Now it's too late, only now are you finally coming over to us.'

'Not me.'

'You! Next you'll be claiming like Rathenau that you have a blond, Teutonic heart, and that the German Jews are a kind of German tribe, somewhere between the North Germans and the Swabians.'

'I certainly wouldn't enter into all that tasteless business about blond, Teutonic hearts, but from a purely intellectual point of view the idea of a kind of German tribe might well apply to the likes of us, I mean people whose mother tongue is German and whose entire education is German. "Language is more than blood!" I can't generally get anywhere with Rosenzweig, whose letters were given me by Privy Councillor Elsa – but Rosenzweig belongs to the Buber chapter, and we are dealing with Herzl.'

'It's pointless talking to you, you don't know Herzl. You must get to know him, that is now an essential part of your education, let me see if I can get something of his for you.' –

The discussion stayed with me for days. Was it really a result of a lack of education that I hadn't read a line of Herzl, and how come he had never been forced on me? Of course I had heard people talk about him for ages, and I had come into contact with the Zionist movement a couple of times in my life. First at the beginning of the century, when a duelling Jewish fraternity in Munich wanted to have me as a member. All I did at the time was shrug my shoulders as if it was something from another world. And then again a few years before the First World War, in Schnitzler's 'Road to the Open', and soon afterwards in a lecture that I held in Prague. In Prague, where I spent a few hours in a coffee house with Zionist students, I told myself it was a specifically Austrian question, with even more conviction, indeed, than I had when reading Schnitzler. There, where people were wont to divide the state up into different, mutually feuding nationalities, who at best only tolerated each other, there may well have been a Jewish nationality; and in the Galician region, where there was still a close-knit petty-bourgeois Jewish population, insisting on voluntary isolation in a ghetto and their own language and customs, just as in neighbouring Polish and Russian Jewish groups, whose oppression and persecution had bred the longing for a better homeland – in these places Zionism was so understandable that there was only one thing about it that needed explaining: why did it only come into being in the final decade of the last century, and why because of Herzl? In fact it had already been in existence much earlier all over the place, in some cases even in an embryonically political form, and it was only the decisive process of drawing out the political component, together with the incorporation of the emancipated Western Jews living under European conditions into the concept of nationhood and into the remigration plan which constituted the new dimension added by Herzl to the existing movement.

But what did all this have to do with me, to do with Germany? I knew perfectly well that Zionism had supporters in the Posen area, and that where we were in Berlin there was a Zionist group and even a Zionist periodical – but in Berlin there were all kinds of eccentric and exotic peculiarities, probably even a Chinese club. What did it have to do with the world in which I moved, and with me personally? I was so confident about being a German, a European, a twentieth-century man. Blood? Racial hatred? Not today, not here – at the centre of Europe! And wars weren't to be expected any more either, not at the centre of Europe . . . at most somewhere in the far reaches of the Balkans, in Asia, in Africa. Right up until June 1914 I believed everything written about the possibility of a return to medieval conditions to be sheer fantasy, and I understood medieval conditions to be anything that could not be reconciled with peace and culture.

Then came the First World War and my faith in the unshakeable strength of European culture certainly took a shaking. And, of course, day by day, I sensed ever more keenly the rising tidal wave of anti-Semitism and National Socialism – I was, after all, in the company of professors and students, and sometimes I think that they were worse than the petty bourgeoisie – (they were undoubtedly more guilty). And of course it didn't escape my notice that even in our area the Zionist movement became increasingly strong as a source of protection and self-defence. But I didn't pay any attention to it, I didn't read any of those special Jewish publications that I later collected with such difficulty in the Jews' Houses. Did I close my mind to it in defiance, or was it stupidity? I don't think it was either. Was it a desperate clinging to Germany, a love which didn't want to accept that it was unrequited? Definitely not, there was nothing histrionic about it, it just came naturally. It is true, the lines of Bab do say it all as far as I'm concerned. (I wonder whether he would stick by them today? Is he still alive? – I knew him when we were both about twelve or thirteen, and never saw him again.) But I am getting bogged down in my diary of 1942 and too far from the philologist's notebook.

No, not really; it is relevant to the theme; because I often asked myself at the time whether I was the only one who had seen things in Germany wrongly or at least not fully; if that was the case, then I also had to mistrust my current observations and was, at the very least, ill-suited to dealing with the Jewish theme. I brought up this question during my customary weekly visit to Markwald. Markwald was a man in his late sixties, almost completely paralysed, but mentally totally alert. Every few hours, when the pain began to torment him too much, his brave wife prepared a morphia injection for him. It had been like this for years and could have gone on for many more. He wanted to see his sons again who had emigrated and get to know his grandchildren. 'But if they send me to Theresienstadt I will bite the dust, because I won't get any morphia.' He was transported to Theresienstadt without his invalid chair and did indeed bite the dust there, along with his wife. To some degree he constituted just as much of an exception amongst those who wore the star as the unskilled worker and employee in the factory: his father had already settled in central Germany as a landowner and he himself, having studied agriculture, had taken over his father's estate and managed it until, during the Great War, he transferred to a high-ranking post in the Ministry of Agriculture in Saxony. On occasion – and this too belongs in the section on Judah – he told me about the slaughter of the pigs which, according to an accusation that was repeated again and again, the Jews had committed in order to starve the Germans to death, and about analogous measures undertaken by the Nazis under a different name: what during the First World War was known as Jewish murder was now called German foresight {*deutsche Vorausschau*} and a planned people's economy {*volksverbundene Planwirtschaft*}. But the discussions with this paralytic did not revolve exclusively around questions of agriculture: both Markwalds were extremely interested and well-read in matters political and literary, and had naturally been forced in recent years to confront the problems facing the German Jews as urgently as I had. And they too had not escaped being affected by the language of the victor. They gave me a lavishly executed and comprehensive manuscript to read, the history of their family in Germany, which could be traced back many hundreds of years; Nazi vocabulary was used widely in it, and the whole thing was a contribution to 'genealogical studies {*Sippenkunde*}', which itself was not ill-disposed to some of the 'authoritarian' laws of the new state regime.

I talked with Markwald about Zionism. I wanted to know whether he had attached great importance to it as far as Germany was concerned. Government officials like to evaluate things statistically. Yes, he had of course come across this 'Austrian movement'; he had also noticed that under the pressure of anti-Semitism it had been on the increase over here since the end of the First World War; but it had never become a movement across the whole of the German Reich, it had always remained just a small minority, a clique. The vast majority of German Jews could not longer be separated from their Germanness. It was not possible to speak of a failed or revokable assimilation; the German Jews could certainly be exterminated, but they couldn't be stripped of their Germanness, not even if they worked at it themselves. Then I related what Seliksohn had told me about Herzl's influence on Nazism . . .

'Herzl? Who was he, or indeed is he?'

'You haven't read anything of his either?'

'This is the first time I've heard the name.'

Frau Markwald confirmed that she too had never heard of him before.

I note this in my own defence. There must have been many, very many people in Germany besides myself for whom Zionism remained something entirely foreign right to the last. And no one can claim that such an extreme advocate of assimilation, a 'non-Aryan Christian', a landowner, is a bad witness in such matters. On the contrary! He is a particularly good witness, especially given that he held a post which offered an excellent overview. *Les extrêmes se touchent:* this proposition is valid insofar as parties at opposite ends of the political spectrum know more about each other than anyone else. When I lay in hospital in Paderborn in 1916 I was provided with an excellent supply of literature from the French Enlightenment by the archiepiscopal seminary . . .

But Hitler spent his years as an apprentice in Austria, and in the same way as he introduced '*Verlautbarung* {announcement}' from over there into the officialese of the German Reich, so he must also have picked up Herzl's ways of thinking and speaking – it is almost impossible to locate the crossover from the one to the other, especially in the case of primitive types – assuming that they were present in him at all. Shortly after these discussions and reflections, Seliksohn brought me two volumes of Herzl, the Zionist writings and the first volume of the diaries, both published, in 1920 and 1922, by the Jewish Publishing House in Berlin. I read them with a dismay bordering on despair. My first diary entry on them reads: 'Lord protect me from my friends! If you are in the right frame of mind, then these two volumes can provide evidence for many of the accusations levelled at the Jews by Hitler and Goebbels and Rosenberg, it does not require any great gift of interpretation or distortion.'

Later, using a number of key words and quotations, I set down clearly the similarities and dissimilarities between Herzl and Hitler. There were, thank God, also dissimilarities between them.

Above all: Herzl is never intent on oppressing, let alone exterminating, other peoples, he never advocates the idea at the root of all Nazi atrocities, the idea of one superior race or people being chosen above all others and having a claim to power over the rest of humanity. He merely calls for equal rights for a group of oppressed people, nothing more than a moderately small safe haven for a group which has been mistreated and persecuted. He only uses the word 'subhuman {*untermenschlich*}' when talking about the subhuman treatment of the Galician Jews. And, moreover, he is not narrow-minded and obstinate, he is not intellectually and spiritually uneducated like Hitler, he is not a fanatic. He would simply like to be one, but only gets halfway there, and cannot quite stifle his reason, equanimity and humanity; he can only believe himself to be the man of destiny sent from God for a few moments at a time, and is always asking himself whether, instead of being a second Moses, he is not merely a feature-writer blessed with a good imagination. He has only one hard and fast objective, and only one aspect of his plan which is clearly worked-out: a homeland must be created for the non-emancipated and truly oppressed eastern Jewish masses, who have remained a people unto themselves. As soon as he touches on the Western side of the problem he ties himself up in contradictions which he then vainly attempts to resolve. The definition of the term *Volk* {people, nation} begins to waver, it's impossible to establish conclusively whether the gestor, who is in charge of government business, is a dictator or a parliament; he doesn't like racial distinctions, but wants to see mixed marriage banned; he clings to German culture and the German language with 'wistful {*wehmütig*}' pleasure and wants to transplant it to Palestine, like everything else from the West, but the Jewish people will be made up of the uniform mass of Eastern inhabitants of the Ghetto, and so on. From all these uncertainties it is clear that Herzl is not a genius, but a warm-hearted and interesting man.

As soon as he elevates himself to the status of someone sent by God, however, and feels the need to live up to his mission, the intellectual, moral and linguistic similarity between the Messiah of the Jews and that of the Germans takes on a dimension which is grotesque one minute and shocking the next. He 'unfurls the national, social flag {*die nationalsoziale Fahne*}' with its seven stars symbolizing the seven hours of the working day, he smashes any resistance, he demolishes any opposition, he is the Führer who has been given his orders by destiny and realizes everything that slumbers unconsciously amidst the masses of his people, the masses that he will turn into a people, and the Führer 'must have a resolute outlook'. He must, moreover, be able to appreciate the psychology and needs of the masses. Notwithstanding his own free-thinking and the furtherance of science, he will create places of pilgrimage pandering to the childish beliefs of the masses and will even exploit his own aureole. 'I watched and listened (he notes after a successful mass meeting) as my own legend came into being. The people are sentimental; the masses don't see clearly. Even now they don't have a clear impression of me. A light mist is beginning to well up around me which will perhaps become the cloud in which I move.' Propaganda is to be made by all possible means: while one can deal with the childlike masses with orthodoxy and places of pilgrimage, in assimilated and educated circles it is possible to 'create propaganda for Zionism out of snobbery', mentioning for example Börries von Münchhausen's 'Ballads of Judah' and Mosche Lilien's illustrations when talking to the Viennese women's association. (If I mention the fact that Münchhausen, who read his own Judah poetry in many Jewish associations before the First World War, was celebrated as a great German writer in Hitler's Reich, and as a *Blubo* man got on extremely well with the Nazis, then I have reached the point I am heading towards; but that is jumping the gun.) Superficial pomp and circumstance and obtrusive symbolism are good and indispensable things, and great importance should be attached to uniforms, flags and festivals. Uncomfortable critics are to be treated as enemies of the state. Opposition to important measures must be broken 'with ruthless severity', there is no need to refrain from casting suspicion on dissenters and insulting them. If the so-called protest rabbis turn against the idea of a political Zionism incorporating the West on decisive spiritual grounds, then Herzl declares: Next year in Jerusalem! 'In the last decades of national degeneration' – he means: of assimilation – some rabbis had given a 'watered-down interpretation' of this age-old motto summarizing their objectives: the Jerusalem of the saying ought really to be London, Berlin or Chicago. 'If you interpret Jewish traditions in this way, then of course there isn't much left of Judaism beyond the annual earnings of these gentlemen.' Enticements and threats should stand side by side in equal doses: no one is to be forced to join in the emigration; however, anyone who hesitates or arrives later, will have a bad time of it on both sides, the people in Palestine 'will seek their true friends amongst those who fought and suffered for the cause at a time when it earned them insults rather than honours'.

While these are simply general expressions and tones the two Führers have in common, Herzl also on many occasions supplies his opposite number with terrible weapons. He wants to force the Rothschilds to use their fortune to benefit the Jewish people, where at present they have the armies of all the major world powers working solely for their own financial advancement. And how will the accumulated mass of the Jewish people – again and again: we are a single entity, we are a people! – assert itself and establish its position? It will intervene as a financial power in the peace agreements between the warring European powers. It will principally be able to do this because following the foundation of the Jewish state there will be enough Jews living abroad in Europe who will want to rely on their own state and serve it from outside. This is open to a wealth of possible interpretations by Nazism!

And again and again the personal affinity, the linguistic accord of the two of them. One should count the number of receptions, speeches and trivialities of the Hitler regime that were referred to as 'historic {*historisch*}'. And when Herzl advances his thoughts to the editor-in-chief of the *Neue Freie Presse* during a walk it is 'an historic hour', and whenever he enjoys the most insignificant diplomatic success it immediately goes down in world history. And there is a moment at which he confides in his diary that his private life has now ceased and his historic life begun . . .

Again and again correspondences between them – intellectual and stylistic, psychological, speculative, political, and how much they mutually encouraged each other! Of all the things on which Herzl bases his idea of a unified people, there is only one which truly fits the Jews: their common opponent and persecutor; seen from this point of view the Jews of all nations certainly unite into 'global Jewry' in their opposition to Hitler – the man himself, his persecution complex and the precipitous cunning of his mania gave a concrete form to that which previously had only existed as an idea, and he converted more supporters to Zionism and the Jewish state than Herzl himself. And Herzl once again – from whom could Hitler have gleaned more crucial and practical ideas for his own purposes?

An accurate assessment of everything that I have brushed aside in the form of this rhetorical question will require more than one doctoral thesis. It is undoubtedly the case that Nazi doctrine was repeatedly stimulated and enriched by Zionism, but it will not be easy in every case to say with certainty what the Führer and any of the co-authors of the Third Reich took specifically from Zionism.

The problem is that Hitler and Herzl feed to a very large extent on the same heritage. I have already identified the German root of Nazism, it is that partial, bigoted and perverted form of Romanticism. If I add Romanticism made kitschy, then I have defined exactly the intellectual and stylistic common ground between the two Führers. Herzl's model, who is referred to lovingly on a number of occasions, is Wilhelm II. The fact that he recognizes clearly the psychological root of Wilhelm's heroic pose – the crippled arm beneath the upturned moustache is no secret to him – merely makes him feel more affectionate towards the Kaiser. The new Moses of the Jews also dreams of a guard in silver cuirasses.

Hitler for his part viewed Wilhelm as a corrupter of the people, but he shared with him the heroic affectations and the penchant for kitschy Romanticism, or rather he outdid him in all of this many times over.

Of course I talked about the theme of Herzl with Privy Councillor Elsa, and of course she knew him. But she couldn't muster up much warmth of feeling towards him, no particular love and no strong aversion. She found him too 'vulgar', not 'intellectual' enough. He meant well when it came to the poor Eastern Jews, and he undoubtedly rendered them a considerable service. 'But he has nothing to say to us German Jews; what's more he is also passé as far as the Zionist movement is concerned. The political tensions over there don't interest me much; neither party is in agreement with Herzl the moderate bourgeois, the extreme nationalists aren't and nor are the communists and friends of the Soviet Union. For me what matters is the purely intellectual leadership of Zionism, and that today rests undoubtedly with Buber. I admire Martin Buber, and if I was not so fanatically – pardon me! – so completely attached to Germany I would have to declare my whole-hearted support for him. What you say about Herzl's kitschy Romanticism is absolutely right, Buber, on the other hand, is a true Romantic, completely pure, completely profound, I would almost say a completely German Romantic; the fact that he ultimately opts for a separate Jewish state – Hitler is certainly half to blame for it, and as far as the rest is concerned – well he came from Vienna for God's sake, and you only become a genuine German over here in the Reich. The best of Buber, in purely German form, is to be found in the writings of Buber's friend Franz Rosenzweig. I'll give you Rosenzweig's letters to take with you' – in fact she later even gave me the valuable volume, of which she had two copies, as a present, and I mourn for it again and again because it provided so many insights into the intellectual history of its age – 'and here are a few things by Buber' . . .

A brief interjection to salve my philological conscience: my conversations in the style of Livy are only very moderately Livyan: they come from my diary, which I really did write day-by-day while my impressions were still fresh, and while the sound of what I'd heard was still ringing in my ears. Buber was not entirely unknown to me, for the previous twenty or thirty years he had been mentioned as one of the philosophers of religion; Rosenzweig, who was less famous and had died young, I had never come across before.

Buber is such an extreme Romantic and mystic that he twists the very being of Judaism into its opposite. Its entire development has shown that the strictest rationalism and a notion of God radically divested of the sensual constitute the heart of this being, and that the Kabbalah and later outbursts of mysticism are merely counter-reactions to this all-powerful and absolutely dominant tendency. For Buber, on the other hand, Jewish mysticism is the most important and creative thing, Jewish ratio merely fossilization and degeneracy {*Entartung*}. He is a far-reaching theologian; Eastern man is the religious person *per se,* but of all Eastern people it is the Jews who have reached the pinnacle of religion. And because for centuries they were in close contact with the vibrant western world, with people of different beliefs, it is now their task to amalgamate the best intellectual strands from the Orient and the Occident and communicate them back and forth. At this point the Romantic, indeed the Romantic philologist, comes into play (not, as in Herzl's case, the politician): in matters religious the Jews have found their meridian in Palestine, they are not nomads, they were originally an agrarian people, all images, all images in the Bible point to this, their 'God was the feudal lord of the field, his festivals were festivals of the field and his law the law of the field'. And 'irrespective of the heights of the universal spirit scaled by the prophets . . . their universal spirit always wanted to lodge in a body from this special soil of Canaan . . .' In Europe, the Jewish soul ('which has passed through all the heavens and hells of the western world'), in particular the soul of the 'conformist' Jews, has sustained serious damage; but 'when it touches its mother earth it will become creative once more'. Buber indulges in the ways of thinking and the feelings of German Romanticism, the linguistic world of Romanticism, and in particular that of Neo-Romantic poetry and philosophy, with its detachment from the everyday and its priestly solemnity and fondness for mysterious gloom.

The situation is similar with Franz Rosenzweig, although he does not get so lost in mysticism, and refuses to give up the geographical link with Germany.

I will stick to the cobbler's last of my LTI. The essence of Judaism, the justification of Zionism are not my theme. (A religious Jew would very probably come to the conclusion that the second, more world-wide diaspora of our own age is as much willed by God as the first; however, neither the first nor the second had its origin in a God of the field, because the real task this God set his people was not to be a people at all, not to be constrained by the confines either of space or the body, but rather to be rootless and serve the unadorned Idea. And dear God, how much time we spent philosophizing about all this, about the function of the Ghetto as a 'fence' around this spiritual identity, and about the fence which became a garrotte, about the way in which the decisive missionaries broke out – the 'great Spinoza' Buber says, in patent contradiction to his own teachings – and about the breaking out and being thrown out of the new national boundaries. And how terrifyingly few of those of us who engaged in this philosophizing are still alive!)

I will stick to my last. The very style which is characteristic of Buber, the very words which in his case have such a solemn polish, words such as '*Bewährung* {proving the worth of something}', '*das Einmalige* {something unique}' and '*die Einmaligkeit* {uniqueness}': how often I have come across all this from the Nazis, in Rosenberg and other lesser writers, in books and newspaper articles. From time to time they were keen to go around like philosophers, from time to time they were keen to direct their attention to the intellectuals; that impressed the masses.

A stylistic affinity between Rosenberg and Buber, a kinship in certain values – cherishing farming and mysticism above nomadism and rationalism is also at the heart of Rosenberg's thinking – isn't this even more disturbing than the affinity between Hitler and Herzl? The explanation for this phenomenon is, however, the same in both cases: Romanticism, not only of the kitschy kind, but also the real one, dominates the period, and the innocent and the mixers of poison, the victims and the henchmen, both draw on this same source.

Chapter 30
The Curse of the Superlative

Once in my life, about forty years ago, I published something in an American paper. To mark the seventieth birthday of Adolf Wilbrandt, the German-language *New-Yorker Staatszeitung* published an essay by me, his biographer. On seeing the specimen copy I immediately got a comprehensive impression of the American press, one which has stayed with me ever since. Probably unjustly, indeed definitely so because generalizations always falsify, and despite knowing this fact, the same image inevitably returns to me with utter clarity whenever I have reason to think of the American press, and regardless of how tenuous the association may be. Right down the middle of my Wilbrandt article, from top to bottom, there was a sinuous line cutting the type in two and advertising a laxative, it began the advertisement with the words 'A man has thirty feet of intestines'.

That was in August 1907. I never thought more deeply about these intestines than in the summer of 1937. Following the Nuremberg Rally it was reported that a column made up of all the German newspapers published on that day would reach 20 km into the stratosphere – which proved that the claims from abroad that the German press was in decline were nothing but lies; and around the same time, when Mussolini visited Berlin, it was reported that the festive decoration of the streets required 40,000 metres of bunting.

'A confusion of quantity and quality, an Americanism of the crudest kind', I noted at the time, and the fact that the newspaper people of the Third Reich were quick to learn from the Americans was demonstrated by the increasing use of headlines in ever thicker type, and the increasing omission of the article preceding the noun that was being highlighted – '"*Völkischer Beobachter*" Builds World's Biggest Publishing House' – thereby compounding the strict concision favoured by the military, sport and business.

But did the Americans and the Nazis really go in for the same kind of intemperance when it came to numbers and figures? I already had my doubts at the time. Wasn't there a bit of humour in the thirty feet of intestines, couldn't one always sense a certain straightforward naivety in the exaggerated figures of American adverts? Wasn't it as if the advertiser was saying to himself each time: you and I, dear reader, derive the same pleasure from exaggeration, we both know how it's meant – so I'm not really lying at all, you subtract what matters and my eulogy isn't deceitful, it simply makes a greater impression and is more fun if it's expressed as a superlative!

A little later I came across the memoirs of an American journalist, Webb Miller's *I Found No Peace*, which was published in German by Rowohlt in 1938. Here the pleasure in figures was clearly totally sincere; breaking records was just part of the job: providing numerical proof that news was transmitted at record speed, numerical proof that the transmission was totally accurate: that earned much greater respect than some profound reflection or other. Miller notes with special pride that he reported in precise detail the beginning of the Abyssinian war (3 October 1935, 4.44, 4.55, 5 o'clock) forty-four minutes before any other correspondent, and an extremely brief sketch of an aeroplane over the Balkans concludes with the sentence: 'The white mass (of the heavy cloud banks) shot past us at a speed of one hundred miles per hour.'

The worst thing that the American cult of numbers could be accused of was naive bragging and an excessive belief in its own worth. Which brings me back to the essay question about elephants set to representatives of different nations. 'How I shot my thousandth elephant', the American reports. With his elephant from the Carthaginian war, the German who appears in the same joke belongs to the nation of thinkers and writers and unworldly scholars of an age dating back a century and a half. Given the same theme, the German from the Third Reich would have finished off the biggest elephants in the world, in unimaginable numbers, with the best weapon on earth.

It may well be that the LTI learned from American customs when it came to the use of figures, but it differs from them hugely and twice over: not only through exorbitant use of the superlative, but also through its deliberate maliciousness, because it is invariably and unscrupulously intent on deception and benumbing. In the Wehrmacht despatches unverifiable figures are strung together one after another detailing spoils and prisoners of war; artillery, planes and tanks are listed by the thousand and ten thousand, prisoners by the hundred thousand, and at the end of the month one is presented with immense lists of even more implausible figures; when it comes to the number of enemy dead, however, the precise figures disappear entirely, and are replaced by expressions of a faltering imagination: 'unimaginable {*unvorstellbar*}' and 'countless {*zahllos*}'. During the First World War we were proud of the sober exactitude of the military despatches. The coquettish modesty of one particular sentence from the first days of the war became famous: 'The stipulated line has been reached.' Of course it wasn't possible to stay as sober as this, but it remained a stylistic ideal to aspire to, and this ideal never became entirely ineffective. The bulletins of the Third Reich, on the other hand, start off in a superlative mode from the very outset and then, the worse the situation, the more they overdo it, until everything becomes literally measureless, twisting the fundamental quality of military language, its disciplined exactitude, into its very opposite, into fantasy and fairy-tale. The fairy-tale quality of the figures detailing spoils is underlined by the fact that there is barely any reference to Germany's own losses, just as in the images of battle which appear in films the bodies piled up in mounds are always enemy losses.

It was frequently noted during and after the First World War that the language of the army, and of the war itself, entered into civilian usage; the characteristic feature of the Second World War is that the language of the Party, the LTI itself, destructively pervaded the language of the army. The complete destruction, which lay in the express abolition of numerical boundaries, the introduction of the words '*unvorstellbar*' and '*zahllos*', was achieved by degrees: initially only the reporters and commentators were allowed to use the extreme words, then the Führer permitted himself to use them when his speeches and entreaties were in full swing, and only then, finally, were they used in official Wehrmacht despatches.

The extraordinary thing was the shameless transparency of the lies revealed by the figures; one of the fundamentals of Nazi doctrine is the conviction that the masses are unthinking and that their minds can be completely dulled. In September 1941 a military despatch reported that 200,000 people were trapped in Kiev; a few days later 600,000 captives were freed from the same encircled area – presumably they were now adding the entire civilian population to the soldiers. In the past, people in Germany liked to laugh about the extravagance of East Asian figures; during the last years of the war it was shocking to see how Japanese and German reports tried to surpass each other in the most senseless exaggerations; it makes you wonder who learned from whom, Goebbels from the Japanese or vice versa.

Exorbitant figures don't only crop up in official war reports: in spring 1943 it is reported in all the papers that 46 million copies of the booklets sent to the soldiers, the so-called forces' postal service editions, have already been dispatched. Sometimes smaller figures are also impressive. In November 1941 Ribbentrop declares that we could continue to fight for a further thirty years; on 26 April 1942 Hitler says in the Reichstag that Napoleon fought in Russia in temperatures of minus 25 degrees, but that he, Commanding Officer Hitler, had fought at minus 45, even at minus 52. Unintended humour apart, this attempt to outdo an illustrious precursor – it was the period when he still liked to be celebrated as a strategist and have himself compared with Napoleon – seems to me to be extremely similar to the American custom of breaking records.

Tout se tient as the French say, everything hangs together. The expression '*hundertprozentig* {100 per cent}' comes directly from America and goes back to the title of a novel by Upton Sinclair which was widely read in German translation; throughout the twelve years it was on everybody's lips and I often heard the adjunct 'Steer clear of that chap, he's a 150-per-center!' And yet, it is precisely this most indisputable of Americanisms that has to be set against that most basic demand and keyword of Nazism – '*total*'.

'*Total*' is also a number of maximum value, and, in its concrete reality, as pregnant with meaning as the Romantic excesses of '*zahllos*' and '*unvorstellbar*'. The terrible consequences for Germany itself of the total war that it declared as part of its own programme are still fresh in everyone's mind. But it is not only in relation to the war that one comes across the ubiquitous 'total' in the LTI: an article in the *Reich* extols the 'total learning environment' in a rigidly Nazi girls' school; in a shop window I saw a board game described as 'the total game'.

Tout se tient. As well as being allied to the principle of totality, the numerical superlatives also encroach on the domain of religion, and one of the fundamental assertions of Nazism is that it is a Teutonic religion taking the place of the Semitic and unheroic religion of Christianity. *Ewig* {eternal, everlasting}, the religious elimination of duration, is often used – the eternal guard, the eternal existence of Nazi institutions – and the 'Thousand Year Reich', an even more conspicuously ecclesiastical and religious name than the Third Reich, is referred to often enough. Of course the round number 1,000 is also popular outside the realm of religion: propaganda rallies intended to raise the spirits for 1941, following the absence of a decisive outcome to the *Blitzkrieg,* are immediately advertised as a thousand.

The numerical superlative can also be arrived at from another angle: 'unique' is just as much a superlative as a thousand. As a synonym for extraordinary, and stripped of its numerical significance, the word became, in Neo-Romantic philosophy and literature at the end of the First World War, a fashionable expression with a whiff of the aesthete about it; it is used by people who set great store by exclusive elegance and stylistic originality, such as Stefan Zweig and Rathenau. The LTI, and particularly the Führer himself, use the word so often and so carelessly that one is reminded in comic fashion of its numerical value. When, following the Polish campaign, a dozen soldiers are promoted to the rank of field marshal for unique acts of heroism, one is forced to ask oneself whether each of them only proved his ability in one single battle, and can but conclude that twelve unique acts and twelve unique marshals make a round dozen.

(Whereupon the devaluing of the *Generalfeldmarschall* {field marshal}, at the time the highest rank, leads inevitably to the creation of the very highest of all, the *Reichsmarschall* {Reich's marshal}.)

However, all these numerical superlatives merely constitute a well-stocked subgroup of the general use of the superlative. This could be referred to as the most prevalent linguistic form of the LTI, which is not surprising given that the superlative is the most obvious means by which a speaker or agitator can achieve a desired effect, it is the quintessential advertising mode. That is why the NSDAP reserved it for its own special use by eliminating all competition and maintaining sole right of disposal: in October 1942 Eger, our neighbour in the next room, the former owner of one of the most respected clothes shops in Dresden, at the time a factory worker and soon to be 'shot attempting to escape', told me that a circular had forbidden him from using superlatives when advertising his business. 'If, for example, you used to write "you will be served by the most highly trained staff", you would now have to write "trained" or, at most, "highly trained".'

In addition to the numerical superlatives and the number-like words, three different usages of the superlative can be distinguished, all three of which are used equally excessively: the regular superlative forms of adjectives, single expressions which inherently contain a superlative value or can have one ascribed to them, and sentence structures completely drenched with superlatives.

The regular superlatives can acquire a special appeal through the effect of accumulation. When I Nazified the elephant joke earlier, I had a sentence ringing in my ear which Generalissimo Brauchitsch used at the time to spice up military commands: the best soldiers in the world are supplied with the best weapons in the world produced by the best workers in the world.

Here, alongside the regular superlative form, is the word filled with superlative meaning which the LTI uttered day in day out. When, on very special occasions, courtly writers solemnly extolled the fame of the Sun King in the florid style of the seventeenth century, they said that *l'univers,* the universe, looked down on him. In every speech and every remark of Hitler's throughout the twelve years – because it was only at the very end that he fell silent – the same headline always appears as a compulsory cliché: 'The World Listens to the Führer.' Whenever a major battle is won it is 'the greatest battle in the history of the world'. 'Battle' on its own is rarely sufficient, it is 'battles of total destruction {*Vernichtungsschlachten*}' that are fought. (Once again the shameless reliance on the forgetfulness of the masses: how often the same enemy, already pronounced dead, is destroyed once more!)

Everywhere *'Welt* {world}' serves as a superlative prefix: Germany's ally Japan advances from a great power to a world power, Jews and Bolshevists are enemies of the world, meetings between the Führer and the Duce will go down in the annals of world history. The word *'Raum* {space, area}' is similar in its superlativeness to the word *Welt.* Of course during the First World War people no longer said 'the battle of Königgrätz or Sedan' but rather 'the battle in the area of . . . {*im Raume von . . .*}', which was simply a result of the escalation of military clashes;

and the science of geopolitics, which so clearly favoured imperialism, is undoubtedly also to blame for the widespread use of the word *Raum*. But there is also something unbounded about the notion of *Raum* itself, and it is this that makes it so seductive. A Reich's Commissioner asserts in his report for the year 1942 that 'for a thousand years the Ukrainian *Raum* has not been governed as justly, generously and progressively as it is now under the leadership of a National Socialist Greater Germany'. 'Ukrainian *Raum'* complements the superlative of a thousand years and the Spanish adverbial triad much better than just 'the Ukraine'. *Großzügig* {generous} and *großdeutsch* {of Greater Germany} are really too old and hackneyed to inflate this sentence with any more hot air. Yet the LTI brought about such a proliferation of the auxiliary syllable *'groß* {great}' – *Großkundgebung* {mass rally}, *Großoffensive* {major offensive}, *Großkampftag* {day of a great battle} – that the good old National Socialist Börries von Münchhausen even protested about it during the Nazi period itself.

The word *'historisch* {historic}' is just as laden with superlative weight and just as common as *'Welt'* and *'Raum'*. Something is historic when it survives in the memory of a people or of mankind as a whole, because it exerts a direct and lasting influence on the population at large or the whole of the human race. Thus the epithet 'historic' applies to all, even the most natural actions of the Nazi leaders in peacetime and of the generals, and the super-superlative *'welthistorisch* {of global historic significance}' is on hand for Hitler's speeches and edicts.

Any kind of bragging can be used to soak entire sentences with the spirit of the superlative. In the factory I hear on the radio a few sentences from an event from the Sportpalast in Berlin. Summer 1943, Speer and Goebbels are speaking. It begins: 'The mass rally is being broadcast across Germany and the Reich, joined by stations in the protectorates of Holland, France, Greece, Serbia . . . in the allied states of Italy, Hungary, Romania . . .' It goes on in this vein for a while. The result was undoubtedly an even more superlative effect on the imagination of the audience than the newspaper headline 'The World Listens', because here they were leafing through the Nazi atlas of the world.

After Speer had delivered extravagant figures about Germany's stockpiles of armaments, Goebbels elevated Germany's achievements to an even higher standing by comparing the exactitude of German statistics with the enemy's 'Jewish numerical acrobatics'. Listing {*aufzählen*} and belittling {*Verächtlichmachen*}. There can't be a single speech of the Führer that doesn't long-windedly list Germany's successes and sarcastically insult the enemy. The stylistic means employed in a rough-and-ready manner by Hitler, are polished by Goebbels into refined rhetoric. He achieves the gruesome apotheosis of this kind of superlative construction on 7 May 1944. The D-Day landings of the English and the Americans are imminent, at which point the *Reich* writes: 'The German people are more worried that the invasion might not come at all than that it might . . . If the enemy really has the intention of starting an operation on which everything depends with something as ludicrous as this, then good night!'

Is this only the gruesome apotheosis for those with hindsight? Surely at the time an attentive reader must have sensed the onset of despair behind the mask of certain victory? Isn't the curse of the superlative all too apparent here?

This curse clings to it of necessity in every language. Because wherever you are, constant exaggeration is always bound to lead to ever greater exaggeration, with the result that a dulling of the senses, scepticism and finally disbelief are inevitable. That is doubtless the case everywhere, but some languages are more receptive to the superlative than others: in Romania, in the Balkans, in the Far East and probably also in North America – in all of these countries a bigger dose of the superlative can be tolerated than with us, and what in our case indicates a fever, is often nothing more than a pleasant rise in temperature. Perhaps this is precisely the reason, or at least a further reason, why the superlative crops up with a vengeance in the LTI; epidemics are supposed to spread like wildfire in places they assail for the first time.

Now it could, of course, be said that Germany had already suffered this linguistic disease once before: in the seventeenth century under the influence of Italy and Spain; but the bombast of that period was harmless, devoid of any of the poison of deliberate mass seduction.

The malignant superlative of the LTI is a new phenomenon in Germany, which is why it has such terrible consequences from the outset, and this is also why it is compelled by its own nature to push itself so far that it becomes meaningless and utterly ineffective, finally bringing about a belief in the very opposite of what it intended. How often I noted down in my diary that some sentence or other of Goebbels's was far too crude a lie, that the man was definitely no advertising genius; on numerous occasions I noted down jokes about Goebbels's big mouth and his effrontery, and on numerous occasions recorded bitter invective about his barefaced lies as 'the voice of the people' from which hope could be drawn.

But there is no *vox populi,* only *voci populi,* and it can only be ascertained in retrospect which of these various voices is the true one – I mean the one which determines the course of events. And even then it can't be said with absolute certainty that all those who laughed at Goebbels's all-too blatant lies actually remained unmoved by them. On countless occasions during my spell as an assistant in Naples I heard people say about some newspaper or other: *è pagato,* it's paid for, it lies for its client, and then on the following day these very same people who had cried *pagato* were absolutely convinced by some obviously bogus piece of news in the same paper. Because it was printed in such bold type, and because the other people believed it. In 1914 I persuaded myself calmly each time that this was a result of the naivety and the temperament of the Neapolitans, after all Montesquieu had written that Naples was more 'of the people' than anywhere else, *plus peuple qu'ailleurs.* Since 1933 I have known incontrovertibly something I had suspected to be the case for a long time and not wanted to admit, namely that it is easy to cultivate such a *plus peuple qu'ailleurs* anywhere; and I also know that a part of every intellectual's soul belongs to the people, that all my awareness of being lied to, and my critical attentiveness, are of no avail when it comes to it: at some point the printed lie will get the better of me when it attacks from all sides and is queried by fewer and fewer around me and finally by no one at all.

No, it's not as simple with the curse of the superlative as logic would have one believe. Certainly, bragging and lies come thick and fast and are finally recognized for what they are, and for some people Goebbels's propaganda ultimately became ineffective inanity. But it is also undeniable that the propaganda exposed as bragging and lies still works if you only have the audacity to continue with it as if nothing had happened; the curse of the superlative is not always self-destructive, but all too often destroys the intellect which defies it; and Goebbels had much more talent than I gave him credit for, and the ineffective inanity was neither as inane nor as ineffective.

Diary, *18 December 1944.* At midday a special announcement came through, the first for years! Totally in the style of the years of the offensive and 'battles of total destruction': 'They unexpectedly fell in from the West Wall for the major attack . . . after brief but intensive preliminary fire . . . first American position overrun . . .' It is out of the question that there is anything more to this than desperate bluff. The end of *Carlos:* 'Let this be my last deceit.' – 'It is your last.'

20 December . . . After all Goebbels has been talking about the strengthening German resistance for weeks now, in the Allied press it is apparently referred to as 'the German miracle'. And it really is miraculous, and the war could go on for years . . .

Chapter 31
From the Great Movement Forward . . .

On 19 December 1941 the Führer and current generalissimo makes an appeal to the Eastern front, the crucial sentences of which are as follows: 'In the wake of their immortal victories against the most dangerous foe of all times – victories the likes of which have never been seen before in the history of the world – the armies in the East must now, following the sudden onset of winter, be redeployed from the great movement forward {*aus dem Zug der Bewegung*} in order to engage in trench warfare on the front line . . . My soldiers! You will . . . understand that my heart belongs to you alone, but that my thoughts and my determination are devoted entirely to the destruction of the enemy, i.e. the victorious ending of this war . . . The Lord will not deny victory to his most courageous soldiers!'

This appeal marks nothing less than the decisive caesura not only in the history of the Second World War, but also in the history of the LTI, and, as a linguistic caesura, it is a twin-headed arrow which rammed into the swollen fabric of that everyday bluster which had been heightened to match the style of Barnum.

It is crawling with triumphal superlatives – but a present tense has become a future tense. From the beginning of the war there had been a poster everywhere covered with flags and bearing the confident message: 'Our flags mean victory!' Up to this point the Allies had been assured over and over again that they were already defeated, and the Russians in particular were told in no uncertain terms that it would be impossible for them to go on the offensive again after so many defeats. And now the absolute victory is being moved into an indefinite future, and God will first have to be petitioned for it. From this point '*der Endsieg* {final victory}', that expression both of longing and stalling, becomes increasingly common, and soon that set phrase crops up which the French clung to during the First World War: *on les aura.* This is translated as '*der Sieg wird unser sein* {victory will be ours}' and written at the bottom of a poster and a stamp depicting the imperial eagle attempting to get the better of an enemy snake.

But the caesura is not only evident in the change of tense. All the great works cannot hide the fact that the forward momentum has shifted into reverse, that they are searching for something to cling on to. A 'movement {*Bewegung*}' has petrified into 'front line trench warfare {*Stellungsfront*}': within the LTI this means considerably more than in any other language. It had been explained in so many texts and articles, in so many different expressions and contexts that trench warfare was a professional error, a weakness, indeed even a sin to which the army of the Third Reich would never succumb, not now or at any time in the future, because *Bewegung* was the quintessence, the unique quality, the very lifeblood of National Socialism which, after the '*Aufbruch* {new departure}' – a sacred LTI word borrowed from Romanticism! – would never be allowed to come to rest. The idea is not to be sceptical, not to be soberly liberal, not to be weak-willed like the previous era; the aim is not to let things dominate you, but to dominate; one wants to act, and never let go of 'the injunction to act {*das Gesetz des Handlens*}' (again a favourite phrase, first used by Clausewitz and quoted ad nauseam during the war until it became an embarrassing absurdity). Or, to put it more grandly and to display one's education, one wants to be '*dynamisch* {dynamic}'.

Marinetti's Futurism had a decisive impact on the National Socialists by way of the Italian Fascists, and it is a German Expressionist, Johst, who will become president of the Nazi academy of writers, despite the fact that the majority of his friends in the early days were communists. *Tendenz* {leaning, bias}, vigorous movement towards a goal, is the elementary and universal order of the day. Movement is the essence of Nazism to such an extent that it unhesitatingly refers to itself as 'the movement', and to its birthplace, Munich, as the 'capital of the movement'. Moreover, it leaves the word unadorned, despite usually searching for mellifluous, exaggerated terms for everything that it deems important.

Its entire vocabulary is dominated by the will to movement and to action. *'Sturm* {storm}' is, as it were, its first and last word: at the beginning there is the training of the SA, the Storm Troopers, and at the end the *Volkssturm* {German territorial army}, a variation of the *Landsturm* {territorial reserve} of 1813 that is literally closer to the people {*volksnäher*}. The SS has its cavalry storm, the army its storm troops and storm artillery, the rabble-rousing anti-Jewish newspaper was called the *Stürmer. 'Schlagartige Aktionen* {abrupt actions}' are the SA's first acts of heroism, and Goebbels's newspaper is called the *Angriff* {attack}. The war must be a *Blitzkrieg* {literally: a lightning battle}, and all kinds of sporting expressions provide fodder for the LTI in general.

The will to action spawns new verbs. They want to get rid of the Jews, so they *entjuden* {dejew}, they want to make sure that all business life is in Aryan hands, so they *arisieren* {aryanize}, they want to re-establish the purity of their ancestral blood, so they *aufnorden* {nordify}. Intransitive verbs, to which technology has assigned new meanings, are reactivated as transitive ones: one flies {*fliegt*} a heavy machine, one flies in {*fliegt*} boots and provisions, one freezes {*friert*} vegetables with new techniques of deep freezing, where one previously had to refer, rather more long-windedly, to making something frozen {*gefrieren machen*}.

Part of the aim is certainly to express oneself more stringently and briskly than is usually the case, and it is this same aim which turns a *Berichterstatter* {a man who makes a report} into a *Berichter* {reporter}, the *Lastwagen* {lorry} into the *Laster*, the *Bombenflugzeug* {bomber plane} into the *Bomber*, and which finally ends up replacing the word with an abbreviation. With the result that *Lastwagen, Laster, LKW*[1] corresponds to a crescendo from positive to superlative. And ultimately the entire predilection for the superlative and, if one looks at the whole picture, all the rhetoric of the LTI can be traced back to the principle of movement.

And now all this is to be displaced from the great movement forward into stasis (and retreat). Charlie Chaplin achieved his most comic effect by suddenly abandoning a headlong dash and freezing like a sculpture cast or carved for some vestibule. The LTI must on no account become ridiculous, it mustn't freeze, it mustn't admit that its upward movement

---

[1] Abbreviation of *Lastkraftwagen,* a further term for lorry.

has become a downward one. The appeal to the forces in the East marks the beginning of the attempt at a cover-up which characterizes the final phase of the LTI. Of course there has been a cover-up from the outset (since the First World War the modern fairy-tale word *Tarnung* {camouflage} has been used for this activity); but up until this point it had been a cover-up of crimes – 'since this morning we have been returning enemy fire', as the first war-time bulletin would have it – and from now on it is a cover-up of powerlessness.

Above all the word *Stellungsfront* {front line trench warfare}, entirely at odds with their principles, has to be covered up, and the unhappy memories of the endless trench warfare of the First World War have to be evaded. It is no more allowed to appear this time than the swedes of yesteryear are allowed to be served up at table. Thus the LTI is promptly enriched with the lasting phrase *'beweglicher Verteidigungskrieg* {a defensive war on the move}'. Even though we have to admit that we have been forced into a defensive position, we can at least preserve the epithet signifying our true nature. And we also don't defend ourselves from the confines of a trench, rather, we fight with much greater freedom of movement within and before an enormous fortress. Our fortress is called Europe, and for a time there was a lot of talk of the *'Vorfeld Afrika* {Africa as the territory in front of the main battle-line}'. From the point of view of the LTI, the word *Vorfeld* is fortunate on two levels: on the one hand it testifies to the freedom of movement we still have left, and on the other it suggests that we may well relinquish the African position, but that this would not be a decisive loss. Later the fortress Europe will become the fortress Germany, and at the very end there is the fortress Berlin – to be sure! there was no lack of movement in the German army to the very last. The fact that this movement was constantly backwards was never said in so many words, the fact was covered up with veil after veil; the words *Niederlage* {defeat} and *Rückzug* {retreat}, and above all *Flucht* {flight} remain unspoken. *Rückschlag* {setback} was used instead of *Rückzug* – that sounds less definitive; rather than fleeing one was simply putting some distance between oneself and the enemy; he never made any *Durchbrüche* {breakthroughs}, they were always just *Einbrüche* {inroads}, at worst *'tiefe Einbrüche* {deep inroads}' which were *'aufgefangen* {cushioned}' and *'abgeriegelt* {blocked off}' because, of course, ours was an *'elastische Front* {elastic front line}'. From time to time, in order to deny the enemy an advantage, we would undertake a voluntary '*Frontverkürzung* {shortening of the front line}' or a '*Frontbegradigung* {straightening of the front line}'.

As long as these strategic measures occurred abroad, the majority of the population didn't need to know how serious they were. Even in spring 1943 (in the *Reich* of 2 May) Goebbels could introduce a charming diminutive: 'We are a trifle susceptible here and there on the periphery of our military activities.' *Anfällig* {susceptible} is the term used for people who tend to catch colds easily, or who have easily upset stomachs, but never of people who are really ill or in a seriously critical condition. And even this susceptibility was disingenuously transformed by Goebbels into mere over-sensitivity on our part and arrogance on the enemy's: the Germans had in effect been so spoiled by a long series of victories that they responded far too emotionally to every setback, whilst the enemy, used to receiving a good thrashing, tended to celebrate inordinately the most insignificant of 'peripheral successes'.

This multitude of cover-up words is all the more extraordinary given that it is in stark contrast to the general, innate and essential poverty of the LTI. Indeed there were even a few modest metaphors here and there, although not original ones of course. Commander Hitler modelled his General Winter on *Général Danube* who had blocked the path of Commander Napoleon at Aspern. General Winter became a much-cited personality and spawned numerous sons – I can only think of General Hunger, but I'm sure I must have come across numerous other allegorical generals. Difficulties that could not be denied were known for a long time as *Engpässe* {bottlenecks}, an expression almost as well-chosen as the *Vorfeld,* because here too there is, right away, the idea of movement (of pushing oneself through). On one occasion a correspondent with a gift for language brought this out neatly by returning the faded metaphor to its original context. He reported that a column of tanks had dared to enter a bottleneck between two minefields.

This circumspect way of describing the crisis was adequate for a very long time because, in complete contrast to the customary German *Blitzkrieg,* the enemy only engaged in 'snail-like offensives' and only made headway at a 'snail's pace'. Only during the last year of the war, when the catastrophe could no longer be concealed, was it given a more explicit name, albeit one that still amounted to a cover-up: defeats were now termed 'crises', but the word never appeared on its own. Attention was always either directed away from Germany to the 'global crisis' or the 'crisis facing western civilization', or alternatively a phrase was used which very quickly became stereotypical – 'a crisis under control'. One brought it under control 'by fighting one's way out of it'. 'Fighting one's way out' was the euphemism for the escape of a few regiments from pincer movements in which whole divisions were lost. The crisis was also brought under control by not allowing oneself to be thrown back over the German border by the enemy, but instead by voluntarily extricating oneself and deliberately 'letting them in' in order that they could be all the more effectively destroyed once they had ventured too far forward. 'We have let them in – on 20 April everything will look very different!', I heard that said as late as April 1945.

And finally, ossified into a scientific formula and turned into a spell, there was the 'new weapon', the magic letter V that could always be heightened. If the V1 wasn't up to it and if the V2 remained ineffective, why shouldn't one keep one's hopes alive by banking on the V3 and the V4?

Hitler's final cry of desperation was as follows: 'Vienna is becoming German again, Berlin is remaining German and Europe is not becoming Russian.' And now, when he is finally beaten, he even effaces the future tense of the final victory, which for so long had replaced the original present tense. Vienna is becoming German again – the believers have to be persuaded that something is dawning in the present which has already been propelled into the farthest reaches of the impossible. Some V or other will make it happen, you'll see!

The magic letter V takes a strange revenge: V was originally the secret code used by the illegal freedom fighters in the occupied Netherlands to identify themselves, V stood for *Vrijheid,* freedom. The Nazis appropriated the sign, reinterpreted it as standing for 'Victoria' and shamelessly forced Czechoslovakia, a country more cruelly tyrannized than Holland, to display this conceited and long-since fraudulent sign of victory on its postmarks, on the doors of its cars and its railway coaches. And then, in the final phase of the war, V became the abbreviation for *Vergeltung* {vengeance}, the emblem of the 'new weapon' which would avenge and bring to an end all the suffering inflicted on Germany. But the Allies advanced inexorably, and there was no chance of sending further V-rockets to England, and no chance of protecting German cities from enemy bombs. When our city of Dresden was destroyed, there was not a single defensive shot fired from the German side, and not a single German plane took off – the retaliation was there, but it hit Germany.

Chapter 32
Boxing

At one point in his letters, Rathenau says that he himself was in favour of a peace based on rapprochement, but that Ludendorff, on the other hand, had wanted, in his own words, 'to fight to win'. The expression derives from the racetrack, where you either bet to win or make a place bet. Rathenau, with his soft spot for aestheticism, puts the phrase in supercilious inverted commas – he clearly considers it undignified to apply such a term to the military context, despite the fact that it comes from a sport long favoured by the aristocracy; racing has always been something for the aristocracy and feudal officer corps, and amongst the amateur jockeys there were lieutenants and cavalry captains with the most noble aristocratic names. For the sensitive Rathenau, however, this does not expunge the enormous difference between a game of sport and the deadly seriousness of war.

In the Third Reich much store was set by covering up this difference. That which to the outside world must appear to be nothing more than an innocent and peaceful game to safeguard the health of the nation, must in fact be a preparation for war, and must also be appreciated in all its seriousness by the population at large. There is now a university for sport and a sports academic is at least on a par with any other academic – undoubtedly superior to them in the eyes of the Führer. The significance of this evaluation is corroborated and encouraged in the mid-1930s by the names given to cigarettes and cigarillos: people smoke '*Sportstudent*' and '*Wehrsport* {military sport}' and '*Sportbanner*' and '*Sportnixe*' {sporting belle}.

The Olympics of 1936 were a further factor in the popularization and glorification of sport. It matters a great deal to the Third Reich that in the eyes of everyone at this international event it should appear as a leading light in the civilized world, and in accordance with its whole outlook – which places physical prowess on a level with intellectual achievement, or rather above it – it surrounds the Olympics with an incredible splendour, to the extent that for an instant even racial differences are forgotten in the glitter: the Jew Helene Meyer, 'blonde He', is allowed to contribute her skill at foil to the victory of the German fencing team, and the high jump of a black American is celebrated as if the leap had been achieved by an Aryan and Nordic man. Thus the *Berliner Illustrierte* can carry the phrase 'the world's greatest tennis genius', and straight after, in all seriousness, compare an Olympic achievement with the actions of Napoleon I.

The reputation of sport is heightened and promoted thirdly through the importance attached to the automobile industry, through the 'Führer's roads' and all the exalted road races held at home and abroad; here all the factors which pertained to military sport and the Olympics also play a part, coupled with the crucial problem of job creation.

But long before military sport and the Olympics and the Führer's roads could make an appearance, Adolf Hitler had a simple and brutal passion. In *Mein Kampf,* when he sets out the 'fundamental principles of education in the *völkisch* {national} state' and discusses sport in detail, he talks more about boxing than anything else. His observations culminate in the following sentence: 'If only our entire intellectual elite had not been educated so exclusively in the refined codes of polite behaviour, had it instead learned how to box properly, the German revolution of pimps, deserters and other such riffraff would never have been possible.' A moment or two earlier Hitler had been defending boxing against the accusation of exceptional brutality – probably with justification, I'm not an expert; but in talking about boxing he turns it into a plebeian activity (neither proletarian nor traditional), accompanying, or resulting from, a furious row.

All this has to be borne in mind when it comes to appreciating the role sport plays in the language of 'our Doctor'. For years Goebbels was known as 'our Doctor', for years he signed every article with 'Doctor', and within the Party his academic qualification was thought of as highly as the qualifications of the ecclesiastical Doctors during the founding years of the church. Our Doctor is the architect of the language and ideas of the masses, even if he does appropriate slogans from the Führer, and even if Rosenberg, in his capacity as philosopher of the Party, is in charge of a special department which incorporates, amongst other things, an 'Institute for Research into Judaism'.

Goebbels spelled out his motto at the 1934 'Party Convention of Loyalty', which had obtained its name to help wipe out and efface the memory of the Röhm revolt: 'We must speak the language that the people understand. Anyone who wants to speak to the people must, as Martin Luther says, listen to the man in the street.' The place in which the conqueror and Gauleiter of the Capital of the Reich – to the last Berlin was referred to in this florid manner in every official report, even when the individual parts of the Reich had long since fallen into enemy hands, and Berlin itself was but a half-destroyed and dying city cut off from the outside world – the place in which Goebbels most frequently speaks to the Berliners is the Sportpalast, and the images which seem to him to be the closest to the people, and to which he most often turns, are those he gathers from sport. It never occurs to him that it could be a disparagement of military heroism to compare it with sporting achievements; the gladiator is both warrior and sportsman, and for him the gladiator is the epitome of heroism.

Any sport will do as far as he is concerned, and one often has the impression that he has become so used to these words that he is entirely immune to the images they conjure up. A sentence from September 1944: 'We will not run out of breath when it comes to the final sprint' – I don't think that in saying this Goebbels really saw in his mind's eye the runner or cyclist making a dash for the line. It is different in the case of the pledge that the victor will be 'he who crosses the finishing tape first, even if only by a short head'. Here the very detail of the image suggests that it is being taken seriously as a metaphor. And if, in this case, racing is alluded to merely by reference to the finish, there is a further example in which an entire sports meeting is invoked, and in which not a single terminus technicus relating to football is shied away from. On 18 July 1943 Goebbels writes the following in the *Reich*: 'Just as the victorious team at a major football match leaves the pitch in a different frame of mind from the one in which it first stepped onto it, so the people will look quite different depending on whether they have finished a war or are just beginning one . . . At this (early) stage the military confrontation could not in any way be described as open. We were fighting exclusively in the enemy's penalty area . . .' And now the Axis partners are told they should capitulate! It is as just 'as if the captain of a losing team were to make the unreasonable suggestion to the captain of a winning team that the game be called off when the score line reaches, say, 9:2 . . . Any team which agreed to something of this kind would deserve to be ridiculed and derided. The team has already won, and all it now has to do is defend its victory.'

On occasion our Doctor mixes expressions from different branches of sport. In September 1943 he holds forth on the fact that strength consists not only in giving but also in receiving, and that no one should ever disclose the fact that they are a bit weak at the knees. Otherwise, he continued, shifting from boxing to cycling, one is soon 'in danger of being shaken off'.

But the vast majority of images, the ones most easily remembered and by far the most brutal, were always taken from boxing. It is futile trying to examine how the connection with sport, and boxing in particular, actually came about – one is still struck dumb by the complete absence of human emotions on display here. Following the catastrophe at Stalingrad, which had devoured so many lives, Goebbels is able to find no better expression of unbroken courage than this sentence: 'We wipe the blood from our eyes in order to see clearly, and, when it is time to enter the ring for the next round, our legs stand firm once again.' And a few days later: 'A people who so far has only boxed with its left hand, and is now in the process of bandaging up its right ready to employ it ruthlessly in the next round, has no reason to be soft.' In the following spring and summer, as German cities everywhere collapsed burying their occupants beneath them, as the hope of final victory could only be kept afloat under the most ridiculous pretences, Goebbels finds the following images to capture the situation: 'On becoming world champion, a boxer does not normally become weaker than before, even if his opponent has broken his nose in the process.' And '. . . what does even the most refined gentleman do when three common thugs attack him, wanting to box him into submission rather than adhere to a strict code of conduct?[1] He takes his coat off and rolls up his shirt sleeves.' This is a precise imitation of the plebeian admiration of boxing peddled

---

[1]The German word is *Komment,* the code of conduct adhered to by students belonging to university fraternities.

by Hitler, and what is behind it, openly for all to see, is an attempt to make people wait patiently for the new weapon which does not adhere to any code of conduct.

I want to give the crassness of Goebbels's propaganda the credit it deserves, in duration and extent its impact speaks for itself. But I simply can't believe that the boxing images really did what was expected of them. They certainly made our Doctor a popular figure, and they also made the war popular – but not in the way they were supposed to: they stripped it of all its heroism, and accorded it the brutality and, ultimately, the indifference associated with the work of the landsknechts . . .

In December 1944 the *Reich* published an encouraging article on the current situation by the author Schwarz van Berk, who was highly regarded at the time. His observations were deliberately bereft of passion. Its title read 'Can Germany Technically Lose on Points? I Bet It Can't'. It would be completely wrong to refer here to the same callousness evident in the sentences uttered by Goebbels following the disaster of Stalingrad. No, the only thing that has disappeared is the sense that there is an immeasurable difference between boxing and waging war – war has lost all of its tragic grandeur . . .

Vox populi – again and again the question of someone who experienced all this as to which of these many voices will be the decisive one! During the final weeks of our flight, and of the war, we met a group of people on the way into an Upper Bavarian village near Aichach who were busy digging deep holes. Next to the diggers stood a number of onlookers, some of them war-wounded in uniform, and with only one leg or one arm, some of them grey-haired civilians of a great age. A lively conversation was under way; it was clear that they were soldiers of the *Volkssturm,* who were to fire their bazookas from these holes at the oncoming vehicles. During these days, as everything was collapsing around us, I had repeatedly heard the most extraordinary professions of faith in the forthcoming victory; what was being aired quite openly here was the conviction, indeed the cheerful conviction, that all resistance was useless, and that this futile war would be over either today or tomorrow. 'Jump down there – into my own grave? . . . Not me!' – 'And if they string you up?' – 'Fine, I'll clamber down, but I'm taking a white handkerchief with me.' – 'That's what all of us should do. Hold it up high as a white flag.' – 'It would be even better, and more impressive (they are Americans after all, sportsmen) if we throw the things their way, just as one throws in the towel . . .'

Chapter 33
Gefolgschaft

Whenever I hear the word *Gefolgschaft* {workforce, entourage, literally: group of followers} I see before me the *Gefolgschaftssaal* {workers' room, hall} at Thiemig & Möbius, and two images spring to mind. On the wall above the door, painted in big, permanent letters, is the word '*Gefolgschaftssaal*'. Sometimes a sign hangs below it, from a nail in the door frame, with the inscription 'Jews!', together with the same warning sign in the WC next door. If this is the case the extremely long room contains a huge table in the shape of a horseshoe and the chairs to go with it, coat-hooks along half the length of one of the long walls, a lectern and a piano on one of the short walls and nothing else other than the same electric clock which hangs in every factory and office. At other times the two signs on the door to the hall and the WC have disappeared, in which case the lectern is draped in a flag bearing a swastika, flags frame a large picture of Hitler above the podium, and the wood-panelled walls are all decked at head height with a garland entwined with little swastika flags. If this is the case – the transformation from bare to festive is normally effected during the morning – then we spend a more pleasant half-hour lunch break than usual because we are then allowed home a quarter of an hour earlier than normal, as immediately after the end of work the hall has to be cleared of Jews {*judenrein*} and re-dedicated to its function as a site for cult practices.

All this is connected with the orders of the Gestapo, on the one hand, and the humanity of our boss, on the other, which has resulted in a lot of trouble and danger for him, and the odd piece of horse-meat sausage from the Aryan canteen for us, and which ultimately did the boss himself some good. The Gestapo had decreed that the Jews were to be strictly segregated from the Aryan workers. At the workplace itself either this could not be achieved at all, or it could be achieved only partially; as a consequence it was adhered to all the more strictly in the cloakroom and canteen. Herr M. could just as well have stuck us in some dingy little room in the cellar; instead he gave us the bright hall.

How many problems and aspects of the LTI went through my mind in this hall as I listened to the never-ending quarrels of the others – one moment, and despite everything, over the basic question of Zionism versus Germanness, the next, and more frequently and bitterly, about the privilege of not having to wear the star, and the next about something totally unimportant. But what bothered me every day afresh, never to be entirely erased by other trains of thought in this hall, or drowned out by any of the quarrelling, was the word *Gefolgschaft.* The whole emotional mendacity of Nazism, the whole mortal sin of deliberately twisting things founded on reason into the realm of the emotions, and deliberate distortion for the sake of sentimental mystification: all of this comes back to me when I remember this hall, just as on festive occasions, after our departure, the factory's Aryan workforce must have crowded together there.

Gefolgschaft! What kind of people were they really who crowded there together? They were blue-collar and white-collar workers who for a certain remuneration carried out certain duties. Everything that took place between them and their employers was governed by rules and regulations; it was possible, but certainly not necessary, and maybe even annoying, that there existed convivial relations between the bosses and certain individuals amongst their number. The regulatory instance governing them all, however, was the impersonal and imperturbable rule of law. And now, in the *Gefolgschaftssaal*, they were all divested of this regulatory instance, only to be dressed up and transfigured by the single word *Gefolgschaft*, which burdened them with the Old Germanic tradition, it turned them into vassals, into weapon-bearing liegemen forced to keep faith with their aristocratic, knightly masters.

Was this dressing up just a harmless game?

Certainly not. It twisted a peaceful relationship into a belligerent one; it stifled criticism; it led directly to the cast of mind expressed in that sentence emblazoned on every banner: 'Führer, command and we will obey {*folgen*}!'

All it takes is just a tiny digression into Old German, which seems poetic on account of its age and the fact it is not longer in everyday use, or perhaps now and then simply the omission of a syllable, and an entirely different mood is summoned up in the person being addressed, his thoughts are channelled in a completely different direction or switched off entirely, only to be replaced by the obligatory faith in what he hears. An Alliance of Defenders of the Law {*Ein Bund der Rechtswahrer*} sounds incomparably more solemn than an Association of Lawyers {*eine Vereinigung der Rechtsanwälte*}, someone who discharges their duties {*Amtswalter*} sounds incomparably more impressive than an official {*Beamter*} or functionary {*Funktionär*}, and if I were to read '*Amtswaltung* {office for discharging duties}' rather than '*Verwaltung* {administration}' above an office door, then the atmosphere is nothing short of sacred. At an office of this kind I would not simply be served as a matter of duty, but rather 'looked after {*betreut*}', and the person who looks after me deserves my gratitude at all times, and I must not in any circumstances offend him by making unreasonable demands or casting doubt on his activities.

But am I not perhaps overstepping the mark here in my condemnation of the LTI? After all, *betreuen* {to look after} is an expression which has always been in common usage, and the Civil Code recognizes the trustee {*Treuhänder*}. Of course, but the Third Reich used *betreuen* inordinately and extravagantly, and integrated it into a system – during the First World War students in the army were provided with study material and attended courses to further their education, in the Second they were '*fernbetreut* {looked after from afar}'.

The focus and goal of this system was *Rechtsempfinden* {the sense of justice}; there was never any mention of *Rechtsdenken* {the concept of justice}, and also never of a sense of justice on its own, rather always of 'a healthy sense of justice'. And healthy meant whatever accorded with the will and interest of the Party. After the Grünspan affair this healthy sense became the motivation for plundering Jewish property, whereby the term '*Buße* {atonement}' once again had a slightly Old German ring to it.

To justify the well-organized arson attacks to which the synagogues fell victim at the time, it was necessary to resort to more robust and far-reaching words, a mere healthy sense of something was not enough. The result was the phase of the *kochender Volksseele* {the raging soul of the people}. Of course this expression was not coined for permanent use, whilst the words *spontan* {spontaneous} and *Instinkt* {instinct}, which had just taken off at the time, became a permanent feature of the LTI, with instinct in particular playing a leading role to the last. A true Teuton reacts spontaneously when there is an appeal to his instincts. After 20 July 1944 Goebbels wrote that the assassination attempt on Hitler could only be explained in terms of an 'eclipsing of instinctual forces by those of a diabolical intellect'.

Here the LTI's preference for everything to do with emotions and instinct is reduced to its lowest common denominator: the herd of rams, blessed with a keen instinct, follows the chief ram even if he jumps into the sea – (or rather, as Rabelais put it, is thrown into it, and who can say to what extent Hitler voluntarily jumped into the blood-bath of war on 1 September 1939, and to what extent his preceding mistakes and crimes forced him into this insane venture?). The insistence on the emotional is always encouraged by the LTI; the association with tradition only serves the LTI on certain occasions. Certain things have to be borne in mind. From the outset the Führer has a strained, adversarial relationship with all that is *völkisch* {national}; even though he later has nothing to fear from it, he can still only make partial use of its conservatism and hyper-Germanness, because he also wants the support of the industrial workers, with the result that technology and Americanisms mustn't get a raw deal, let alone be spurned altogether. Without doubt the glorification of the farmer, wedded to the earth, steeped in tradition and hostile to all things new, remains constant to the last, and the declaration of faith expressed in the formula BLUBO (*Blut und Boden* {blood and soil}) is aimed directly at him, or rather derived from his very way of life.

From summer 1944 a Low German word that had long since dropped out of use in Germany gained a new and tragic currency: the *Treck* {trek of people}. Previously we had only known about the treks of Boers in Africa searching for land. Now resettlers and refugees being led back home {*heimgeführt*} into German territory from the East were trekking along every country road. Of course this 'home {*heim*}' is itself something of an affectation, indeed a very old one, which brings us back from the period of misfortune to the glorious beginnings. Back then the slogan was: Adolf Hitler is bringing the Saar back home!, and cheerful Berlin cockiness could still have Goebbels travel to Germany's former colonies to teach the Negro children there to chant in unison 'We want to return to the Reich!' And now uprooted settlers, with at most a few possessions they had been able to rescue, were being brought home to the most unstable conditions imaginable.

In mid-July I read in a Dresden newspaper (oh yes, alongside the Party paper proper, the *Freiheitskampf* {Battle for Freedom}, there was only one other newspaper, which is why I haven't bothered to note its masthead) an article from some correspondent or other: 'The Trek of 350,000 People'. This description, which must undoubtedly have appeared in numerous papers with at most minor variations, is exemplary and interesting for two reasons: it sentimentalized and glorified the farming community yet again, just as it had been celebrated in peacetime during the harvest festivals on the Bückeberg, and it heaped up quite unscrupulously all the choicest morsels of the LTI, unearthing in the process a fair number of decorative terms which, in those dreadful times, had dropped out of use. These 350,000 German settlers, who were being transferred from southern Russia to the Warthegau, were 'German people of the best Germanic stock, upright Germans through and through', they were of 'biologically unadulterated productivity' – under German leadership the number of live births had risen during the period 1941 to 1943 from 17 to 40 per thousand – they were, 'incomparably enthusiastic as farmers and settlers', they were 'filled with a fanatical enthusiasm for their new homeland and national community {*Volksgemeinschaft*}', etc. The final observation, that on account of all this they deserved to be recognized as 'Germans of equal status', especially given that their young people had long been members of the Waffen-SS, suggested, however, that everything was not quite as it should be when it came to their ability to speak German and their level of German acculturation; be that as it may: in this 'unique' trek of people the farming community is once again romanticized with what had initially been a rather one-sided enthusiasm for all that is traditional.

However, from the master of propaganda himself, and the LTI as a whole, it can be ascertained quite clearly how, for the sake of the whole, he was able to dissolve the original alliance between tradition and emotion. It was as apparent to him as to the Führer that the people could only be got controlled by working on their emotions. 'Does a bourgeois intellectual understand the first thing about the people?' he writes in his diaries *From the Kaiserhof to the Reich Chancellery* (doubtless cleverly polished for public consumption). The obligatory, universal and interminable emphasis on the link between every object, relationship or person and *das Volk* {the nation, people} – you are either a *Volksgenosse* {national comrade}, *Volkskanzler* {national chancellor}, *Volksschädling* {national pest}, *volksnah* {close to the people}, *volksfremd* {an enemy of the people}, *volksbewußt* {responsive to the people}, etc. *ad infinitum* – this alone makes for an abiding emotional intensity which to some extent always sounds hypocritical and shameless.

So where does Goebbels seek out the people, to whom he claims to belong, and about whom he knows so much? This question can be answered *ex negativo*. The fact that, according to the same diary entries, the theatres in Berlin are only populated 'by an Asiatic horde on the sands of the Mark Brandenburg' doesn't tell us anything, it is merely a manifestation of the usual anti-intellectualism and anti-Semitism; more revealing is a word which he uses repeatedly in *Battle for Berlin,* and always in a pejorative sense. This book was written before the takeover of power, but at a time when he was already sure of victory; it depicts the years 1926/27, the period during which Goebbels, having left the Ruhr, begins to conquer the capital for his party. The word used over and over again to express aversion is '*Asphalt*'.

Asphalt is the man-made surface which separates the city-dweller from the natural soil. It was first used metaphorically in Germany (around 1890) in the poetry of Naturalism. At that time an 'asphalt flower' was a Berlin prostitute. It implied little or no censure, because in these poems the prostitute was a more or less tragic character. In the case of Goebbels an entire asphalt flora blossoms, and every one of its flowers is poisonous and proud of the fact. Berlin is the asphalt monster, its Jewish newspapers, sorry efforts of the Jewish yellow press, are asphalt organs, the revolutionary flag of the NSDAP must be vigorously 'rammed into the asphalt', the path to ruin (Marxist attitudes and statelessness {*Vaterlandslosigkeit*}) is 'asphalted by the Jews with hollow phrases and hypocritical promises'. The breathless speed of this 'asphalt monster has made people heartless and unfeeling'; as a result, the inhabitants are a 'formless mass of anonymous, global proletarians' and the Berlin proletarian is 'a thing without a real home {*ein Stück Heimatlosigkeit*}'.

What Goebbels felt was missing completely in Berlin at the time was 'any kind of patriarchal bond'. He himself came from the Ruhr; he had been in direct contact with industrial workers there too, but they are different and special: they have been 'rooted to the soil since time immemorial', the bedrock of the local population consists of 'long-established Westphalians'. Thus at the beginning of the 'thirties Goebbels still adheres to the traditional *Blubo* cult and sets the soil off against the asphalt. Later he becomes more cautious in expressing his preference for the farmers, but it was to be twelve years before he would take back the defamation of the asphalt people, and even in this retraction he remained a liar, refusing to admit that he himself had taught people to despise the city-dwellers. 'We have great respect', he writes on 16 April 1944 in the *Reich* having experienced the terrible bomb damage at first hand, 'for the indestructible rhythm of life, and the rugged will to live demonstrated by our metropolitan population. They have not become as rootless on the asphalt as we were led to believe by many a well-meaning but overly theoretical book . . . The vital energy of our people is as dependable here as it is amongst the German farmers.'

Of course it isn't the case that the emotional exaltation and courting of the working classes was delayed until this point; efforts had been made to woo them with sentimental overtures as well. When Jews were banned from driving cars in the wake of the Grünspan affair, Himmler, Minister of Police at the time, justified the step not only on the grounds of the 'unreliability' of the Jews, but also because their driving was an insult to the 'German driving community {*deutsche Verkehrsgemeinschaft*}', especially since they had had the impertinence to drive on the 'motorways of the Reich, built by the hands of German workers'. Yet the mixture of emotion and traditionalism leads first and foremost to the farmers and country customs – '*Brauchtum* {customs}' is also one of those sentimental words with a poetic, Old German root. In March 1945 I racked my brains every day to understand a picture in the display window of the *Falkensteiner Anzeiger.* It showed what was undoubtedly a very pretty half-timbered village house and, below it, a quotation from Rosenberg to the effect that one old German farmhouse accommodates more 'spiritual freedom and creative potential than all the skyscraper cities and corrugated iron huts put together'. I have attempted in vain to find an explanation for this sentence; it can only be found in Nazi-Nordic hubris and its substitution of emotion for thought. In the realm of the LTI the sentimentalizing of things is not, however, necessarily coupled with the urge to fall back on some tradition or other.

It can also associate itself quite freely with the everyday, it can turn to commonplace, colloquial expressions and even jocular terms, it can also make use of what appear to be highly sober neologisms. Right at the beginning I noted the following on the same day: 'Kempinski advert: "Gourmet Hamper Prussia 50 M., Gourmet Hamper Fatherland 75 M." and in the same paper official instructions for making an "*Eintopf* {stew, literally: single pot}". What a crude and provocative technique – used initially during the First World War – to advertise some delicacy or other by arousing patriotic feelings; how clever and evocative to give food regulations a name of this kind! The same dish for everyone, a national community {*Volksgemeinschaft*} rooted in the most everyday and essential of things, a uniform simplicity for rich and poor in the service of the fatherland, the most momentous thing encapsulated in a plain and simple word! *Eintopf* – all of us eat what has been frugally cooked together in a single pot, we all eat from one and the same pot . . .' The word *Eintopf* may well have been widespread for a long time as a culinary *terminus technicus*: introducing it, loaded with emotional associations, into the official language of the LTI is, from a Nazi point of view, a stroke of genius. The expression 'Winter Charity {*Winterhilfe*}' is on a par with the *Eintopf*. What in reality was an obligatory contribution was disingenuously turned into something voluntary, an emotionally prompted donation.

And it is also a case of sentimentalism when official statements talk of schools for *Jungen und Mädel* {lads and lasses} (rather than *Knaben und Mädchen* {boys and girls}), when the '*Hitlerjungen* {Hitler youths}' and the '*deutschen Mädel* {German lasses, girls}' (of the BDM) play their fundamental role in the education system of the Third Reich. Of course, in this case it is a sentimentalizing with a deliberate minus sign attached to it: *Junge* and *Mädel* don't only sound more traditional and hearty than *Knabe* and *Mädchen,* but also earthier. *Mädel* in particular clears the way for the subsequent term '*Waffenhelferin* {female military auxiliary}', which itself is a smoke-screen of a word, or at least half a one, and should under no circumstances be confused with *Flintenweib* {gunwoman, female enemy soldier} – if it were one might just as well confuse the *Volkssturm* with the partisans.

When, however, at the very last minute – 'the final hour' is not the right phase for it any more – the decision is made to go over quite openly to gang warfare, a name is chosen for this activity which evokes the terror associated with the gothic horror story: on the official radio station the warriors refer to themselves as 'werewolves'. This amounted to yet another link with tradition, with the oldest of them all in fact, with mythology. And thus, at the very end, an extraordinarily reactionary outlook was exposed yet again through language, the notion of falling back entirely on the primitive, most predatory beginnings of mankind, which thus revealed Nazism in its true colours.

Clearly in a more harmless form, but still mixed with a good dose of hypocrisy, sentimentalism made its presence felt when in political geography, for example, reference was made to the 'heartland of Bulgaria'. Ostensibly this merely referred to a central location, to the central importance of the country in relation to its neighbours in an economic and military context; but behind it, implicit yet also to some extent explicit, lay an attempt to court friendship, an expression of sympathy with a 'heartland {*Herzland*}'. Finally, the word utilized most powerfully and most commonly by the Nazis for emotional effect is '*Erlebnis* {experience}'. Normal usage draws a clear distinction: we live {*leben*} every hour of our lives from birth to death, but only the most exceptional moments, those in which our passions are aroused, those in which we sense the workings of fate, can be deemed real experiences. The LTI deliberately draws everything into the realm of experience. 'Young people experience Wilhelm Tell' announces a headline which, out of many similar examples, has stayed with me. The true purpose behind this use of the word was exposed by a remark made to the press by the provincial head of the Reich's Literary Chamber in Saxony apropos a week-long book festival in October 1935: *Mein Kampf,* he claimed, is the bible of National Socialism and the New Germany, one must 'experience {*durchleben*}' it from beginning to end . . .

All of these things, first one and then another, went through my mind as I entered the *Gefolgschaftssaal*, and it is true: they all follow on from this one word, they all owe their existence to the same tendency . . .

Towards the end of the time I spent working in the group at the factory, I came across the novel *Eine Zeit stirbt* (An Age Comes to an End) by Georg Hermann, author of *Jettchen Gebert.* The book appeared in the Jewish Book Club and showed clear signs of having been influenced from its very conception by the ideas of fledgling Nazism. I have no idea why there are no detailed comments on the book as a whole in my diary; I merely noted a single sentence from one particular scene: 'Gumpert's wife quickly leaves the cemetery chapel before the funeral service for his mistress begins, "and, with less haste, but at a brisk pace, her *Gefolgschaft* does precisely what a *Gefolgschaft* is supposed to do, and follows her".' At the time I took this to be straightforward irony, for that Jewish irony which the Nazis so hated because it invariably has a go at hypocritical emotions; I told myself that he was stabbing the inflated word and letting it shrivel up pathetically. Today I see this passage differently. I think that it is full of profound bitterness rather than irony. For what, after all, was the ultimate purpose and eventual success of all these overblown emotions? Emotion was not itself the be-all and end-all, it was only a means to an end, a step in a particular direction. Emotion had to suppress the intellect and itself surrender to a state of numbing dullness without any freedom of will or feeling; how else would one have got hold of the necessary crowd of executioners and torturers?

What does a perfect group of followers do? It doesn't think, and it doesn't even feel any more – it follows.

Chapter 34
The One Syllable

I only actually saw and heard Nazi marches directly, rather than in newspapers and on the radio, during the last year. Because even before I wore the star – and afterwards it was a matter of course – I used to escape quickly into the safety of a side street whenever such a march made its presence felt; otherwise I would have had to greet the dreaded flag. In the last year, however, we were stuck in one of the two Jews' Houses on the Zeughausplatz, where the hall and kitchen windows looked out directly onto the Carolabrücke. Whenever a ceremony took place on the splendidly adorned Königsufer on the other side – a speech of Mutschmann's perhaps, or even an address by Streicher, the leader of the Franconians – columns of SA and SS, of the HJ and the BDM would march over the bridge with their flags and songs. Whether I liked it or not, it made an impression on me every time, and every time I said to myself in desperation that if this was the case, then it must make an enormous impression on others with a less critical mentality.

Just a few days before our *dies ater,* 13 February 1945, they marched over the bridge in this manner, perfectly in step and singing vigorously. It sounded rather different from the marching songs that the Bavarians had sung during the First World War, rather more clipped, more of a bark and less melodic – but the Nazis had always exaggerated anything and everything militaristic, and thus it was still their old sense of order and conviction which was marching and singing down below. How long was it since Stalingrad fell, since Mussolini was deposed, how long since the enemy had reached the borders of Germany and crossed them, how long since the Führer's own generals had wanted to kill him? – and still they marched and sang away down below, and the legend of final victory lived on, or at least everyone succumbed to the pressure to believe in it!

I knew a few of the texts having caught the odd snippet here and there. It was all so brutal, so pathetic, as remote from art as it was from the authentic voice of the people – *'Kameraden, die Rotfront und Reaktion erschossen / Marschiern im Geist in unsern Reihen mit* {Comrades shot by (or: who shot) the Red Front and the Reaction, / March in spirit amongst our ranks}': that is the poetry of the Horst Wessel Song. One has to be good at tongue twisters and solving cryptic clues. Perhaps *Rotfront* and *Reaktion* are in the nominative, and the murdered comrades are present in the spirit of the marching 'brown battalions'; or perhaps – the 'new German song of initiation', as it was referred to in official school song books, was penned by Wessel as early as 1927 – and this would come rather closer to the objective truth of the matter, perhaps the comrades are in prison for having started some gun battle or other, and are longingly marching in spirit with their friends in the SA . . . But who amongst those marching or watching would think about such grammatical or aesthetic matters, who would worry about the content? The melody and the marching step, a few individual expressions or phrases in isolation invoking the 'heroic instincts': 'Hold the flag high! . . . Clear the street for the Storm Trooper! . . . Soon Hitler's flags will wave . . .': isn't that sufficient to stir up the mood that's wanted?

I was unexpectedly reminded of the period when German confidence in the forthcoming victory was dealt its first blow. With immense skill Goebbels's propaganda had managed to turn the serious and appalling defeat if not quite into a victory, then certainly into the most glorious triumph of the military spirit. At the time I noted down in particular a report from the front; like all the old pages from my diary it had been out in Pirna for a long time by now, but I could visualize it quite clearly: in response to the Russian invitation to surrender, the soldiers on the very front line had answered by chanting, reaffirming their unshakable faith in Hitler and their mission.

In the early days of the movement chanting was very much in vogue, and had reappeared out there during the catastrophe of Stalingrad; they were hardly ever to be heard at home any more, and banners, like dormant notes, were the only reminders that they had once existed. I have often asked myself, and it crossed my mind again now, why it is that chanting sounds so much more powerful and brutal than communal singing. I think the reasons are as follows: language is an expression of thought, chanting hits out with a bare fist at the good sense of the addressee, and endeavours to subjugate it. In the case of a song, the melody is a soothing mantle, and good sense is won over in a roundabout way via the emotions. Moreover, the song of people marching past is not really sung directly to the listeners on the wayside; they are simply captivated by the roaring of a river flowing past for its own sake. And this river, the communality of the marching melody, can be achieved more easily and naturally than the communality of chanting, because in song, in the melody, there is a meeting of moods, but in a communally spoken text there is supposed to be a convergence of thought within a group. Chanting is more artificial, more rehearsed and promotes its cause more violently than song.

Soon after their takeover of power the Nazis were able to dispense with it in Germany, they didn't need it any more. (Clearly there is generally little to distinguish the ritualistic chanting of the kind used from time to time at Party rallies, and other ceremonial occasions, from the clipped sentences uttered during marches such as *'Deutschland erwache!* {Germany awake!} *Juda, verrecke!* {Judah perish!} *Führer befiehl!* {Führer command!}'*, and so on.)

It particularly depressed me that no one deemed it necessary at any point to depart from the tried and trusted brutal songs: it was not felt to be necessary either to exorcize the chanting or to tone down in any way the endless showing-off and threats in which the song texts indulged. By this point the *Blitzkrieg* had become a war of nerves, and victory had become a final victory, and by now the last great offensive had begun to flag, and by now . . . but why go on forever listing all the things that had gone wrong? They continued to march and sing as before, and it was accepted as before, and nowhere in all this shameless singing was there the slightest hint of surrender to draw hope from . . .

And yet there was just such a glimmer of hope, and it would have made the philologist happy if only he had known it was there. But I only got to know about this one-syllable consolation afterwards, at a point when it was only of academic importance to me any longer.

It is worth going back to the beginning.

During the First World War the Allies wanted to read Germany's will to conquest between the lines of our anthem *'Deutschland über alles'*.

That wasn't fair, because *'über alles in der Welt* {above everything else on earth}' doesn't refer to an appetite for expansion, but rather to the esteem in which the patriot's feeling towards his native land is held. More embarrassing was the army song *'Siegreich woll'n wir Frankreich schlagen, Rußland und die ganze Welt* {Triumphantly we want to defeat France, Russia and the entire world}'. However, even here you can't really establish conclusively the presence of true imperialism: it could be argued for the defence that this is patently a war song – those who sing it see themselves as defenders of the fatherland, they want to assert themselves by 'triumphantly defeating' the enemy, irrespective of how many of them there are – it is not a question of appropriating foreign territory.

This has to be set against one of the characteristic songs of the Third Reich, which as early as 1934 passed from a special collection into the 'Song Companion {*Singkamerad*}, School Song Book of the German Youth, published by the Reich Central Office of the National Socialist Confederation of Teachers', thereby earning an official and universal significance. *'Es zittern die morschen Knochen / der Welt vor dem roten Krieg. / Wir haben den Schrecken gebrochen /für uns war's ein großer Sieg. / Wir werden weitermarschieren, / wenn alles in Scherben fällt, / denn heute gehört uns Deutschland / und morgen die ganze Welt.* {The brittle bones tremble / worldwide, fearing a red war. / We have allayed the terror / for us it was a great victory. / We will march on, / when everything is smashed to pieces, / for Germany is ours today / and tomorrow the entire world.}' This was in vogue immediately after the political victory at home, after Hitler took power that is, and at the time when he was stressing in every speech his desire for peace. And yet here immediately there is talk of everything from 'smashing to pieces' to the conquest of the world. And in order to dispel any doubt about the unequivocal nature of this will to conquest, the next two verses repeat, first that we will smash *'die ganze Welt zu Hauf in Trümmern* {the whole world to smithereens}', whereupon 'worlds' (in the plural) will pit themselves against us in vain, and the refrain reminds three times over that tomorrow the entire world will be ours. The Führer delivered one speech about peace after another, whilst his *Pimpfe* and Hitler Youths were forced to sing this loathsome text year in and year out. This song and the national anthem about 'German loyalty' . . .

When I first spoke publicly about the LTI in Autumn 1945. I referred to the 'Song Companion', which I had by then managed to get hold of, and quoted the song about the trembling brittle bones. After the lecture an aggrieved member of the audience came up to me and said: 'Why do you quote something as crucial as this incorrectly? Why do you want to accuse the Germans of a greedy desire to rule the world which they didn't have even in the Third Reich. There is nothing in the song to say that the world should be ours.' – 'Come and see me tomorrow,' I replied, 'then you can have a look at the school song book.' – 'You're definitely wrong, Herr Professor, I'll bring the correct text along.' The following day the 'Song Companion' arrived – 6th edition 1936, published by Franz Eher, Munich, 'approved and strongly recommended by the Bavarian Ministry of Education and the Arts for use in schools'; but the preface is dated Bayreuth, March {*Lenzing*} 1934 – the song-book was already open at the relevant passage. '*Heute gehört uns Deutschland, und morgen die ganze Welt*' – there were no ifs and buts about it.

Oh yes there were. The man showed me a pretty little miniature song book with a thread so that it could be carried from a buttonhole. 'German Songs; Songs of the Movement, published by the Winter Charity of the German People, 1942/43.' All the Nazi emblems – swastika, SS-rune, etc. – adorned the cover, and amongst the songs there were the brittle bones, brutal enough, but with the decisive passage touched up. The refrain now read: '. . . *und heute, da hört uns Deutschland, und morgen die ganze Welt* {and today Germany listens to us, and tomorrow the entire world}.'

That sounded much more innocent.

But because a whole world was lying in ruins as a result of German rapacity, and because, after the winter of Stalingrad, it no longer looked as if Germany was going to win a 'great victory', the touching up had to be reinforced and annotated. A fourth verse had been added, in which the conquerors and oppressors tried to disguise themselves as friends of peace and freedom fighters, and bemoaned the malicious interpretation of the original song. The new verse ran as follows: '*Sie wollen das Lied nicht begreifen, sie denken an Knechtschaft und Krieg. /Derweil unsre Acker reifen, du Fahne der Freiheit flieg! /Wir werden weitermarschieren, wenn alles in Scherben fällt. /Die Freiheit stand auf in Deutschland, und morgen gehört ihr die Welt!* {They refuse to understand the song, they think of slavery and war. /Whilst our fields are ripening, fly you flag of freedom! /We will march on, when everything is smashed to pieces. /Freedom arose in Germany, and tomorrow the world is hers!}'

What kind of nerve did it take to distort the truth to such an extent! And what desperation to risk such a lie! I can't imagine that this fourth verse ever came to life; it is far too contorted and imprecise compared with the crude simplicity of three previous ones, whose original savagery couldn't really be covered up completely. But the retraction of the claws, the coy omission of the ominous syllable, appears to have won through.

This should be remembered. The borderline of Nazi self-confidence runs precisely between '*gehören* {belong}' and '*hören* {hear}'. As projected onto the surface of this Nazi song, the omission of this syllable represents Stalingrad.

Chapter 35
Running Hot and Cold

After the elimination of Röhm, and the minor blood-bath which followed amongst his supporters, the Führer had his Reichstag confirm in writing that he had acted 'lawfully {*rechtens*}'. A distinctly Old German expression. But the crushed *Aufstand* {uprising} or *Aufruhr* {rebellion} or the *Meuterei* {mutiny} or the *Abfall* {demise} of the Röhm brigade – that event for which so many German terms were available – was called the *Röhmrevolte* {Röhm revolt}. Unconscious or semi-conscious sound associations undoubtedly played a part in this – language which writes and thinks for you! – just as was the case with the Kapp Putsch, although here the association could, after all, be extended to incorporate the idea implied by the word '*kaputt* {broken}': it is still peculiar, however, that with regard to one and the same thing, and without any obvious pressure, a distinctly German word is enlisted on one occasion, and a decidedly foreign one on another. In exactly the same way, the hyper-German term '*Brauchtum* {customs}' is often used, whilst Nuremberg, the city of the Party Rallies, is officially the suburb of the 'traditional *Gau* {*Traditionsgau*}'.

Some germanizations of commonplace foreign words are popular: *Bestallung* {appointment} is used for *Approbation* {licence to practise}, *Entpflichtung* {retire, literally: be relieved of duties} for *Emeritierung* {to be given an emeritus status}, and it is *de rigueur* to say *Belange* {concerns} for *Interessen* {interests}: '*Humanität* {humanitarianism}' is tainted by the stench of Jewish liberalism, German '*Menschlichkeit* {humanity}' is, however, something altogether different. On the other hand, things can be dated '*im Lenzing* {obsolete: in March}' only in connection with Wagner's town of Bayreuth – the Old German names for the months of the year were not able to gain a foothold in common usage despite all the runes and shrieks of *Sieg Heil.*

I touched on some of the reasons for the limited spread of hyper-German language in my reflections on the word *Gefolgschaft.* However, this limit can at most explain the retention of common foreign words. If, however, the LTI effects an increase in the number and frequency of use of foreign words in comparison with the period which preceded it, then there must be special motives. That there was an increase, both in number and frequency of use, is without doubt the case.

In every speech and every bulletin the Führer delights in two entirely superfluous foreign words which were by no means widespread or generally understood: *diskriminieren* {discriminate} (he regularly says '*diskrimieren*') and *diffamieren* {defame}. '*Diffamieren*', a word generally used in polite society, sounds all the more strange coming from his mouth since he is otherwise, and as a matter of principle, a match for any drunken menial when it comes to swearing. In his address to the Winter Charity 1942/43 – all the signposts along the LTI measure the distance to or from Stalingrad – he refers to the ministers of the enemy powers as 'numbskulls and nonentities indistinguishable from one another'; a lunatic governs in the White House and a criminal in London. Turning to himself, he declares that there is 'no longer any education in the traditional sense, just the standing of the determined warrior, of a bold man well-suited to being his people's Führer'. But as far as foreign words are concerned, he does make some further borrowings, and, as I said before, not as a result of the lack of a German equivalent. In particular he is again and again the *Garant* {guarantor} (and not the *Bürge* {supporter}) of peace or of German freedom or of the independence of the small nations or of all the other noble things that he has betrayed; again and again anything which enhances or reflects the splendour of the Führer is said to have 'eternal {*säkulare*}' significance, occasionally he is tempted by a turn of phrase in the style of Frederick the Great, and he threatens unruly officials with common cashiering {*gemeine Kassation*}, where he could just as well dismiss them without notice {*fristlos entlassen*} or – in the German of the Hitlerian menial – throw them out {*hinauswerfen*} or send them packing {*fortjagen*}.

Of course the raw material of Hitler's words is polished by Goebbels and prepared for repeated ornamental use. The war subsequently enriched the Nazi lexicon of foreign words quite decisively.

A very simple rule can be drawn up governing the sensible use of foreign words. It should read roughly as follows: use a foreign word only when you are unable to find a simple and completely satisfactory substitute in German; if this is the case, use it.

The LTI breaks both parts of this rule; one moment (and, indeed, for the reason stated above, increasingly rarely) it uses approximate germanizations, the next it turns without good cause to a foreign word. When it speaks of *Terror* (terror from the skies, the terror of bombs, and, of course, counter-terror) and *Invasion* it is on well-trodden ground, but the *Invasoren* {invaders} are new and the *Aggressoren* {aggressors} are completely superfluous, and for *liquidieren* {liquidate} there are a frightful number of options available: *töten* {to kill}, *morden* {murder}, *beseitigen* {do away with}, *hinrichten* {execute} etc. Another word that was repeatedly used, *Kriegspotential* {military potential}, could easily have been replaced either by *Rüstungsgrad* {military scope} or *Rüstungsmöglichkeit* {military capacity}. Particularly given that an effort had been made in the case of the sin of *Defaitismus* {defeatism}, after dressing it up to look a little more German by changing the spelling to *Defätismus,* to prepare the neck for the guillotine by calling it '*Wehrkraftzersetzung* {military subversion}'.

So what are the reasons for this predilection for resonant foreign words, as demonstrated here by only a small number of examples? First and foremost their very resonance, and, if you look at the different motifs down to the last detail, it is invariably both this resonance and the desire to drown out certain undesirable things.

Hitler is an autodidact, and not so much half-educated as at most one-tenth educated. (You only have to listen to the unbelievable farrago of his Nuremberg speeches on culture; the only thing more dreadful than the rubbish of this Karlchen Miesnick is the grovelling way in which it was admiringly received and quoted.) As the Führer he is proud not to be weighed down by 'education in the traditional sense' and in the same breath proud of the knowledge he has gathered for himself. Every autodidact shows off with foreign words, and somehow they always manage to take their revenge on him.

But one would be doing the Führer an injustice if one were to explain his fondness for foreign words solely in terms of vanity and an awareness of his own shortcomings. What Hitler invariably knows frighteningly well, and exploits to his advantage, is the psyche of the unthinking masses, who are to be kept from thinking at all costs. A foreign word impresses all the more the less it is understood; in not being comprehended, it confuses and stupefies and, in addition, drowns out thought. Everyone would understand *schlechtmachen* {to run down} whilst fewer understand *diffamieren* {to defame}, but its impact on absolutely everyone is more impressive and more powerful than *schlechtmachen.* (One only has to think of the impact of the Latin liturgy in the Catholic mass.)

Goebbels, who defines his supreme stylistic principle as listening to the man in the street, also knows all about the magic of foreign words. The people like to hear them and also like to use them themselves. And it expects to hear them from its 'Doctor'.

'Our Doctor', this title from Goebbels's early years, brings us to another issue. Regardless of how often the Führer stresses his disdain for the intelligentsia, educated people, professors, and so on – an abiding hatred of thinking born of a bad conscience is always behind all these terms and specifications – the NSDAP still needs this most dangerous social stratum. It is not enough to have our Doctor and propagandist on his own, there needs to be Rosenberg the philosopher, who indulges in philosophizing and stylistic profundity. Our Doctor will also take on board a little philosophical jargon and some popular philosophy; what could be more natural to a political party that calls itself 'the movement' *per se* than to invoke the spirit of dynamism and confer on the word '*Dynamik* {dynamism}' a prominent status amongst its scholarly words?

And in the realm of the LTI there are not simply, on the one hand, scholarly reference books and, on the other, deliberately folksy literature decorated with a mere sprinkling of erudition serving as beauty spots. Rather, in all the serious newspapers (I am thinking of *Das Reich* and the *DAZ,* the heir to the *Frankfurter Zeitung*) one often comes across articles written in the most florid language of profundity, in the precious and arcane style of snobbish pomposity.

One example, chosen almost at random from a superabundance: on 23 November 1944, i.e. towards the end of the day as far as the Third Reich was concerned, the *DAZ* finds ample space for the self-advertisement of a certain Doctor von Werder, who had probably only recently been appointed, and who had written a book on 'emigration from the countryside to the city as a spiritual reality'. What the author has to say has already been said innumerable times before, and can be summarized very simply: anyone who wants to counteract the migration of the rural population to the cities can't do so just by improving income, but rather he must look at the spiritual factors in two different ways, first by bringing something of the spiritual stimuli and advantages of the city to the village (through films, radio, libraries, etc.) and second by asserting through education the hidden benefits of country life. This young writer and, more importantly in the present context, journalist, uses the language of his Nazi teachers. He emphasizes the need for a 'psychology of country folk' and holds forth as follows: 'For us today a person is no longer merely a separate economic entity, but rather a being comprising a body and a soul, someone who belongs to a people and behaves as a bearer of certain racial and spiritual predispositions.' It was therefore necessary to gain 'authentic insights into the real character of migration to the cities'. Modern civilization 'with its characteristic, extreme hegemony of reason and consciousness' undermines the 'once integrated lifestyle of country people', whose 'natural bedrock rests securely on instinct and feelings, on the primordial and the unconscious'. The 'loyalty to the soil' of these country people has been weakened 1. by 'the mechanization of rural labour and materialization, i.e. the radical commercialization of their products, 2. through the isolation and dying out of traditions and local customs, 3. by the objectification and rational process of urbanization of social life in the country'. The result is 'migration to the cities, which must be recognized for what it is, a psychological deficiency disease' if taken seriously as a 'spiritual reality'. Which is why material assistance in this case must inevitably remain 'superficial', and why spiritual remedies are needed. These included, in addition to the folk-song, traditions, etc., also the 'modern cultural media of film and radio, as long as the principles of inner urbanization are eliminated'. It continues in this vein for a good while. This is what I call the Nazi *Tiefenstil* {stylistic profundity} as applied to every scientific, philosophical and artistic discipline. It is not read from the lips of the man in the street, it cannot be and should not be understood by him, rather, it is smeared around the lips of the intellectuals struggling to be superior.

But the consummate and most characteristic feature of the Nazi art of language lies not in this kind of segregated book-keeping for the educated and the uneducated, and also not simply in impressing the masses with a few learned scraps. Rather, the real achievement – and here Goebbels is the undisputed master – lies in the unscrupulous mixture of heterogeneous stylistic elements; no, mixture isn't quite the right word – it lies in the most abruptly antithetical leaps from a learned tone to a proletarian one, from sobriety to the tone of the preacher, from icy rationalism to the sentimentality of a manfully repressed tear, from Fontane's simplicity, and Berlin gruffness, to the pathos of the evangelist and prophet. It is like an epidermal stimulation under the impact of alternating cold and hot showers, and just as physically effective; the listener's emotions (and Goebbels's audience always comprises listeners, even if it only reads the Doctor's essays in the newspaper) never come to rest, they are constantly attracted and rebuffed, attracted and rebuffed, and there is no time for critical reasoning to catch its breath.

In January 1944 articles appeared to celebrate the tenth anniversary of Rosenberg's department. They were intended to be a hymn in praise of Rosenberg, the philosopher and herald of the pure doctrine, who dug deeper and aspired to greater heights than Goebbels, who was merely in charge of mass propaganda. But in fact these reflections ended up celebrating our Doctor much more than Rosenberg, because in all these comparisons and delimitations it was clear that the latter only had one distinctly profound register, whilst Goebbels, on the other hand, had command of this and all the other registers of a resounding organ. (And, with the best will in the world, even the greatest admirers of the *Myth* could not speak of a philosophical originality which would place Rosenberg beyond compare.)

If one were to look for a precedent for the tension in Goebbels's style, one might find an approximation to it in the medieval church sermon, in which an intrepid realism and verism of expression is allied with the purest pathos of ecstatic prayer. But this medieval style of preaching issues from a pure soul, and is directed at a naive audience which it aims to elevate from the constraint of spiritual poverty straight into transcendental realms. Goebbels, on the other hand, is cunningly intent on deception and benumbing.

Following the attempted assassination of 20 July 1944, at which point no one could any longer have any serious doubts as to the mood and general awareness of the public, Goebbels writes in the most casual of tones: only 'a handful of hoary old grandads from a bygone age' could doubt that Nazism constitutes 'the greatest, and also the only, hope of salvation for the German people'. On another occasion he manages to make a pleasant everyday idyll, one which the LTI would call *volksnah* {close to the people}, out of the misery of cities devastated by bombing: 'From the rubble and the ruins the stovepipes are playing with fire once again as they inquisitively poke their noses out of the wooden sheds.' You almost begin to long for such romantic quarters. And at the same time one is supposed to feel a yearning for martyrdom welling up inside: we are in the middle of a 'holy people's war', we find ourselves – the intellectual must be included, the Rosenberg register mustn't be overlooked – in the 'greatest crisis of Western civilization' and must discharge our historical 'task {*Auftrag*}' (where *Auftrag* sounds much more imposing than the hackneyed foreign word *Mission*), and 'our burning cities are beacons on the path to realizing a better world order'.

I have already outlined in a special section the role played in this alternating series of hot and cold baths by that most popular of sports. Goebbels undoubtedly achieved the most offensive apogee of his – to use a Nazi expression once again – totalitarian style in his *Reich* article of 6 November 1944. There he wrote that everyone must see to it that 'the nation remains standing on its own two feet and never falls to the ground', and then, immediately following the boxing image, he continues by claiming that the German people are waging this war 'like a divine judgement'.

But perhaps this particular passage, which could be joined by quite a few similar ones, only seemed to me to be so exceptional because I was repeatedly reminded of it in the most drastic way. Because anyone from outside Berlin who has work to do at the *Zentralverwaltung für Wissenschaft* {Central Office for Science} in the Wilhelmstraße will discover that the most comfortable accommodation can be found in the Adlon opposite (or at least what remains of the former splendour of this Berlin hotel). The windows of the dining room look straight out onto the ruins of the Propaganda Minister's villa, in which his corpse was discovered. I have stood by these windows at least half a dozen times, and standing there I have been reminded again and again of that divine judgement which he and he alone conjured up, only to steal away from the world before its final scene.

Chapter 36
Putting the Theory to the Test

On the morning of 13 February 1945 the order came to evacuate the last remaining bearers of the star in Dresden. Spared deportation up until this point because they were living in mixed marriages, they now faced certain death; they would have to be done away with *en route* because Auschwitz had long since fallen into enemy hands and Theresienstadt was in grave danger.

On the evening of 13 February the catastrophe overtook Dresden: the bombs fell, the houses crumbled, the phosphorus poured down, the burning timbers fell on Aryan and non-Aryan heads alike, and one and the same firestorm drove Jews and Christians to their death; for any of the seventy or so remaining bearers of the star who survived this night, however, it meant salvation, because they were able to evade the Gestapo in the general chaos.

For me the adventurous flight provided conclusive evidence to put my philological examples to the test: up to this point everything that I knew about the LTI, in its oral form at least, was derived from the limited perspective of several Jews' Houses and factories in Dresden, along with the Dresden Gestapo of course. Now, during the final three months of the war, we passed through innumerable towns and villages in Saxony and Bavaria, and in countless railway stations, in countless barracks and bunkers, and again and again on interminable country roads, we came into contact with people from every region, every nook and cranny, every municipality in Germany, people of all classes and ages, of every imaginable educational background or lack of it, of every persuasion, with every shade of enmity towards and – as ever! – resolute faith in the Führer: and all of them, without a single exception, spoke exactly the same LTI that I had heard at home in Saxony, sometimes with a southern or western accent, sometimes with a northern or eastern one. All that I had to add to my notes during this flight were additions and confirmations.

Three distinct stages stood out.

The middle stage covered three weeks in March – every day the spring colours grew more vivid in the forest, although it still looked Christmassy because both the branches and the ground gleamed with the strips of silver paper dropped by the enemy squadrons to confuse German detection equipment, and day and night they roared above us, often heading for the unfortunate neighbouring region of Plauen – this Falkenstein stage imposed a period of calm which enabled me to undertake some study.

It was not a matter of being in a calm state of mind, however; rather the reverse, and more than ever before my study of the LTI served me now as a balancing pole. For the one and only new Nazi word I came across here was written on the arm-bands of some of the soldiers – 'Volksschädlingsbekämpfer {people's pest control}'. A large number of Gestapo officers and members of the military police had been deployed because the whole area was crawling with soldiers on leave who had become deserters and civilians who were evading service in the Volkssturm. Of course it was obvious from my appearance that I was no longer of an age to be liable for military service, but there was still the Volkssturm riddle which ran 'What has silver in its hair, gold in its mouth and lead in its legs?' And in the vicinity of Dresden there was always the danger that someone would recognize me, given that I had, after all, stood behind my lectern for fifteen years, had trained teachers during the whole period and conducted Abitur examinations in various places across the region. Moreover, if I was apprehended, my own death would not be the end of it, my wife and our faithful friend would also have paid the penalty. It was invariably a torture to walk down the street, and in particular to enter a restaurant; as soon as someone caught my attention I was barely capable of returning his gaze with any degree of composure. If it wasn't for the fact that we would have had to venture out into total nothingness, we wouldn't have stayed another day in this dangerous hide-out. But this back room in the 'Pharmacy on

Adolf Hitler Square', under whose portrait of the Führer we slept, was our last refuge after we had had to leave our dear Agnes. Thus, when we were not out in search of quiet forest paths, I spent as much time as I could quietly in my room, forcing myself to read anything with which I could hope to further my knowledge of the LTI.

Or rather, I read whatever I could catch sight of, and everywhere I saw traces of this language. It was truly totalitarian; here in Falkenstein this became abundantly clear to me.

I found a little book on Sch.'s writing desk, he told me that it had appeared at the end of the 1930s: 'The Medical Recipe for Tea, published by the German Association of Pharmacists'. Initially I saw it as a comic document, then as a tragi-comic one, and finally as a truly tragic one. Not only because it expressed in non-committal phrases the ugliest form of obsequiousness towards the prevailing, universal doctrine, but also because it toned down a necessary protest in the most servile manner, thereby rendering it null and void as soon as it was uttered, and revealing in the process the full extent of the conscious sleaziness of a scientific future. I noted down for myself a few sentences *in extenso.*

'Across wide sections of the population there is an unmistakable reluctance to take chemo-therapeutic medications. In contrast, the desire for prescriptions of natural remedies untouched by laboratories and factories has arisen again in recent times and has met with approval. Herbs and herbal mixtures from our meadows and woods undoubtedly have something reassuring and wholesome about them. Their medicinal use is supported by traditional and successful cures from the dim and distant past, and the idea of the kinship of blood and soil reinforces the confidence in native herbs.' Thus far, the comic element holds sway in these remarks, because it is comic how the universal slogans and tenets of Nazism have worked their way into this specialist scientific text. At this point, however, after the humble genuflection and *captatio benevolentiae*, a spirited defence in the interests of both business and medicine cannot be avoided. Under the guise of Teutonic traditionalism, the fellowship with nature and anti-intellectualism, together with the 'recurrent, insidious rumours about the toxicity of chemicals', quackery flourishes, making money out of 'uncritically' concocted medicinal German teas, driving customers away from the factories and patients away from their doctors. But how this attack is toned down through apologies and compliance, and how deep are the steadfast author's repeated obeisances to the tenets and the will of the ruling party! After all, we registered pharmacists, chemists and doctors also use native medicinal herbs, but not exclusively and indiscriminately! And now 'the desire on the part of the medical profession to expand therapies using herbs and teas, and the endeavour, wherever feasible, to accommodate the wishes and natural sensibilities of the people, is evident amongst all progressive practitioners. Therapies using herbs and teas, otherwise known as phytotherapy, are only one aspect of the whole medicinal therapy, but a factor which cannot be underestimated if the trust of the patient is to be maintained and secured. The people's trust in their doctors, who in turn have always been at pains to foster a methodical, conscientious approach to their work based on sound knowledge, must not under any circumstances be shaken by insinuations of the above-mentioned kind . . .' The initial *captatio* has become a barely disguised capitulation.

I came across individual issues of pharmaceutical and medical journals, and in all of them I hit upon the same style and the same stylistic howlers. I made a note to myself: 'Remember the Nordic mathematics, which on one occasion in the early days the *Freiheitskampf* quoted from our colleague Kowalewski, the first Nazi vice-chancellor at our Institute of Science and Technology; don't forget to investigate the spread of the LTI epidemic to other branches of science.'

I came back from science to my own discipline when Hans brought me recent literary publications from his own private library. (He was still a man of the humanities and of philosophy, just as he had been thirty years before; the pharmaceutical business and Party badge – the latter in order to steer clear of the inevitable harassment – were simply prerequisites for a quiet life; but of course, if a friend was in need of help one had to take the odd risk and threaten the quiet life – it is just that that would have been too much to ask for the sake of politics in general.) He brought me a new history book and a new volume of literary history; in the case of both of these entirely serious works it was clear from the number of copies published that they were counted among the privileged and highly influential textbooks. I studied and annotated them from the point of view of the LTI. 'The mere banning of reading matter of this kind for the general public (I noted) will in future not be sufficient; it will be necessary to tell future teachers in detail about the characteristic features and the sins of the LTI, I am noting down examples of how to teach this to a historian and a Germanist.'

First, Friedrich Stieve's *Geschichte des deutschen Volkes* (History of the German People). This thick book was published in 1934, and by 1942 had reached its twelfth edition. Since summer 1939 (the preface to the ninth edition) events up to the annexation of Czechoslovakia and the reclamation of the Memel region had been included. If there was in fact a later edition (which I think highly improbable), it is unlikely to have incorporated the historical events that followed, because one month before the beginning of the new world war the author concludes with the triumphant cheer that 'this whole incomparable upturn' had been 'achieved without spilling a single drop of blood', followed by a frighteningly ominous simile, in which the German Reich rises up 'out of the current of history as a stronghold of composure and stability, a resplendent promise to the future, just like the buildings of Adolf Hitler'. The printer's ink on my copy must barely have had a chance to dry before the first of these buildings, 'which in their imposing, harmoniously structured form embody the glorious union of strength and order' – ('highlight this architectural flexing of muscles which is also LTI') – began to collapse under the bombs of the enemy planes.

Stieve's book is like a good bait, its poison is wrapped up in innocent scraps. Amongst the 500 printed pages of this work there are lengthy chapters which, despite the all-pervading pathos, are written with a degree of composure and are free of violent distortions of style and content, with the result that even a thoughtful reader could begin to trust it. But when the opportunity to use a Nazi inflection arises, all the registers of the LTI are called upon. All – which is not synonymous with many; it is, quite simply, impoverished, it has no desire or facility to be otherwise, and it achieves emphasis merely through repetition, through repeatedly hammering home the same thing.

At solemn moments, both positive and negative, blood must of course be called upon. If it was indeed the case that 'even someone like Goethe' felt 'deep respect' for Napoleon, then it must be the case that 'the call of the blood had atrophied'; when the Dollfuß government turns against the Austrian National Socialists, then it is turning against 'the call of the blood'; and when Hitler's troops subsequently march into Austria the 'hour of the blood' has finally come. At which point the old

Ostmark 'has found its way home to everlasting Germany {*zum ewigen Deutschland heimgefunden hat*}'.

Ostmark, ewig {everlasting} and *heimfinden* {to find one's way home}: these are entirely neutral words *per se,* words which had belonged to the German language for many centuries prior to Nazism and which will belong to it for ever more. And yet in the context of the LTI they are decidedly Nazi words belonging to a special linguistic register, a register for which they are both characteristic and representative. *Ostmark* in place of *Osterreich* {Austria}: this represents the link with tradition, reverence for the ancestors, who, rightly or wrongly, are invoked, whose legacy one claims to honour and whose testament one professes to fulfil. *Ewig* points in the same direction; we are links in a chain stretching back into the misty past, one which is supposed to pass through us into the distant future, we always were and always will be. *Ewig* is simply the most forceful special case amongst the numerical superlatives, which are themselves but a special case in the midst of the ubiquitous LTI superlatives. And *heimfinden* was one of the very first expressions emphasizing feeling that was to gain notoriety, it derives from the glorification of blood and itself precipitates an exuberance of superlatives.

Tradition {*Tradition*} and duration {*Dauer*} are two concepts that are so familiar and fundamental to historiography that they cannot really have any notable effect on a historian's style. Stieve however virtually legitimizes himself as a faithful and orthodox nationalist by his constant array of words accenting feeling.

'Unbridled {*unbändig*}' power drives the Cimbri and Teutoni, with whose invasion of Italy this history opens, 'unbridled' desire drives the Teutons on 'to fight to the bitter end'; 'unbridled' passion explains, justifies, indeed ennobles the worst excesses of the Franks. *Furor teutonicus* is rated a lofty and honourable title of the 'native children of the North': 'What heroism and glory accompanied them as they stormed across the land, unaware of the perfidy of their surroundings, entirely geared {*eingestellt*} to the power of overflowing feeling, to the power of that inner momentum which permitted them to shout out with joy when it came to taking on the enemy.' I refer only in passing to the word *'eingestellt',* which had already begun to lose its original technical meaning prior to the emergence of the LTI. Be that as it may: something of the Nazi insensitivity about, or indeed positive affection for, the abrupt juxtaposition of mechanistic and affective expressions can also be found in Stieve; he writes of the NSDAP: 'It fell upon the Party to be the powerful motor at the heart of Germany, the motor of spiritual improvement, the motor of active devotion, the motor of constant awakening in the spirit of the newly created Reich.'

In general, however, Stieve's style is characterized entirely by a one-sided insistence on feeling, resulting from the fact that he traces anything and everything back to this celebrated, privileged and pre-eminent characteristic of the Teutons.

It determines political structures because the competence of a leader is judged by the size of his following {*Gefolgschaft*}, and the following relies 'exclusively on voluntary, heart-felt devotion, and its establishment is thus categorical proof of the fundamental role that feeling played amongst the Teutons'.

Feeling endows the Teuton with imagination and a religious inclination, it enables him to idolize nature, makes him 'close to the earth', and allows him to adopt a sceptical attitude towards the intellect.

Feeling propels him towards the infinite, and it is this which constitutes the fundamentally Romantic quality of the Teutonic character.

Feeling makes a conqueror out of him, furnishes him with the 'German faith in his own calling to world domination'.

However, the predominance of emotion also give rise to a situation in which 'alongside the craving to dominate the world was a desire to escape it', which explains the fact that for all the cult of vitality and activism there is a special predilection for Christianity.

Whenever the passage of history allows – and the fact that he doesn't do it forcibly at an early point is what distinguishes him from the unadulterated propagandists of his Party – Stieve brings in the Jew as the distorted counterpart to the man of feeling, and from here on the specifically Nazi expressions accumulate, or rather they are amplified in a negative direction. '*Zersetzung* {subversion}' is now a central word. It began with *Junges Deutschland*. 'Two Jewish writers, Heine and Lion Baruch, known as Ludwig Börne following his baptism', are the first demagogues from the ranks of the 'chosen' people. (I believe *auserwählt* {chosen} to be the word from which the LTI's ironic inverted commas first sprung.) The materialistic spirit of the age suits the hereditary characteristics of the members of this foreign race and the traits they acquired whilst in exile, and is itself encouraged by them.

Now the Nazi vocabulary can blossom: *'niederreißende Kritik* {destructive criticism}', *'zerfasernder Intellekt* {hairsplitting intellect}', *'tödliche Gleichmacherei* {deadly levelling down}', *'Auflösung* {dissolution}, *'Unterhöhlung* {undermining}', *'Entwurzelung* {rootlessness}', *'Durchbrechung der nationalen Schranke* {undermining national boundaries}'; 'Marxism' for socialism, because real socialism is the prerogative of Hitlerism, and the false one must be marked out as the heresy of the Jew Karl Marx. (The Jew Marx, the Jew Heine, not simply Marx or Heine, is a special technique for hammering something home stylistically which had already occurred in the ancient *epitheton ornans.*)

Defeat in the First World War lends further weight to this branch of the LTI: now there is talk of *'teuflischen Giften der Zersetzung* {the diabolic poison of subversion}', of *'roten Hetzern* {malicious red agitators}' . . .

The third intensification derives from the belligerent position taken against bolshevism and communism: the 'sinister hordes' of the red front battalions crop up.

And finally – the crowning achievement of the whole work and its stylistic apogee, the ultimate crescendo of the Nazi linguistic organ: the saviour, the unknown soldier, the man from Greater Germany, the Führer appears. Now all the slogans from both categories come together in one confined space. And the terrible prostitution of the language of the Gospels in the service of the LTI culminates in the following: 'Through the exhilarating power of his own faith, the man at the top was able to rouse the sick man, prostrate on the ground, with the primordial spell "arise and walk".'

I called the LTI impoverished. But how rich it is in the hands of Stieve in comparison with the linguistic skills demonstrated by Walther Linden in his *Geschichte der deutschen Literatur* (History of German Literature) of 1937, a book which can certainly be described as representative – it was published in the popular {*volkstümlich*} Reclam publishing house, despite being a good 500 pages in length it had seen four editions, it encapsulated the prescribed, universally valid literary judgements of the Hitler period in such a prescriptive style that it undoubtedly constituted an essential handbook for pupils and students. During the 'twenties its author, who had the good fortune to die before the collapse of the Third Reich, had been the editor of a thoroughly scholarly *Zeitschrift für Deutschkunde* (Journal for German Studies) in which I myself had published a number of articles. Since then he had undergone a thorough re-education, although it has to be said that he made this re-education as easy as possible by explaining everything from a single perspective, and expressing it in no more than two words at a time, usually coupled together and practically made synonymous by the LTI (which would itself describe them as having been brought into line {*gleichgeschaltet*}).

Every current, every work, every author is either '*volkhaft* {national, of the people}' and '*arthaft* {characteristic}' or it isn't; and anyone refused this rating by Linden is denied both ethical and aesthetic value, indeed even the right to exist. This is the case in paragraph after paragraph, sometimes even page after page.

'Following the heroic Teutonic poetry of the royal courts a second, inspired high culture, characteristic of the race {*arteigen*}, came into being with the Age of Chivalry.'

'Outside Italy, humanism has become the antithesis of all that is national {*volkstümlich*} and characteristic of the race {*arteigen*}.'

'It was only the eighteenth century that was finally able to transform the inherited wealth of spiritual and sensory resources into an organic unity and totality of life characteristic of the race {*arteigen*}: in the national {*volkhaft*} rebirth of the German Movement since 1750.'

Leibniz is 'a characteristic {*arthaft*}, global philosopher who thinks of himself as a German'. (His successors 'infiltrate his teachings with too many foreign ideas {*überfremden*}'.)

Klopstock's 'Teutonic, characteristic sense of universal oneness {*germanischarthaftes Alleinheitsgefühl*}'.

Winckelmann's interpretation of Ancient Greece 'brought together two kindred {*artverbunden*} Indo-Germanic peoples'.

In *Götz von Berlichingen* 'an indigenous way of life borne of the earth {*bodenentstammte Volksart*} and native justice' succumb to 'a foreign {*volksfremd*} order based on slavish obsequiousness', which asserts itself 'by means of alien {*artfremd*}, Roman laws . . .'

'Löb Baruch (Ludwig Börne)' and 'Jolson (Friedrich Ludwig Stahl)', also a baptized Jew, are both, the liberal and the conservative, equally guilty of the abandonment of the 'Germanic concept of order', and of the 'move away from the characteristic {*arthaft*} notion of statehood'.

Uhland's 'national {*volkshaft*} lyric poetry and balladry' contributes to 'the reawakening of a conscious awareness of nativeness {*Artbewußtsein*}'.

'In mature realism the characteristic, Teutonic {*arthaft-germanisch*} sensibility is victorious once again over French *esprit* and newfangled Jewish, liberal literature.'

Wilhelm Raabe puts up a fight against 'the gradual loss of the German soul under alien {*artfremd*} influences'.

Fontane's novels mark the end 'of realism, a characteristic {*arthaft*}, German movement'; Paul de Lagarde strives to achieve 'a characteristic {*arthaft*} German religion'; Houston Stewart Chamberlain is even 'more true to kind {*artechter*}' than the Rembrandt German {*Rembrandtdeutsche*}, he brings 'spiritual heroes characteristic of the race {*arteigen*}' home to the Germans once again, rouses 'the Teutonic outlook on life once again in order that it may become a productive, national {*völkisch*} force'; all of these examples are crowded together in just under sixty lines, and in listing them I have overlooked the 'nervous degeneration' and the 'battle between superficial literature and eternal, characteristic {*arthaft*} writing', together with the endeavour to 'constitute a characteristic {*arthaft*} intellectual life and thereby anchor national {*volkhaft*} culture'.

With Bartels and Lienhard there begins around 1900 'the national {*volkhaft*} counter-current'. When it then comes to the 'great pioneers of national {*volkhaft*} writing', to Dietrich Eckart and all the others directly beholden to National Socialism, it is hardly surprising that everything constantly revolves around *volk-* and *blut-* and *arthaft*.

A strain played on the one and only, most national {*volkstümlichst*} string of the LTI! I had heard it resound long before reading this Nazi literary history and truly *de profundis*. 'You racial traitor {*Du artvergessenes Weib!*}' Clemens the Hitter said to my wife every time he searched the house, and Weser the Spitter added, 'Didn't you know that it says in the Talmud that "a foreigner is of less value than a whore"?' This is repeated every time word for word like a messenger's brief in Homer. 'You racial traitor! Didn't you know . . .'

Again and again during these years, and with particular fervour during the weeks in Falkenstein, I asked myself the same question, and am still today unable to find an answer: how was it possible for educated people to betray their entire education, culture and humanity to such an extent?

The Hitter and the Spitter were primitive beasts (despite holding the rank of officer); you have to put up with that sort of thing until you can kill it. But you don't have to rack your brains over it. But an educated man like this literary historian! And behind him I discern a multitude of literary figures, writers, journalists, a multitude of academics. Betrayal as far as the eye can see.

Then there's a certain Ulitz, who tells the story of a tormented Jewish sixth-former {*Abiturient*} and dedicates it to his friend Stefan Zweig, and who then, in the hour of the Jews' greatest need, draws a distorted portrait of a Jewish usurer merely in order to demonstrate his enthusiasm for the prevailing line. And then there's Dwinger, who in his novel written in Russian captivity and during the Russian revolution knows nothing whatsoever about the crucial influence of the Jews and about Jewish atrocities; instead the only two occasions on which Jews are mentioned in the entire trilogy relate to acts of humanity, one performed by a Jewish woman, the other by a Jewish businessman; and then, during the Hitler era, the bloodthirsty Jewish commissar crops up. Then there is Hans Reimann, the joker from Saxony – I found this in an essay published in what had once been the entirely distinguished *Velhagen-und-Klasing-Hefte* {Velhagen & Klasing books} (of 1944) – who discovers the peculiarities of the Jews in general and their sense of humour in particular: 'The Jewish faith is superstition, their temple is a club bar and their god an almighty department store owner . . . The tendency of the Jewish brain to get carried away is so rampant, that it is often difficult to differentiate between the monstrous products of ramshackle intellectualism and flat-footed stupidity.' (Note the close proximity of hot and cold: ramshackle intellectualism and flat-footed stupidity!)

All I am doing here is giving an indication of the kind of things I read during my days in Falkenstein. Perhaps more interesting than this endlessly repeated and invariably inexplicable fall into betrayal, more explicable at least and more tragic – for intellectual sickness and unexpected criminality are not tragic *per se* – is the half-innocent slide into betrayal of the kind that can be observed, for example, in the case of Ina Seidel, who with a pure heart descends the slippery slope of Romanticism, ending up with her late paean of greeting to the German Messiah Adolf Hitler, who is already up to his neck in blood. But I can't do that properly in my notebook, one day I shall have to study it carefully . . .

Amongst the traitors I also came across a good old friend from the days of the First World War – amongst German political journalists he was at one time a respected name for friends and foes alike: Paul Harms. I well remember our discussions in the Café Merkur, the former Leipzig literary café, which lasted for hours. Harms had just moved a few steps from left to right, from the *Berliner Tageblatt* to the *Leipziger Neuesten*

Nachrichten, but he was no rabble-rouser and he was averse to any kind of inflexibility. And he was thoroughly decent, he had learned a good deal and was possessed of a clear head. He knew what a terrible thing war was, and was fully capable of judging the insanity of Germany's plans to master the world by the strength of the opposing forces. For many years I had not heard anything from him and, immersed in my subject, I had restricted my newspaper reading to the local paper. If alive at all, Harms must by now have been nearer eighty than seventy, and long since gone into retirement. And then I saw the *Leipziger Neuesten* again. And every three or four days there was a political article in it with the old signature P.H. But it was not 'Paul Harms' any more, it was just one of many hundreds of variations of Goebbels's weekly texts, which were to be found every day in every newspaper of Greater Germany, there was global Jewry and the steppe, there was the British betrayal of Europe, there was the Teutonic world fighting selflessly for the freedom of the West and the world at large, there was the entire LTI – putting my theory to the test. A sad test for me, because these particular lines spoke to me with an individual voice, with a familiar intonation behind the equally familiar, in fact all-too-familiar, words – words which, coming out of this mouth, were quite unexpected. When I heard during the following summer that Harms had died a few days before the entry of Russian troops into Zehlendorf, it came to me almost as a relief; at the very last minute he had been, as the pious saying goes, put beyond the reach of mortal judgement.

And it was not only from books and papers and the fleeting exchange of words during agonizing restaurant visits that the LTI besieged me: the good burghers in my pharmaceutical surroundings spoke it without exception. Our friend, who, with advancing years, was increasingly disposed to see everyday things, even the most appalling, with faintly scornful forbearance and as unimportant in relation to the Eternal – I do believe he really said 'matters Eternal {*den ewigen Belangen*}' – even he made no effort to steer clear of the poisonous jargon; and for his filial helper it wasn't even jargon at all, but remained the language of the faith in which she had been brought up, and which no one could have shaken even if they had dared to try. Even the young Lithuanian pharmacist – but I have already spoken about her in 'The Jewish war'.

And on one occasion, during a major air-raid warning – the wings of death were thrashing again, roused from their phraseological torpor into the real world, low over the roofs of the cowering little town before the bombs crashed into Plauen – the district vet stopped over with us. He was a talkative man, but not a gossip, he was considered very capable and good-humoured, and he would make every attempt to reduce the customers' alarm at air-raid warnings by distracting their attention. He talked about the new weapon, or rather the new weapons, which were now ready and would certainly come into play in April and secure victory. 'The single-seat plane is far more efficient than the V2, it will definitely see off even the largest bomber squadrons; it flies at such a fantastic speed that it can only shoot backwards because it is faster than the projectile; it brings down the enemy bombers before they can drop their load; the final experiments are complete and mass-production is under way.' It's true! He really did tell it exactly like this, and it was apparent from his tone that he believed this fairy-tale, and it was equally apparent from the faces of those listening to him that they were convinced by this storyteller – at least for a few hours.

'Do you think this man is a deliberate liar', I asked our friend later, 'and are you yourself absolutely sure that what he is saying is a fairy-tale?' – 'No,' Hans replied, 'he's an honest man, he must have heard someone talking about this weapon – and why shouldn't there be some truth in it after all? And why shouldn't the people comfort themselves with the idea?'

The following day he showed me a letter that had just arrived from a friend who was a headmaster somewhere near Hamburg: I would like him much more than the vet yesterday, he was a sound philosopher and a pure idealist entirely devoted to humanitarian ideas and not an admirer of Hitler in any way. I have forgotten to report that the vet not only talked about the wonder weapon yesterday but also, in a similarly devout manner, about a repeatedly observed phenomenon, namely that whole buildings had collapsed except for the 'wall with Hitler's portrait', which had been left standing. The philosophical, anti-Nazi friend from near Hamburg, on the other hand, did not believe in any wonder weapon or myth and professed himself to be in despair. 'Yet (he wrote) despite the desperate situation one still wants to believe in a turn-around {*Wende*} or a miracle, because our culture and idealism can't just succumb to the united onslaught of global materialism!'

'All that's missing is the onslaught of the steppe!' I said. 'But don't you find that your friend is pretty much in tune with contemporary Germany?

Even if someone is praying for a *Wende* to Hitler's disadvantage – *Wende* is a very popular made-up word amongst Hitlerites.'

*

The bourgeois district of the Falkenstein pharmacy is bordered on the map of our escape by two rural areas. Initially we had turned to the Wendish village of Piskowitz near Kamenz. It was there that our faithful Agnes lived as a farmer's widow with her two children. She had worked for us for a number of years and subsequently continued to send us replacements from her region when one of the girls got married. It was certain that she would receive us warmly, and it was highly likely that neither she nor anyone else in the village would know that I was affected by the Nuremberg Laws. We wanted to tell her about it now to be on the safe side; it would mean that she would take extra care of us. Barring a terrible stroke of misfortune we expected to be able to drop out of sight in the seclusion of this hide-out. Particularly given the fact that the population was, as we knew, strongly anti-Nazi. If her pious Catholicism was not enough, then her Wendishness would certainly have immunized her: these people were very attached to their Slavonic language, which the Nazis wanted to stop them using for their local customs and in religious education, they felt themselves to be allied to the Slavonic peoples and insulted by the Teutonic self-deification of the Nazis – we had heard that often enough from Agnes and her successors. And, what was more, the Russians were on the outskirts of Görlitz; soon they would be in Piskowitz or we would manage to get across to them.

My optimism was founded on the elation following our fairy-tale deliverance and the burning heap of rubble that was all that remained of Dresden when we left, because on the basis of this destruction we felt that the end of the war was imminent. My optimism was dealt a first blow, or rather turned into its complete opposite, when the head of the village – my papers had of course been 'burnt' – asked me whether I had any non-Aryan relations. It cost me an enormous effort to utter a nonchalant 'no', I felt he was suspicious of me. Later I discovered that this had been an obligatory question, and in fact the man never suspected anything throughout. But from that point on I always had the same terrible whispering and murmuring in my ear, sometimes louder, sometimes more quietly, a sound I had got to know in 1915 when the bursts of fire from the machine guns swept over the people lying on the ground, a sound which affected me far more than the honest explosions of the grenades; in Falkenstein the feeling became even more harrowing, and it only finally stopped on the day the Americans swallowed us up in Bavaria. I wasn't afraid of the bombs or the hedgehoppers, nor even of death – it was simply the Gestapo. Constantly the same fear that someone would come up behind me, or meet me head-on, or wait for me at my house to take me away {*holen*}. ('*Holen!*' Now I'm using this language as well!) All that matters is that I don't fall into the hands of my enemies! was what I said to myself every day with a deep sigh.

But now and again there were also peaceful hours in Piskowitz, because it was a quiet world all of its own, a world that was thoroughly anti-Nazi, and even in the case of the village leader I had the impression that he would have preferred to be a little more dissociated from his Party and his government.

Of course Nazi political science had found its way into this place as well. On the tiny writing desk in the communal living-room of the little half-timbered house, between bills, family letters, a handful of envelopes and writing paper, there were the children's schoolbooks.

Above all the German School Atlas, which Philipp Bouhler, the man from the Reich Chancellery, had published with a facsimile signature in September 1942 for use in all German schools, and which had reached every last village. The true hubris of this venture only becomes apparent when one considers the advanced date: already by this point the imaginary German victory had become an impossibility, already it was merely a matter of trying to avoid total defeat. And at this point one hands children a map in which 'The lebensraum of Greater Germany' includes the 'General Government[1] with Warsaw and the Lemberg District', the 'Reich Civil Administration for Occupied Soviet Territories in the East' and the 'Reich Civil Administration for the Ukraine', a map in which Czechoslovakia, referred to as 'the protectorate of Bohemia and Moravia', and 'Sudetenland' are identified by a special colour as the actual property of the Reich, a map in which German cities proudly sport their honorary Nazi titles – alongside the Capital of the Movement and City of the Rallies there are 'Graz, City of the Popular Uprising', 'Stuttgart, City of Expatriate Germans', 'Celle, Home of the Reich Court of Hereditary Law', etc. – a map in which instead of Yugoslavia there is

---

[1]*General-gouvernement* was the official name for Nazi-occupied Poland.

a 'Region of the Military Commander in Serbia', and in which a special map shows every Nazi *Gau,* another the German colonies, and it is only at the foot of the page, not on the colonies map itself, that there is a note in tiny print (and, what's more, in brackets) 'under mandatory administration'. How must the world look today in the mind of someone who in an earlier, defenceless stage of their childhood had all these things impressed on them in such a colourful manner!

Together with the atlas, which linguistically added up to a special LTI vocabulary of considerable proportions, there was a German arithmetic book, the exercises of which were derived from the 'Versailles Diktat' and 'The Führer's Job Creation Scheme', and a German reader in which sentimental anecdotes glorified Adolf Hitler's fatherly love of animals and children.

Yet in the same cramped space there were also antidotes to all this. There was the holy corner, its saviour (like almost all crucifixes in the village streets) was accompanied by a text in Wendish, and there was also a Wendish Bible. I am not sure whether one could have considered Catholicism on its own as an entirely safe antidote were it not for the stress on their own language. I say this because, apart from the Bible and the schoolbooks that I found in the house, my principal reading matter was a fat, very well-thumbed folio volume of the 'City of God {*Stadt Gottes*}'. This was an illustrated *Journal for the Catholic Community* from 1893/94. It was brimful of attacks on the 'Judaified lodge', on 'liberal, social democratic slaves of the Jews', it defended Ahlwardt's standpoint for as long as was humanly possible, and only turned its back on him at the very last minute. It had no knowledge of racial anti-Semitism, however, although I was struck once again how unerringly demagogical – or, to use his own term, *volksnah* {close to the people} – the Führer had been in subsuming the multitude of elements hostile to him under the heading of Judaism.

But I was hardly entitled to draw any conclusions about contemporary Catholic anti-Semitism from attitudes in the 1890s. Anyone who took their Catholic faith seriously stood alongside the Jews in mutual, mortal conflict with Hitler.

And what is more: the domestic library contained a further, equally old, thick and well-thumbed book from whose politics it was also impossible to draw any conclusions about the attitudes of the house's current occupants. The late farmer had been a very active beekeeper, and this final work in the house was a beekeeping yearbook by Baron August von Berlepsch. The author, whose introduction is dated Coburg, 15 August 1868, is evidently not only an expert, but also a moralist and scholarly citizen. 'I know many people (he writes) who before becoming beekeepers used every minute of their free time (who indeed took time off at their own expense) in order to head to the nearest pub for a drink, to play cards or get into a lather over futile political disputes. But as soon as they became beekeepers they stayed at home with their families; when the weather was fine they spent their leisure hours with their bees, and when it was inclement they read magazines about beekeeping, made hives, repaired their beekeeping equipment – in short they enjoyed home life and hard work. "Staying at home" is of course the shibboleth of the responsible citizen . . .'

Agnes and her neighbours thought quite differently about such things. For every evening the room we called the Wendish spinning-room – being admitted meant that we were genuinely trusted – was chock-full. Everyone met at the house of Agnes's brother-in-law, a man of wide interests who, incidentally, despite being a Catholic and ardent Wend – 'we stretched as far as Rügen, and that's how far our realm should extend now!' – was a member of the *Stahlhelm* until it was absorbed into the NSDAP, but not a minute longer. There was a lot of coming and going in the warm, spacious kitchen-cum-living-room; women sat at their needlework and men stood around smoking. Children ran in and out. The centre of attention was the impressive wireless, around which a group was always huddled. One tried to find the stations, others made suggestions, discussed what they had just heard and forcefully asked everyone to be quiet when something important was announced or was imminent.

The first time we entered the room there was a good deal of noise and no one was paying much attention to the broadcast. The brother-in-law explained to me almost apologetically, 'It is only Goebbels – we seem to have tuned into him for the moment, the other programme is on in ten minutes.'

It was on that day, 28 February, that I heard the Doctor for the last time. In terms of content it was exactly the same as all his speeches and articles during the final period: brutal sporting imagery and final victory and ill-concealed despair. But his manner of speaking seemed to me to have changed. He dispensed with any variations in modulation; he uttered the individual words slowly, in a uniformly emphatic tone, beat by beat, pause by pause, just like a pile-driver.

'The other' – this was the general, all-inclusive term for the entire range of prohibited programmes, for Beromünster, for London and Moscow (who transmitted news in German), for the Allied radio stations, the independent stations, and anything else that was illegal. Everyone knew about all this listening, a prohibited activity punishable by death, knew the times, wavelengths and specialities of the individual stations and thought us rather unworldly for never having had any contact with 'the other'. No one dreamt of hiding this proscribed listening from us, or in any way surrounding it with secrecy and circumspection. Through our friend Agnes we belonged to the village, and the attitude of the village was uniform: everyone was waiting for the certain end of Hitlerism, everyone was waiting for the Russians.

Every Allied success, every action and every plan was discussed at length, even the children had something to add; they also didn't have to rely exclusively on the news from 'the other' – they brought home news from outside as well, because here it didn't just rain chaff, as was later the case in Falkenstein. As well as this silver paper, which, together with the vestiges of the winter snow, also made the forests of fir and pine look far more festive than the springlike mixed woodland of the Erzgebirge, there were also leaflets, which were keenly collected and studied. For the most part they repeated what was said in the broadcasts of 'the other': appeals to renounce a criminal and insane government intent on continuing to fight an irretrievably lost war until Germany was totally destroyed. The children were certainly told that it was strictly forbidden to collect these pieces of paper, but all anyone did was repeat the injunction whilst everybody read them avidly and agreed with what they said. On one occasion Agnes's Juri turned up brandishing an open pamphlet: 'We don't have to burn this one, we've already been given it at school!' It was a booklet: 'Goebbels's Treatises on War' with a typical Nazi warrior's head on the cover (half-eagle, half-rowdy). On the left were the sentences which had been impressed on the schoolchildren, on the right a point-by-point refutation of them by the Allies. There was a particularly detailed and informative rejoinder to the assertion that the war had been 'forced {*aufgezwungen*}' on the peace-loving Führer. (The notion of the war 'forced' on the Führer is pre-eminent amongst stereotypical expressions of the LTI.)

There were two other sources from which the village apprised itself of the state of things: the pathetic treks of country people fleeing from Silesia who were permitted a brief stopover in the 'Maidenlager', the sprawling green-painted camp of the former Women's Labour Service {*weiblicher Arbeitsdienst*}, and a number of Bavarian artillerymen on horseback, but with no weapons, who were allowed to have a breather here on their way back from the front.

Finally, on very rare occasions, these thoroughly modern and informative discussions were supplemented by a very different source of enlightenment: passages from the Bible were quoted – Agnes's elderly but very sprightly father spoke at great length about the Queen of Sheba – which unequivocally prophesied the arrival of the Russians. Initially I wanted to categorize this impact of the Bible on the LTI as an exclusively rural phenomenon, but then in good time I was reminded of our Babisnau poplar along with the widespread fondness for astrology amongst the leadership and the nation as a whole.

Despite all this, the mood in Piskowitz was in no way despairing. To date they had not suffered especially from the war, and not a single bomb had fallen on this inconspicuous village – it didn't even have its own siren; and when the distant alarm sounded, as it repeatedly did day and night, no one allowed their sleep to be interrupted, and by day they watched with interest what, in a purely aesthetic sense, was often a beautiful spectacle: at an immense height swarms of silver arrows the length of a finger crossed the blue sky, emerging from the clouds only to disappear behind them again. And then every time, without fail, one of the onlookers would remind everyone, 'And Hermann said his name would be Meier, if a single enemy plane reached Germany!' And someone else would add, 'And Adolf wanted to wipe out {*ausradieren*} the English cities.'

These two expressions really were perennials both in the cities and the countryside, whilst other topical phrases, faux pas and jokes had to make do with a single day of fame; and in this case, by which I mean the brilliance of their aura, there was a temporal delay between the village and the city.

Just like all the other people in the village, we had pig slaughters; because, although nobody otherwise had any real fear of the Russians, they still preferred to eat up the prime pork rather than hand it over to their liberators. The meat inspector took out his microscope, the butcher and his assistant stuffed sausages, neighbours came round for quick visits to scrutinize and make comparisons, and all the time everyone told jokes to rooms full of people and set riddles. I then experienced something I had already encountered during the First World War: in 1915 I heard *'Sous les ponts de Paris'* in a village in Flanders, a song which two years previously had been the hit of the season in Paris, and which in the meantime had been replaced by more topical *chansons.* In a similar way the people of Piskowitz and their meat inspector enjoyed a riddle which in Dresden, and doubtless in every German city, had done the rounds soon after the beginning of the war with Russia: what is the real meaning of *Ramses* cigarettes. Answer: *Rußlands Armee macht schlapp Ende September* {Russia's army will collapse at the end of September}. But back-to-front: *sollte England siegen, muß Adolf 'raus* {if England wins, Hitler must go}! I made a note to myself to the effect that migrations of this kind should be investigated in temporal, geographical and social terms. Someone once told me that the Gestapo had spread a rumour in Berlin and then studied how long it took to reach Munich and how it got there.

I took part in the pork feast {*Schlachtfest*} in a very depressed and, regardless of how much I laughed at myself, in a fairly superstitious frame of mind. The pig should have been slaughtered the week before; at that time the Allies were 20 kilometres outside Cologne and the Russians were in the process of taking Breslau. The butcher, inundated with jobs, had been forced to cancel and the pig had survived. I had read it as an omen; I said to myself: if the pig lasts longer than Cologne and Breslau, then you will live to see the end of the war and your butchers. Now my tasty boiled pork had been somewhat soured because Cologne and Breslau had not yet fallen.

For lunch the following day we had pork again, during which the head of the village came in: the order had just arrived to clear the village of outsiders by the evening, because by tomorrow combat troops would be stationed here; at five o'clock a vehicle would take us to Kamenz, from where a refugee transport would bring us to the Bayreuth region. At that point, standing crushed between men, women and children in an open cart, as sleet fell on us, I really felt our situation was hopeless; but three weeks later and our situation really was hopeless. Because at the counter in Kamenz we could still say 'We have been bombed out and need private accommodation in Falkenstein' – there really was still something we could set our hopes on; the 'reception centre', that wretched but yet reassuring concept from the dying days of the Third

Reich, was still valid for us as well. But when we also had to leave Falkenstein – Hans had been forced to take in two pharmacists who had studied in Dresden and who might well have recognized me; the danger of being discovered was too great, and the end of the war had still not come – where were we to find a safe reception centre to stay? Everywhere we were in danger of being discovered.

The next twelve days on the run were full of exertions, of hunger, of sleeping on the bare stone floor of a railway station, of bombs dropped on the moving train and on the waiting room where we were supposed to be fed at last, of walking at night along the bombed railway line, of wading in streams alongside smashed bridges, of cowering in bunkers, of sweating, of freezing and shivering in sodden footwear, of rattling bursts of fire from hedgehoppers – but much worse than all that was the ceaseless and agonizing fear of being challenged and imprisoned. Hans had given us ample money and means of support, but had refused to give us the poison I had begged for in case of dire emergency – 'Don't let us fall into the hands of our enemies, they are a hundred times more terrible than any death!'

At last we were so far from Dresden, at last the paralysis and conflict were so far advanced in Germany, at last the end of the Third Reich was so close at hand, that the fear of being discovered abated. In the village of Unterbernbach near Aichach – to which we had been sent as refugees, and which strangely housed no one from Saxony, only from Silesia and Berlin – we, along with all the other inhabitants, only had to fear the interminable hedgehoppers and the day on which the Americans, who at the time were approaching Augsburg, would overrun {*überrollen*} us. I think *'überrollen'* is the last military coinage that I came across. It was undoubtedly tied up with the supremacy of motorized troops.

In Dresden in August 1939 we had witnessed how the army was gathered together in a secret and undignified manner; now we saw it trickle home in a secret and undignified manner. Small groups and individuals broke away from the disintegrating front line, crept out of the forests, sneaked through the village, sought food and civilian clothing, looked for a quiet place to spend the night. Some of them still believed in victory. Others were entirely convinced that everything was coming to an end, yet loose scraps of the former triumphalist language still entered into their conversation.

However, amongst the refugees billeted here and the local inhabitants there was no longer anyone who believed there was even the slightest chance of victory or of Hitler retaining power. In their total and embittered condemnation of Nazism, the villagers of Unterbernbach were absolutely indistinguishable from those of Piskowitz. The only difference was that the Wends had displayed this animosity from the outset, whilst the Bavarian farmers had initially sworn by their Führer. At the beginning he had promised them so much, indeed he had even kept some of the promises. But now it had been raining nothing but disappointments for ages. The people of Unterbernbach could have visited the Wendish spinning-room, and the people of Piskowitz could have gone to Unterbernbach: they wouldn't have understood what the others were saying even if the people of Piskowitz had all spoken German (which they never did amongst themselves), but as regards their opinions, they would very soon have been of the same mind: they all rejected the Third Reich.

Amongst the farmers of Unterbernbach I discovered enormous moral disparities and contritely noted to myself: 'Make sure you never again say The Farmer or The Bavarian Farmer, don't forget The Pole and The Jew!' In his abiding willingness to help every refugee, whether in uniform or not, and in his goodwill towards them, the head of the village farmers, a man who had long since fallen out of love with the Party but had not been allowed to relinquish his post, was a spitting image of that paragon of goodness portrayed by the priest in his Sunday sermon – (Note on the sermon of 22 April: *Stet Crux dum volvitur orbis.* Entirely unimpeachable in its timelessness, and yet what a revenge on the Nazis! A special task: the sermon in the Third Reich, the cover-ups and open declarations, the connection with the style of the Encyclopaedia.) – And on the other hand the bloke we were allocated to for the first night and who refused us water to wash in; he claimed that the pump in the barn was broken (which later turned out to be a lie), and told us to get lost. – And between these two extremes there were so many shades, including our landlord and landlady who were nearer to the bad extreme than the good one.

But in terms of their use of the LTI it was always the same: they cursed Nazism and did so using its own expressions. Everywhere there was talk of the *Wende,* be it hopeful or despondent, serious or sarcastic, everyone was fanatical {*fanatisch*} about something or other, and so on.

And of course everyone discussed in detail the Führer's final appeal to the Eastern Front, and quoted from it the 'countless new units' and the Bolsheviks who 'have murdered your old men and children, degraded your women and girls by turning them into army whores – the rest are marching to Siberia'.

No, despite the fact that there was so much to be experienced during the final days of the war (and afterwards on the journey home) – and these were real experiences, not the false kind promulgated by the language of the Hitler regime – I didn't find anything to add to the LTI or any departure from what I had observed from the restricted vantage point of our particular place of suffering. It really was total, it truly encompassed and contaminated the whole of Greater Germany in its absolute uniformity.

All that remains to be recorded here are two visible signs of the end of its reign.

On 28 April wild rumours spread about the direct proximity of the Americans; towards evening what remained of the military units stationed in or near the village marched off and withdrew, mainly the HJ, unkempt boys rather than soldiers, and higher-ranking officers who had occupied the attractive, modern administrative building at the entrance to the village. During the night there was an hour of heavy artillery fire, and shells roared over the village. The following morning in the lavatory there lay a document bearing stylish red and black lettering, torn in two; it remained there for a number of hours because it was too thick for its new purpose. It was a certificate of allegiance belonging to our landlord. It bore witness to the fact that 'Tyroller Michel' had sworn 'absolute loyalty to the Führer Adolf Hitler and his chosen deputies on the Königsplatz in Munich, in the presence of Rudolf Heß, the Führer's representative. Drawn up within the traditional *Gau* of Munich on 26 April 1936.'

There followed a number of eerie hours around midday; a few shots sounded from the edge of the forest, now and then we heard the whistling of bullets close by, somewhere there was still a skirmish going on. Then we saw a very long trail of tanks and automobiles on the country road which passed by the village – we had been overrun {*überrollt*}.

The next day, when we complained to him once again about our miserable living conditions and lack of food, our kind friend Flamensbeck suggested we move into the now empty administrative building. Most of the rooms had a cast-iron stove on which breakfast could be cooked, we could find pine cones to fuel it in the forest, and he certainly had enough lunch for us as well. That very afternoon we celebrated our move into our new accommodation. Along with many other comforts, these lodgings afforded us a very special pleasure. For a whole week we didn't have to worry about pine cones and brushwood – we had better fuel. During better Nazi times the HJ and the like had lived in this house, and the rooms had been chock-full of beautifully framed portraits of Hitler, the movement's wall banners, flags and wooden swastikas. All of this, together with the huge swastika above the door and the display case for the *Stürmer* from the hallway, had been removed and taken to the loft, where it formed a huge, jumbled heap. Next to the loft there was the bright attic which we had chosen for ourselves, and in which we spent a number of weeks. For the whole of the first week I kept the room warm with portraits of Hitler and their frames, with swastikas and flags bearing swastikas and yet more portraits of Hitler, and each time it was bliss.

Once the last picture had been incinerated the display case was due to come a cropper. But it had been made of heavy, thick planks and I couldn't manage it by kicking or brute force. In the house I found a little hatchet and a small handsaw. I tried with the hatchet and I tried with the saw. But the frame refused to give. The wood was much too thick and solid, and after all that had happened my heart couldn't take too much strain any more. 'Let's go and collect pine cones in the wood instead,' my wife said, 'it's more enjoyable and more healthy.' So we moved over to different fuel and the display case for the *Stürmer* remained intact. Now, when I receive letters from Bavaria, I am sometimes reminded of it . . .

''Cos of Certain Expressions' (An Afterword)

Now that the pressure had been lifted from us, and it was only a question of time before I would be able to return to my job, I began to ask myself which work I should turn to first. Back then they had taken my 'Eighteenth Century' away from me. My wife had saved both this and my diaries by sending them to our friend in Pirna; perhaps our friend and the manuscripts had survived – indeed there was good reason to assume that this was the case, not only because, of all places, a clinic is liable to be spared wherever possible, but also because there was no evidence that Pirna had suffered any great damage from the bombing. But where would I be able to get hold of the necessary library material to continue working on my Frenchmen? And what's more: I was so preoccupied with things to do with the Hitler period, which had transformed me in so many ways. Had I too also once thought too readily about THE German and THE Frenchman, rather than keeping in view the diversity of the Germans and the French? Had it perhaps been a luxury and egotistical to bury oneself exclusively in academia and avoid worrying about politics? There were a number of question marks in my diaries, certain observations and experiences in them which could teach one a thing or two. Perhaps I should first deal with all the things that I had accumulated during these years of suffering. Or was that a conceited, pompous plan? Regardless of how often I thought about these things whilst collecting pine cones, and whilst resting against my full rucksack, I was always reminded of two people who tugged me back and forth from one decision to another.

First there was the tragi-comic figure of Käthchen Sara, at first entirely comic and even at the last, when her destiny had slid entirely into the realm of tragedy, shrouded in a gentle humour. She really was called Käthchen, the name was recorded at the register office and on her certificate of baptism, to which she remained ostentatiously faithful by always wearing a little cross on her necklace alongside the compulsory Jewish star and the supplementary name Sara. And somehow the fond children's name was not entirely inappropriate to the 60-year-old with her slightly fatty heart, because she laughed and cried quickly and in quick succession, like a child whose memory is like a slate that can easily be wiped clean. For two bad years we were forced to share the flat with Käthchen Sara, and at least once a day she stormed into our room without knocking, and sometimes on a Sunday morning we woke to find her sitting on our bed, and each time she said: 'Write it down – you must write it down!' And then, with the same emotion, she would report on the latest house search, the latest suicide, the latest cut in ration cards. She believed in my role as chronicler, and in her childish eyes it was as if no other chronicler of the age would appear other than me, whom she so often saw sitting at the writing desk.

But hard on the heels of Käthchen's childishly over-enthusiastic voice I heard the half-sympathetic, half-sarcastic tones of good old Stühler, with whom we had been brought together following a new rounding-up. It occurred much later, by which time Käthchen Sara had long since disappeared for ever in Poland. Stühler also didn't live to see the day of salvation. He was allowed to stay in the country and die a natural, Gestapo-free death, yet he too is a victim of the Third Reich, because, but for the preceding suffering, the young man would have had more power of resistance. And he suffered much more than poor Käthchen, because his soul was not a slate, and because he was tormented by worry for his wife and son, a highly gifted boy who was robbed of any school education by Nazi law. 'Stop doing all that writing and have an extra hour's sleep', was invariably his reaction on noticing that I had got up too early; 'Your writing is merely putting you in danger. And do you really think that you are experiencing anything special? Don't you realize that thousands of others are suffering thousands of times more than you are? And don't you think that in time there will be more than enough historians to write about all this? People with better material and a better overview than you? What can you see, what can you record from your confinement here? Everyone has to go to the factory, many are beaten, and no one makes a fuss about being spat at any longer . . .' He often went on in this vein for a long time as we stood together in the kitchen when we had time off and helped our wives with the washing up or scrubbing vegetables.

I didn't let myself be led astray at the time, I got up each morning at half-past three and noted down what had happened during the previous day before starting work at the factory. I told myself: you hear with your own ears, and what matters is that you listen in specifically to the everyday, ordinary and average things, all that is devoid of glamour and heroism . . . And moreover: I kept hold of my balancing pole, and it kept hold of me . . .

But now, with the danger gone and a new life opening up in front of me, I ended up asking myself how I should initially fill it up and whether it wouldn't be conceited and a waste of time to bury myself in my bulging diaries. And Käthchen and Stühler fought over me.

Until a single word made up my mind for me.

Amongst the refugees in the village there was a worker from Berlin with her two little daughters. I don't know how it came about that we got talking to one another even before the Americans marched in. By that time it had already given me pleasure for a day or two, on passing her by, to hear her speaking with an unadulterated Berlin accent in the heart of Upper Bavaria. She was sociable, and recognized immediately that we were kindred spirits politically. She told us almost at once that her husband had spent a long time in prison for being a communist and, if he was even still alive, was now God knows where in a punishment battalion. And she herself, as she proudly reported, had also been locked up for a year, and would still be there today but for the fact that the prisons were overcrowded and that they needed her as a worker.

'Why were you in prison?' I asked. 'Well, 'cos of certain expressions {*wejen Ausdrücken*} . . .' (She had insulted the Führer along with the symbols and institutions of the Third Reich.) For me this was the revelation. It was this word that made me see clearly. 'Cos of certain expressions. That was the why and the wherefore of my setting to work on the diaries. I wanted to separate the balancing pole from the mass of other things, and just sketch in the hands that held it. That is how this book came about, less out of conceit, I hope, than 'cos of certain expressions.

Index

The original edition of *LTI* did not include an index. The following, compiled by the Press for this edition, is intended as an aide to research. It does not, of course, lay any claim to completeness.

CPSIA information can be obtained
at www.ICGtesting.com
Printed in the USA
LVHW080248050719
623114LV00019B/61/P

9 781472 507211